The Cultural Capital of
Asian American Studies

The Cultural Capital of Asian American Studies

Autonomy and Representation in the University

Mark Chiang

NEW YORK UNIVERSITY PRESS

New York And London

NEW YORK UNIVERSITY PRESS
New York and London
www.nyupress.org

Library of Congress Cataloging-in-Publication Data

Chiang, Mark.
The cultural capital of Asian American studies : autonomy and
representation in the university / Mark Chiang.
p. cm.
Includes bibliographical references and index.
ISBN-13: 978-0-8147-1700-4 (cloth : alk. paper)
ISBN-10: 0-8147-1700-4 (cloth : alk. paper)
ISBN-13: 978-0-8147-1701-1 (pbk. : alk. paper)
ISBN-10: 0-8147-1701-2 (pbk. : alk. paper)
1. Asian Americans—Study and teaching (Higher) 2. Education,
Higher—Political aspects—United States. 3. Asian Americans—Ethnic
identity. 4. Ethnicity—Political aspects—United States. 5. Autonomy.
6. Asian Americans—Politics and government. 7. Ethnology—Study
and teaching (Higher)—United States—Case studies. 8. Minorities—
Study and teaching (Higher)—United States—Case studies. I. Title.
E184.A75C494   2009
371.829'95073—dc22   2009019753

New York University Press books are printed on acid-free paper,
and their binding materials are chosen for strength and durability.
We strive to use environmentally responsible suppliers and materials
to the greatest extent possible in publishing our books.

Manufactured in the United States of America

10 9 8 7 6 5 4 3 2 1

Contents

Acknowledgments

This book is the product of a long and somewhat tortuous evolution, and it has benefited greatly from the influence of a number of people, either directly or indirectly. First I would like to thank Eric Zinner for his sustained commitment to the project almost from its inception, as well as Ciara McLaughlin for shepherding the manuscript through the editorial process, and the anonymous readers for New York University Press whose incisive comments helped reshape and clarify my arguments.

Because my book is so centrally concerned with moments of origin, it seems only appropriate to acknowledge the importance of the Asian American Reading Group at the University of California at Berkeley to my own entry into the field of Asian American studies. This group consisted of Juliana Chang, Jeannie Chiu, David Eng, Candace Fujikane, Daniel Kim, Cynthia Liu, Karen Su, Theresa Tensuan, and Dorothy Wang, and they will forever be associated with my discovery of the field that has provided an intellectual home for me in the academy. Special thanks must go to Candace Fujikane for sharing with me her unique insight into local cultural politics in Hawai'i and her personal archive of materials on the *Blu's Hanging* controversy, both of which were crucial to the development of my analysis in this book.

David Lloyd and Sau-ling Wong, the cochairs of my dissertation committee, have had a profound impact on my subsequent work, and I would especially like to thank Elaine Kim for the example of her pioneering work in the field as well as for her professional guidance. I must also acknowledge my colleagues at the University of Pennsylvania: Rosane Rocher, Grace Kao, and Eiichiro Azuma in the Asian American Studies Program; and Eric Cheyfitz, Herman Beavers, and John Richetti in the English Department. John Huntington, Walter Benn Michaels, Madhu Dubey, and Mark Canuel have been both supportive colleagues and mentors in the English department at the University of Illinois at Chicago (UIC). I also am grateful to my colleagues who have worked to bring Asian American studies to UIC: Helen Jun, Gayatri Reddy, Kevin Kumashiro, Anna Gue-varra, and Eric Tang.

A fellowship from the Institute for the Humanities at UIC provided essential time to write, and I am grateful to its director, Mary Beth Rose. The last chapter of the book benefited from the comments and suggestions of the participants in the Junior Faculty Publication Workshop held at the Center for Ethnic Studies and the Arts at the University of Iowa. I thank in particular the director, Lauren Rabinowitz, and Kent Ono for their detailed responses to the chapter. Josephine Lee offered extremely helpful feedback on the manuscript in her role as the director of the Asian American Studies Consortium of the Committee on Institutional Cooperation (CIC).

Finally I must thank my parents, Han and Grace Chiang, who have been waiting too long for this book. Most of all, I want to express my appreciation to Karen Su for her support and sacrifices during the writing of this book, and especially to Miya and Zeno, who provided the raison d'être.

Introduction

Institutionalization and the
Crisis of Representation

The development of Asian American studies as an academic field offers an intriguing case study in the history of the American university over the last three decades of the twentieth century. Emerging from the mass movements of the 1960s, Asian American studies has undergone major transformations over its rather brief time span. The first Asian American studies programs were established at San Francisco State College (now University) and the University of California at Berkeley in 1969, as a result of the Third World Strike, a boycott of classes by a multiracial and cross-class coalition of students, activists, and labor and community members. After protracted struggles to consolidate its presence in the university throughout the 1970s, new graduate students entered the field, and new programs began to appear at schools in places outside the West Coast in the 1980s. But then during the 1990s, tensions began to develop in the field, tensions between theory and practice, between political work and intellectual work, and between the community and the academy.[1] They finally erupted in 1998 with the conflicts over the Association for Asian American Studies (AAAS) fiction award given to Lois-Ann Yamanaka's novel *Blu's Hanging*.

Although the protests over the fiction award nearly led to the dissolution of the association itself, this event has already begun to be forgotten.[2] The award was featured in several books and articles published shortly afterward, but scholarly commentary on both the event and Yamanaka's novel has been notably sparse to date, now almost a decade later. This forgetting clearly has something to do with the traumatic nature of the conflicts, as well as with the uncertainty of what they signaled or what lessons might be drawn from them. The controversy was, in a sense, both too obvious and not obvious enough. That is, the debates over the fiction award before it was revoked raised issues such as cultural nationalism, the politics of representation, internal conflicts in the panethnic Asian American coalition, and the nature of the aesthetic and of literary value. In the wake of these events, however, it is not readily apparent what the controversy means or even why it is important to the history of the field or of Asian American politics in general. This book seeks to rectify that neglect on both counts, by arguing that the episode was significant not only as an instance of popular struggles over cultural politics, but that it also reveals certain basic lacunae in the theory and methods of Asian American studies. These absences call for a reflexive analysis of the political-intellectual project of the field, and, more specifically, for a concrete assessment of its location in the academic field and the university.

I use the historical context of the crisis around *Blu's Hanging* as a point of entry into the larger project of my book, an analysis of the development of Asian American studies as a field. This book seeks to produce a genealogy of Asian American studies from its origins in the Third World Strike of 1968 to the events surrounding the AAAS fiction award in 1998, particularly with regard to the role of culture and cultural studies in the development of the field. My intention is not to produce an intellectual history or even an institutional history, although the book encompasses aspects of both; rather, it is an excavation of certain fundamental dynamics that have driven the field's institutionalization over its brief, though eventful, life span. To that end, I am guided by two questions. First, what is the relation between the academic work of producing conceptual or theoretical representations and the political project of representing particular individuals or groups? And second, how should we understand the politics of academic work in the university if we take seriously the contention that one of its primary functions is the (re)production of cultural capital? Whereas the first question speaks to the purpose of establishing ethnic studies as a project of institutional transformation, the second addresses the ways in which this project had to acquire institutional legitimacy in order to survive.

In my investigation, I hope to provide a more detailed analysis of "institutionalization" and the ways that ethnic studies and the university have transformed each other. What happens when the radical politics of a mass movement enter the university and become institutionalized as a field of study? What does it mean to engage in political struggle within the university? This book explores the history and evolution of what is understood as politics in the field of Asian American studies, and it argues that the politics of the field needs to be understood in the context of struggles over the particular forms of capital that circulate both inside and outside the academy. Higher education has always been an object of political struggles in American society, but the student strikes of the 1960s and the demand for black studies and other ethnic studies marked a qualitatively new stage in the evolution of the university. For the first time in the history of American higher education, students sought to intervene in processes of university governance that had previously been closed off to them, and in doing so, they came to challenge the foundations of the university itself.

The *Blu's Hanging* controversy was widely regarded as a manifestation of the "crisis of representation" that engulfed many parts of the university, but the nature of the crisis and how it was related to representation were not as clear. *Race and Resistance: Literature and Politics in Asian America*, by Viet Nguyen, and *Imagine Otherwise: On Asian Americanist Critique*, by Kandice Chuh, two books published after the event, feature the crisis as a central part of their theoretical arguments. Both books agree that the crux of the event was the lack of correspondence between the representations and the objects they were intended to represent. In this case, it was the discrepancy between the AAAS's claim to represent Asian Americans and the complaint of some Asian Americans that the organization was not in fact properly representing them. Both also assert their critiques of (mis)representation in the name of the represented. Apart from this, however, the two books' arguments proceed in different (if not opposed) directions. Nguyen, for example, attributes the discrepancy to the representatives' interests, which he sees as distorting their perception of those whom they claimed to represent. In contrast, Chuh calls into question representation as such by arguing that any act of representation inevitably neglects and thus suppresses differences in the group being represented.

Although both these accounts offer important insights into the controversies over Yamanaka's novel, I find it striking that they proceed as if on parallel tracks with almost no points of intersection between them, especially since both sets of questions had already circulated in debates around the controversy. Besides construing the source of the conflicts in dramatically different fashion, these accounts also imply different solutions, essentially either greater accountability or no representation at all. This dichotomy, however, only replicates the "paradox" of representation identified by Hannah Pitkin, which is that representation is often gauged in relation to two ideals, those of perfect instruction—in which the representative acts only in accordance with the directives of the represented—or complete independence—in which the representative pursues the best interests of the represented, irregardless of what their actual wishes might be. As Pitkin argues, neither of these two ideals can be said to constitute political representation at all. If representation proper operates only between those two poles, however, the *Blu's Hanging* episode marks an instance in which there was apparently no possibility of reconciling them.

Given the immense conflicts that surfaced over the book, perhaps it is neither surprising nor coincidental that the two main responses to the "crisis of representation" would bifurcate along exactly this division. The mutually exclusive relation of the two books reveals the gulf between the opposing sides in the revocation of the fiction award, a gap that persists and that underlies, I argue, this episode's resistance to analysis. In focusing on the actions of the representatives, Nguyen implicitly adopts the perspective of the protesters, whereas Chuh, by calling for the rejection of representation and essentially severing any relation of obligation between Asian American studies practitioners and the Asian American population, opposes those who would make political claims on academic institutions. Although correlating the two accounts in this way may help illuminate the opposing sides of this conflict, unless we can bridge the gap between them, we will not understand the issues any better. Instead, we must seek to recombine the two theoretical models and restore to each what has been excluded. In particular, I argue that the *Blu's Hanging* episode raises questions regarding how judgments about the best interests of those they represent might have been affected by representatives' own unacknowledged interests, unacknowledged because they are not personal but collective interests, that is, the interests of those in the university.

To supply the missing link between the two theoretical models, we must confront one of the most persistent and vexing questions in Asian American studies, that of institutionalization, or what it means for the field to become an integral part of the very institution that it initially opposed and sought to transform. Even though this issue is hardly unique to Asian American studies, I contend that an investigation of the *Blu's Hanging* incident can help illuminate this problematic in ways that lead to new conceptual frameworks for the field. Indeed, institutionalization is intractable because it is almost always comprehended only in terms of contradiction, partly because of the way that ethnic studies originally conceived of itself as being opposed to the university. Once ethnic studies entered the university, this self-conception could be maintained only by regarding itself as a site of extraterritoriality, somehow figuratively outside of the institution despite being literally inside. This was, to say the least, not only an inadequate model of institutionalization, but it was also predicated on a monolithic and reductive account of the university and how it functions. My intention is not to examine the institution in all its manifold complexity, but to concentrate on one aspect that is salient to the questions raised here, the structures that produce and sustain the autonomy of the university.

For example, after President George W. Bush ordered the invasion of Iraq, several petitions and resolutions began to circulate on the Internet. Most were calls for faculty to take action against the war, but one was addressed to members of the AAAS, calling on the association to "form a task force to produce and disseminate educational resources as an alternative to the propaganda of U.S. multinational, corporate media" as well as to "build alliances with other academic, legal, policy and community-based organizations to protect civil liberties and human rights, and fight for social justice." What caught my attention was not these two injunctions but the one that preceded them in the list, which urged the AAAS "to defend the academic freedom of its members' research, teaching and professional services in challenging this imperial 'War on Terror.'" Clearly, the authors of this resolution viewed academic freedom as a prerequisite to taking political action, but for those who were not academics, the defense of academic freedom might have seemed, at best, like a rather indirect response to military conflict. Although freedom of speech is certainly at stake here, couching the matter as academic freedom slants it more toward faculty autonomy rather than the First Amendment. To push the issue a bit further, we might ask how the defense of faculty autonomy would respond to the political exigencies of war.

What makes this document even more interesting is that it was proposed by the Critical Filipino Studies Collective, a group that grew out of (and several of whose members were involved in) the Filipino American Studies Caucus, which played a central role in the call to rescind Yamanaka's fiction award. As chapter 5 of my book demonstrates, autonomy became one of the central issues in the debate because the AAAS's board refused to interfere in the decision by the three-person award committee in the name of academic freedom. The question, then, is how we conceive of autonomy in relation to the political aims of Asian American studies as an academic field. While the institutional structures that produce the autonomy of the university arguably are the main obstacles to any political movements that seek to transform it, once that movement gains entry to the university, autonomy apparently becomes something it can use to its own advantage. Does this mean that autonomy is simply a neutral bureaucratic apparatus that can be manipulated for radically different political purposes and hence something to be conquered and seized? Or is autonomy itself integral to the institution's ideological or political functions? Put more succinctly, is the defense of academic freedom and faculty autonomy a precondition for effective opposition to domination, or does it in fact indirectly sustain domination? Although that is one of this book's central questions, it cannot be answered easily. Rather, I contend that the question of autonomy must be raised in order for Asian American studies to have any coherent political agenda at all, whether inside or outside the academy.

The term *Asian American* was formulated by activists in the 1960s to denote a new identity for Asians in the United States, one that insisted on "claiming America." The emphasis on a national identity and belonging, however, was soon challenged by developments occurring simultaneously with the Asian American movement. Major changes in U.S. immigration law in the 1960s and the rise of Japan and the Four Tigers (Taiwan, South Korea, Singapore, and Malaysia) as sites of capital accumulation in the global economy significantly transformed the Asian American population. Before the 1960s, the main factor in the demographics of Asian American communities was the series of immigration laws, beginning with the 1882 Chinese Exclusion Act, that restricted the entry of almost all Asian immigrants to the United States. It was only with the Immigration Act of 1965 that the United States finally equalized the quotas for all nations, thereby ending almost eighty years of legal exclusion. One impetus for immigration reform at this time was government reports forecasting a shortage of skilled and technical labor in the U.S. economy. Even though the 1965 Immigration Act expressed a preference for immigrants with these skills, legislators thought that this preference would be filled by European immigrants. As a result of certain transformations in the international division of labor, however, it was largely Asians who met this preference.[3]

These changes had three major consequences for Asian American communities. The first was a dramatic rise in the number of first-generation Asian immigrants, so that they now outnumber the second generation and later, who had previously constituted the majority of the

Asian American population during the exclusion era. The second was the enormous expansion of new ethnic groups, so that the Asian American population has changed from being mostly Chinese, Japanese, and Filipino, to being a heterogeneous grouping of East Asians, South Asians, and Southeast Asians, with Pacific Islanders and West Asians (or those from the Middle East) as the most recent and controversial inclusions.[4] Finally, both the immigration preferences and the gains of the civil rights movement have created a new Asian American middle class, contributing to a widening class division in Asian American communities. It has thus become increasingly difficult not only to say who Asian Americans are in any singular way, but to locate them either geographically or politically.

These dramatic demographic changes are generally agreed to be the underlying factors of the recent crisis in the field, which has been described by a number of scholars as a crisis of representation. Whom or what does Asian American studies represent, and how does it represent them? This is, above all, a question regarding the field's political aims, and it also speaks to the assumptions that guide its intellectual and scholarly work. One of the field's primary imperatives, for example, was to "serve the community." After the 1965 Immigration Act, though, Asian American diversity increased to an extent that it now is nearly impossible to say who or what the "community" is. The crisis of representation also has produced a crisis of identity. What does it mean to engage in Asian American literary criticism or Asian American studies in general? If it is no longer possible to know the community, then what principles or politics can give the field of Asian American studies some kind of coherence? To pose the question in these terms already indicates the divergence of Asian American studies (or any minority studies in general) from the "traditional" academic disciplines. If there is a crisis of literary studies, for example, it is not because English departments have lost a sense of whom they represent.[5]

This book offers a critical analysis of Asian American studies as one particular case that illuminates the situation of the American academy at the beginning of the twenty-first century. My analysis is based on the problematic of representation, a term that is used in many ways but raises a number of issues confronting ethnic studies, literary studies, and the academy in general. More specifically, the book examines the development of Asian American studies in its social, historical, and institutional contexts by focusing on Asian American literary and cultural studies as the nexus of the crisis of Asian American studies, on the one hand, and the crisis of literature (or the "canon"), on the other. While the former is seen as a crisis of representation, the latter is generally understood as a crisis of value. Asian American literary studies is one node where these two crises intersect. The relation between them, I believe, offers an intriguing map of the current state of literary studies, insofar as the two oppose each other in many respects despite deriving from the same social and historical matrix.

Historically, representation has been conceived in two main senses, political and aesthetic. The question is whether these two are related and, if so, how. In liberal political philosophy, culture is construed as a domain separate from politics and economics; hence the two meanings of representation are seen as distinct. Others scholars see them as being connected in various ways, as, for example, in the wide-ranging debates over the relation of culture to politics. If one position is that political and aesthetic representation are fundamentally different, the other extreme holds that they are simply the same or that all aesthetic representations reflect a particular structure of political representation. Debates in Asian American literary studies have tended to mirror these larger disagreements, from those who argue that Asian American cultural production must serve primarily a political function to those who seek to defend the autonomy of the aesthetic. This book proposes an alternative understanding of the relation between political and aesthetic representation that seeks to preserve the relative autonomy of the field of cultural production even as it explicates the complex articulation that nevertheless links it to the political field. Drawing on the work of Pierre Bourdieu, I argue that the connection between the two forms of representation must be understood as the relation between political capital and cultural capital. In other words, both political and aesthetic representation operate in distinct ways in more or less discrete spaces, but the effectiveness of both fundamentally depend on forms of capital. It is only in elaborating this linkage that we can begin articulating the connection between Asian American studies as a project within the university and the Asian American movement in the political field.

The Cultural Capital of Asian American Studies argues that among the key features of the modern research university are the structures of autonomy that produce a relation of representation between the academy and the world—a relation that we might refer to as simply the ideology of "research." This institutional structure becomes evident in the history of Asian American studies at San Francisco State College, since the necessary condition for incorporating the program in the university was

eliminating community control in order to establish a representative relation to the community. The most radical aspect of Asian American studies at SF State, as chapter 2 shows, was that it based the governance of the
program on the principle of "community autonomy." What was not suf-
ficiently recognized was that *community* autonomy was directly opposed
to the principle of the research university, which is *faculty* autonomy. Subsequently, as the field's institutional situation has evolved, those changes
have been reflected in myriad ways in its intellectual work, perhaps most
strikingly in the "cultural turn" that took place during the 1980s. Initially,
Asian American studies was largely concentrated in history and the social
sciences, but during the 1980s, those core disciplines began to be displaced
by a new surge of interest in literary studies, and in literary and cultural
theory in particular. The question of theory has become one of the central
issues in the field, but the debate over theory has tended to focus on the
political implications of different theoretical paradigms. I offer instead a
historical and institutional account of this disciplinary reconfiguration of
the field.

In this book, I contend that one of the features distinguishing Asian
American studies (and other branches of "minority" studies) from the
"traditional" disciplines is its claim to a kind of political representation
that contrasts in many ways with the forms of theoretical or descriptive
representation seen as legitimate in the academy. The problem of reconciling these two antagonistic modes of representation motivates much of
the theoretical work in what I call *Asian American cultural studies*. The
broader argument of my book is that shifting the theoretical focus of Asian
American literary and cultural studies from the thematics of identity to
those of representation can dispel certain persistent theoretical quandaries and, more important, can lead to new political-theoretical questions.
To that end, the book develops a theory of representation using Pierre
Bourdieu's elaborations of cultural and symbolic capital, since the credibility and verisimilitude of any representation are functions of the capital
that they mobilize. In particular, I argue that Asian American literary and
cultural studies are sites in the academy for the conversion of political and
cultural capital and that the interplay between these two forms of capital
reveals how the field is shaped by its relations to the Asian American political field, on the one hand, and the university, on the other.

Although the impact of theory may simply appear to reflect the rise
of literary theory in the American academy in general during the 1980s
and 1990s, its impact on the various forms of "minority studies" takes a

specific trajectory that must be understood in relation to their political dynamics, which are distinct from those of the "traditional" disciplines. Responses to theory in Asian American studies have largely been divided between those who remain committed to identity politics and the proponents of difference, but I propose that this dichotomy is itself a product of the relations of representation that structure the university. While the main thrust of theory in Asian American studies has been the political critique of identity and essentialism, I contend that the importation of literary and cultural theory into the field has also brought with it political agendas derived from other institutional conflicts. As the theoretical critique of identity expanded, it began to call into question the basis of the Asian American category itself. Theories of difference, for example, propose that as an identity category, Asian American necessarily subsumes heterogeneity and so perpetuates domination and inequality. It is, moreover, a category of the state and thus is implicated in the reproduction of hegemony. I contend that the history and subsequent development of Asian American studies as an academic field cannot be fully grasped in terms of identity or its theoretical critique. Rather, in order to advance beyond some of the theoretical cul-de-sacs to which the anti-identitarian critique has led, political work in Asian American studies (as well as in other fields) needs to investigate the conceptual and institutional structures of representation constituting one of the links between the academic field and the political field in liberal democracy.

I argue that it is possible to resolve many of the difficulties currently plaguing efforts to produce a nonrestrictive and nonessentialist account of the group when we recognize that the object of such efforts is not a community or a people but, first, a *category* and, second and more important, a *field*, in Bourdieu's conception of the term. As I discuss in chapter 1, to conceive of the Asian American category as a field eliminates at one stroke many of the theoretical difficulties leading to the necessity of pronouncements such as the imperative to redefine Asian American studies as a "subjectless discourse." This and other similar theoretical formulations are drawn from the political-intellectual project of reconciling identity with difference, but I suggest that the apparent conflict between these two terms has more to do with a logical than a political contradiction. The logical contradiction arises in part from a conceptualization of difference that dictates the refusal of representation as an essential component of the mechanism of identity. But this necessarily gives rise to a situation in which theorists seek simultaneously to resolve the antinomy of identity and difference even as they reject representation.

The first point to be made about such arguments is that there is no possibility of refusing representation per se because that would result in a purely idealist discourse. Given that we are talking about the study of *Asian Americans*, we would have to say that something is being represented. The question that we must ask, then, is what kind of representation is being refused and what kind of representation is being retained. Clearly, it is *political* representation that is being rejected in favor of a purely theoretical or conceptual representation. These terms are somewhat misleading, however, because I am not implying that the representations produced in academic work are not political but that they are political in a way that is different from the kind of representation operating in the political field. This difference can be understood according to the disparate principles of legitimacy of the academic and political fields; that is, political representation bases its legitimacy (at least in theory) on consent, whereas conceptual representations are assessed according to the standards and methods of academic work. In other words, the difference is one between *accountability* and *autonomy*. Political representations are accountable to those they represent, whereas academic work is accountable only to the academy.

The disparity in these rationales was one of the sources of the conflicts between ethnic studies at its origins and the university. In addition, this disparity also lies at the root of the tension between Asian American studies and Asian and area studies. If a rapprochement between those two fields now seems possible, it is largely because Asian studies has come increasingly to assume a political stance as speaking for—rather than simply studying—Asians. In contrast, Asian American studies has become increasingly distant from the constituencies that it was originally created to serve. How and why that distance was created are questions central to this study. My argument is that the attempt to reconcile identity with difference can be read as the theoretical work to produce a rationale for the field capable of reconciling community autonomy with faculty autonomy, or at least of making them appear continuous rather than antithetical. Theorizations of difference, then, are impelled by various institutional as well as political agendas, and the effort to bring incompatible and conflicting impulses more or less into alignment has produced the particular theoretical device that I call *nonrepresentative representation*.

In its most elementary form, nonrepresentative representation simply hypostatizes contradiction, as exemplified in theoretical constructions of subjectlessness, difference, catachresis, or what is arguably the ur-trope of these formulations, strategic essentialism.[6] My discussions of these "concept-metaphors" (Gayatri Spivak's term) is not intended to dismiss or disprove them. Rather, it seems to me that they are overdetermined and thus revelatory of the extraordinarily complex entanglements of political-institutional agendas and interests that lie at the core of the academic field. Indeed, the AAAS fiction award and the controversy it provoked can be regarded as a sort of empirical test of the theoretical claims made for the politics of difference or strategic essentialism. As I elaborate in chapter 5, the fiction award became a point of articulation between the academic and political fields, but one whose functioning depended on certain kinds of obfuscation. For example, one question repeatedly asked during the episode was why the AAAS handed out literature awards in the first place, since they seemed anomalous given the association's academic constituency. If the fiction award was intended to link Asian American studies to Asian American politics or communities, it did so only by displacing political representation into cultural representation, in that it fostered the *political* representation of Asian American *culture* rather than *people*. Once the protests exerted pressure on this rather fragile conceptual apparatus—one motivated as much by the exchange of capital as by political advocacy—it quickly began to break apart.

Indeed, the controversy over the fiction award was an especially good reason to investigate the problematic of representation in the Asian American category, because it shows that whom or what the award is supposed to represent cannot be divorced from the value that it is meant to either recognize or bestow. What is missing from this argument that the "Asian American" rubric contains normative and exclusionary criteria is the distinction between intellectual categories and political categories. That is, the former refers to Asian Americans as a nominal class, or a purely theoretical classification, whereas the latter denotes the realized class, or the group mobilized for political purposes. Asian American politics, we might say, is the effort to join these two categories. But while the first concerns definitions of identity, the second, I believe, depends on identification. To conceive of the Asian American category as a field requires shifting our investigation from the former to the latter because belonging in a field is defined by investments, not boundaries. Thus, rather than constructing a purely theoretical unity, I suggest that disparate individuals and groups are held together under the Asian American designation only by an interest. This interest, however, is not a "common" one insofar as that implies a unitary and homogeneous subject. Instead, it is a *competitive* interest signifying both acting *against* but also *with* others in the pursuit of some object or end, which in this instance is the specific capital of the Asian American field, or what I call the *political capital of representation.*

Although the term *Asian American* has been sanctioned as official state terminology for three decades now, studies have repeatedly shown that only a relatively small minority of Asians in the United States would identify themselves first and foremost as "Asian American."[7] Of course, the exact percentage is difficult to quantify, given the ways that identity can shift depending on context and circumstance. Nevertheless, most nominal Asian Americans identify themselves primarily in terms of their nationality or ethnicity. The Asian American category, then, is a spectrum extending from those who identify as Asian American to those who do not, with most falling somewhere in between. Why this is the case is a matter of some debate, but the important point here is that Asian American identity remains largely unnaturalized, meaning that unlike "primordial" ethnic identities—the fiction of consent notwithstanding—one must more or less consciously *choose* to become an Asian American via an act of identification. Therefore, it seems to me that the question is *not* why so few "Asian Americans" identify as such, but why anyone would choose to do so at all.

One of the main objectives of the Asian American political movement was the production of Asian American subjects by means of politicization or, to use the original term, *consciousness raising.* The primary motivation for identifying with the movement was largely understood to be the struggle against racial inequality and exclusion from full status as American citizens, but racism proved to be less than a completely unifying force, as it affected various Asian Americans in sometimes dramatically different ways. Moreover, besides the differential impact of race, major disagreements arose over how best to oppose racial oppression. Theories of difference respond to a historical context in which a monolithic racism no longer provides a foundation for "the" Asian American subject, but they do so in ways that tend to obscure even further the question of why someone might choose to become Asian American.

I argue that to identify oneself as Asian American is to stake a claim of belonging in the Asian American field or—what is essentially the same thing—to stake a claim to the capital of the field as one who has the ability to represent or to speak for Asian Americans as a group. What, after all, is politicization if not an investment—of belief and of interest—in Asian American politics? This investment, or identification, is motivated by an interest in the accumulated capital of the field, which is the material or economic capital possessed by all those in the field and, more important, the symbolic capital into which it can be transformed. It is part of the un-naturalized condition of Asian American identity—or, put another way, the weakly institutionalized status of the Asian American field—that there are almost no mechanisms for the popular selection of legitimate repre-sentatives, which means that one can become a representative simply by identifying oneself as Asian American and that representatives select one another by mutual recognition. Understanding constructions of Asian American identity as strategies of capital accumulation offers a different gloss on the notion of "strategic essentialism." At the same time, the con-cept of the Asian American field reinserts academic work into the larger social and political fields by showing that academic theorization about identity also engages in struggles over the political capital of representa-tion, albeit in collective rather than individual ways.

In order to situate Asian American studies in the Asian American field as a whole, the book does not debate its theories or methods but inves-tigates the sources of its academic legitimacy or capital. Asian American studies as an academic enterprise does not derive its intellectual capital solely from the traditional disciplines. Ethnic studies, for example, began as a challenge to what activists perceived as the educational institution's lack of representation and accountability. Thus the initial capital for Asian American studies came from the political mobilization of the mass move-ment. This "primitive accumulation" was the basis of the political capital of representation, or the specific capital of the Asian American field. The strictures enforcing the disinterestedness of academic work, though, pre-clude the direct accumulation of political capital in the academic field, which means that one of the primary tasks of ethnic studies has been to produce the theoretical mechanisms for converting political capital into cultural and academic capital. Ultimately, I argue that the problematic of representation in Asian American studies needs to be understood in terms of strategies of capital accumulation and field formation and that these concepts provide the basis for a revisionary account of the trajec-tory of the field that also helps illuminate the history of the modern re-search university.

. . .

Because I have devoted a great deal of attention to the study of narrative, I am sensitive to the ways in which readers may unwittingly impose conventional or formulaic narratives on sequences of events, thereby transforming them into chains of causation. One narrative that this book seems readily to conjure up is the narrative of decline and fall. This is a narrative that I have sought rather strenuously to avoid in writing this book. It is not that I necessarily disagree with this interpretation, but I wanted to pose the questions in this book as openly as possible, especially since they are among the most politically divisive and contentious issues in the field. Other narratives that may be evoked are those of "selling out," "the return to origins," "betrayal of the community," and "seduction by capital." As dramatic as they may be, these are not the stories this book intends to tell. I am skeptical of any return to the past in a context of radically changed historical circumstances. Rather, one of the aspirations of this book is to revisit the questions originally posed by the Asian American movement in order to see what kinds of answers we might arrive at in the present.

Some readers have urged me to state more clearly my own position on these conflicts or to assess the interests and investments that led to this book. Others may want me to take a more polemical position or adopt a programmatic agenda regarding future directions in the field. Certainly this is a polemical book: raising the question of interest in the academic field is always somewhat threatening, since it requires confronting the various denials, prohibitions, and other forms of censorship that maintain its objectivity and disinterestedness. Those immersed in postmodern and poststructuralist forms of skepticism may take this statement as confirming the ideological and thus illusory quality of those values, but that is not the point. Instead, I follow Bourdieu in maintaining that only by recognizing and accounting for those denials can we even begin to analyze objectively the structure of relations in fields constituted by symbolic capital, which is "symbolic" only in that it is economic capital denied. Indeed, I regard the central insight of Bourdieu's work, which inaugurates his entire analysis of symbolic capital, as the realization that denial is a mechanism that does not simply negate or suppress but is transformative and might be said to produce the social as such.[8]

The issue of the self-interestedness of academic work is hardly new; in some branches of literary theory, disclosing one's privilege or "positionality" was, at a certain point, a prerequisite. One of the major deficiencies of such forms of reflexivity, though, was their circumscription by the limits of the personal and the individual, at times making it seem to be almost a kind of confession or mea culpa. As I have argued, interest in academic work cannot be grasped in terms of the personal, but only at the level of the academic field as a whole, which also requires situating it within the larger social field. The interests driving academic work are not personal. This is not to say, however, that there are not personal motivations—for recognition, prestige, reward—but that these are subject to the strictures of the academic field, which means that they can be pursued only through indirect strategies. Academic work in general encodes multiple levels of legitimacy, from that of the educational system as a whole through particular institutions, to college-level transdisciplinary formations (liberal arts, sciences, engineering, the professions, and so on), to the disciplines, and to subdisciplinary specializations. It is only by identifying with the collective interests of the field (either implicitly or explicitly) at each of these larger social and institutional levels that it is possible to accrue *individual* capital.

The foregoing may help explain why this book aims at a certain impersonality and why I resist calls to position myself more explicitly in relation to the issues that I examine.[9] The reason is not simply the protocols of academic discourse but also the awareness that the basic form of capital in the academic field is the taking of positions. Because the central issue in this book is the difficulty of separating interest from disinterest in academic work, it seemed advisable to refrain as much as possible from commingling analysis with any attempt to advance a political agenda. Indeed, this is, as I argue, where John Guillory runs into problems. Since all work in the academy must engage in capital accumulation, any academic work that reflects on those processes must confront the ways in which its own strategies of accumulation may distort its analyses, a problematic to which Bourdieu was always acutely attuned. To restate the question, this book asks what it means when academic work that strives to be political instead becomes cultural capital. We could say that this is simply an inevitable condition of academic work, but that does not mean it should not be subjected to analysis and reflection. Indeed, without a thorough investigation, how can we know whether it is inevitable? This is the question that my book addresses.

How are the Asian American political field and the academic field of Asian American studies connected? Chapter 1, "From Cultural Politics to Cultural Capital," proposes that whatever the ideological relation is between them, the two fields are united by a circuit of capital and that Asian American literature is one node of exchange between them. In this chapter I ask what value Asian American literature might have in the academy and how it is related to the "crisis of literature" that forms the primary context of John Guillory's monumental *Cultural Capital*. Although Guillory's analysis is important and provocative, I take issue with his critique of minority literature in relation to the "canon wars" of the 1980s. His argument derives from what he perceives as the contradiction between integrationist and separatist constructions of minority literature, in which that literature is construed simultaneously as both canonical and non- or anticanonical. What Guillory fails to consider is whether the "noncanonical" in fact names a different kind of value, which I argue is the political capital of representation. The academic field of Asian American studies, then, is structured by the ratios and mechanisms of exchange between the political capital of the Asian American field as a whole and the cultural or academic capital of the university.

The second part of this chapter contrasts articulations of difference in Asian American cultural studies with the model of relational analysis at the heart of Bourdieu's ideas of field and capital. Although both conceive of social relations as operating in a dynamic system of negative differences, they are opposed in that the former is committed to an antirealist and antirepresentational epistemology whereas the latter seeks to decipher the inequalities of a social order constituted by the structure of distribution of capital. I argue that one detrimental consequence of Asian American cultural studies' rejection of the abjected troika of identity-essentialism-representation is that it obscures the relations of capital linking the university to the polity by attempting to (re)construct that relation as one of *nonrepresentation*. As a conceptual device, nonrepresentation (in its various permutations) offers a means of resolving the numerous contradictions of institutionalization, but it does so, of course, only in theory.

Chapter 2, "Contradictions in the Emergence of Ethnic Studies," returns to the birth of Asian American studies at San Francisco State College. Emerging from the Third World Strike, the most radical aspect of the SF State program was an institutional structure predicated on the slogan of "community autonomy," which meant that Asian American communities should control the programs that were intended to serve their needs. Community control, however, is necessarily antithetical to the principle of the modern research university, which is faculty control. In order to establish itself in the university, therefore, the program had to eliminate community control in favor of academic autonomy. This transformation was made at a practical rather than a theoretical level, though, since the question of program governance was never subjected to critical examination. As this chapter demonstrates, the question of autonomy was fundamental to the formation of black studies in particular, since that was the paradigmatic model on which the other ethnic studies programs were based. One of the principal demands of the Black Students Union (BSU) at SF State was autonomy for the black studies department, but as statements by various BSU members and other students illustrate, that autonomy could be and was conceived in entirely opposing ways.

This chapter then situates the emergence of the Asian American identity within a historical trajectory of capital accumulation in order to introduce new perspectives on the political history of resistance to racial oppression. I propose that to revise our understanding of the Asian American movement as engaged in constructing a field may enable us to displace the dual motifs of resistance, on the one hand, and "claiming America," on the other, in favor of an active agency that cannot be inscribed in the nationalist dichotomies of resistance or accommodation. For example, I suggest that one project of Asian American studies in the university was converting the political capital of the Asian American field into a form of cultural capital whose value could be institutionally guaranteed. Indeed, given the obstacles Asian Americans confronted in the political sphere, the conversion of political capital into cultural capital in the university was quite likely the most efficient means of conserving that capital. This helps explain why university and college campuses were central focal points of the Asian American movement and why they were among the main sites of political struggle.

Chapter 3, "Disciplinarity and the Political Identity of Asian American Studies," defines the institutional location of Asian American studies as both an academic and a political project by asking why ethnic studies has historically defined itself as an interdisciplinary field rather than establishing a disciplinary status for itself. In this chapter I examine the debates over the impact of postmodern and poststructuralist theory in Asian American studies in a special issue of the journal *Amerasia* entitled *Thinking Theory in Asian American Studies*. One of the most salient aspects of these debates was the way in which the division over theory fell largely along disciplinary lines, with literary and cultural studies being opposed to history and social sciences. The other major aspect of the debates was that even though they concerned theoretical paradigms and methods, the essays in the issue, whether pro or con, justified their positions based less on intellectual or academic criteria than on *political* criteria. In this way, the debate over theory was overdetermined by two somewhat different sets of dynamics: political struggles in the Asian American field and academic struggles in the university. My argument is not that theory marks the site where these two fields converge but that Asian American studies as a whole is constituted by that convergence and that its constitution as a "permanent interdiscipline" allowed the field to contain these multiple, overlapping political and intellectual antagonisms.

This chapter extends an analysis of the space of Asian American studies as an interdisciplinary field by examining the interface between two closely related disciplines, literature and history. Despite the long history of traffic across this border, I find that work in Asian American cultural studies that aspires to historicist modes of cultural analysis must continually confront the antithetical epistemological and methodological assumptions of the two academic disciplines of literary studies and history, assumptions derived directly from how each field defines the terms of its academic legitimacy. Finally, I return to the pivotal moment in Asian American literary history of the critical revaluation of Theresa Cha's *Dictée*. Although the explicit political rationale for this revisionary reading was the demographic transformations of the Asian American population following the immigration reforms of the 1960s, I advance an alternative argument. That is, I locate the primary impetus for this critical intervention in the field of Asian American studies by arguing that *Dictée* facilitated a reconfiguration of the Asian American literary field in order to enable new modes of capital accumulation.

Chapter 4, "The Political Economy of Minority Literature," revisits the origins of the Asian American literary field in the writings of two of its most influential figures, Frank Chin and Maxine Hong Kingston. Although the polemics of Chin and the other editors of *Aiiieeeee!* are now identified with the formation of Asian American literature, some serious misconceptions have become sedimented in the critical responses to them and have been compounded by the ways in which cultural nationalism is construed in critiques of identity politics. At the most general level, for example, it is almost axiomatic that cultural nationalism in *Aiiieeeee!* sought to subordinate art to politics, and the editors' own self-representation as the "radical" pole of Asian American cultural production is often simply accepted at face value. In contrast, I argue that the *Aiiieeeee!* editors actually tried to articulate a political rationale justifying why art needed to be *free* from politics. In this way, they attempted to extract some of the political capital of the mass movement in order to construct an autonomous Asian American literary field.

Chapter 4 then juxtaposes this analysis with a rereading of *The Woman Warrior*, arguing that the dilemma motivating the narrative is not the anxiety of influence, as in the dominant literary tradition, but the anxiety of representation. In other words, only within and against the writer's relation of representation to the community can she become a representative, or an author. In this chapter I demonstrate in an extended reading of *The Woman Warrior* how the political problematics of representation become sublimated in and reworked through the formal structures of Kingston's narratives. In particular, I argue that the problem of political representation in the book (that is, its relation to Chinese Americans) is divided across two opposing modes of aesthetic representation, which are, roughly speaking, form and content, or fiction and nonfiction. Although the book tries to liberate the former from the latter, thus pitting them against each other, it states over and over again their interdependence. Ultimately, I contend, the book's pervasive motif of "translation" must be read as a trope for the conversion or exchange of capital.

Chapter 5, "Asian American Cultural Capital and the Crisis of Legitimation," describes the events regarding Lois-Ann Yamanaka's novel *Blu's Hanging*. These conflicts encapsulate most of the issues covered in this book. Although the debates over the award encompassed a number of theoretical and material issues regarding the field, these issues were tied to questions regarding what constituted a legitimate interpretation. Rather than rehearsing those debates, my analysis focuses on the main charge directed against the book itself, that it replicated stereotypical and racist depictions of Filipinos, especially given the location of Yamanaka's narrative in Hawai'i. Literary and cultural studies, however, have almost entirely abandoned stereotype analysis because of a number of conceptual difficulties, perhaps chief among them being the impossibility of deciding what is or is not a stereotype. Consequently, in regard to *Blu's Hanging*, it became impossible to refute the charge of stereotyping because there was no way to define what is *not* a stereotype. I propose an alternative approach to this problem by asking who perceived the book as stereotypical and who did not, but these perceptions were linked to divergent constructions of Asian American identity, or political capital. Ultimately, I argue, one of the main underlying factors in the conflict, which contributed substantially to its intractability, was that it opposed those who possessed

Asian American cultural capital (the book's defenders) against those who did not (the protesters).

The second part of the chapter offers an extended reading of *Blu's Hanging* that reconstructs it as a response to the protests against Yamanaka's earlier work. One of the factors that may lead to an impression of stereotypicality is the somewhat mysterious antagonism between the protagonist, Ivah Ogata, and her Filipino neighbors, the Reyes family, and especially their cousin, Uncle Paulo. I contend that this antagonism serves as the displaced staging of the conflict between Yamanaka and the protesters and that the narrative responds to the complaints of the protesters through a series of events revolving around the central issue of whether Ivah can be considered a legitimate representative of the local community. One of Yamanaka's primary aims in the narrative is defining this legitimacy not in political but in cultural terms. In this respect, the pervasive violence in the narrative expresses the anxieties of representation that permeate the book, so that the degraded figure of Uncle Paulo reflects those in the community who resist Ivah's representation as well as the underlying violence of that representation.

Blu's Hanging and the controversies surrounding it exemplify the questions that this book raises because they dramatize the tensions and complications of the Asian American field, which is structured by the polarities of autonomy and representation. To return to the specific locus of the university, I ask again, what function does the system of higher education play in reproducing structures of social inequality? More specifically, what relation does academic autonomy have to the expansion of democratic participation? Is autonomy necessarily tied to the concentration of cultural capital, and if so, can that capital be used for radical social transformation, or is it an obstacle to such transformation? What are the interests of a field like Asian American studies in this context, and what role can or does it play in those processes? These are the questions that animate every part of this study and that it hopes to illuminate in some small way.

1

From Cultural Politics
to Cultural Capital

In order to describe the struggles that take place in the disparate fields of culture, politics, and the academy, we must specify the particular forms of capital at stake in each field, as well as the ratios of exchange by which the specific capital of one field can be transferred to another. The model of capital developed by Pierre Bourdieu provides a framework that preserves the relative autonomy of different sectors of the social formation while simultaneously enabling us to grasp the dynamics of capital underlying the struggles both within and across fields. As part of the political-intellectual project of Asian American studies, literary and cultural studies have theorized in various ways the relation of culture to politics and the role of culture in the political life of Asian Americans and the academic work of Asian American studies. This chapter establishes the foundation for a model of cultural production attuned to the dynamics and relations characterizing the fields of Asian American politics, Asian American culture, and Asian American studies.

This analysis relies in particular on the concepts of field and cultural capital, but it heeds Bourdieu's own injunction that we can arrive at the most general principles only by attending to the particularities of specific cases and by excavating the structural principles and mechanisms that reproduce a field or social space. A field is constituted by a form of capital specific to it, and it consists of a set of objective relations expressed in a structure of positions. This space of positions defines a set of possible position-takings. Agents occupy particular positions in strategic efforts to maximize their share of the specific capital at stake in the field, but they can take positions only against other agents and other positions, thereby reconstituting the field. In the cultural field, occupying a position means seizing the field's legitimate definitions and thus controlling who is or is not included in the field as well as the criteria by which value is recognized. Every social formation is composed of a hierarchical structure of fields, which are relatively autonomous from one another and, more important, from the economic and political fields. The degree of a field's autonomy is directly related to the extent to which it is able to function solely with regard to its own internal logic and rules.

To locate Asian American literary studies in relation to the "community" and the university, this chapter expands on the notion of a symbolic capital of race proposed by Viet Nguyen. The first half of the chapter asks what it would mean to think of Asian American literature or culture as constituting a new kind of cultural capital, and it does so by engaging with John Guillory's influential book *Cultural Capital*. Guillory offers a brilliant and sweeping account of literature's evolution as cultural capital across the history of "Western culture," but I take issue with his critique of minority literature in relation to the debates over the canon and the culture wars of the 1980s. Guillory argues that it does not make sense to conceive of minority literature as noncanonical or as constituting an alternative canon because that simply means that it has no value and is therefore not worth teaching. I will demonstrate that the plan he proposes is fraught with contradictions. My argument is that the construction of a separatist minority literary field participates in a larger politics of struggle to transform the dominant cultural capital. The second half of the chapter takes up recent work in Asian American cultural studies centering on questions of identity and difference. I am especially interested in theoretical efforts in Asian American studies to negotiate the apparent contradictions between identity politics and various articulations of the poststructuralist politics of difference. I argue that Bourdieu's model of relational analysis resolves many of these contradictions but that it also allows us to situate Asian American studies (as well as the related fields of ethnic studies, women's/gender studies, queer studies, and so forth) within the larger academic field in a way that helps illuminate the complex interests and forces motivating these forms of academic work.

As part of his response to the "crisis of representation" surrounding the controversy over Lois-Ann Yamanaka's *Blu's Hanging*, Nguyen proposes the concept of a symbolic capital of race. He raises the question of how the material interests of Asian American intellectuals affect their articulations of Asian American identity and their political representations of the group:

Asian American literary critics are part of a larger class of Asian American intellectuals, broadly defined here to include academics, artists, activists, and political leaders. As an intellectual class, we share a certain set of assumptions about the object of our collective work, Asian America. . . . I argue that this consensus can be seen through the work of Asian American literary critics, particularly in the theory of value that literary critics use to assess literature. These critics have been inclined to see Asian American literature as a body of texts that demonstrates opposition to, or accommodation with, the various kinds of oppression that Asian Americans have had to endure.[1]

Nguyen critiques the ways that Asian Americanist critics have tended to evaluate Asian American literature in terms of a reductive binary of resistance or accommodation, and he contends that the literature actually deploys much more flexible strategies than the criticism is willing to admit. Nguyen suggests that the rigidity of Asian American literary criticism stems from the disavowal of its own flexible strategy for institutional survival, which he identifies as "panethnic entrepreneurship."[2] Asian American studies, in other words, has become "an enterprise of panethnic entrepreneurship within academia, reaping the particular and peculiar rewards of academia by using the symbolic capital of race and resistance."[3] On this reading, the ideological predisposition toward oppositionality of Asian American intellectuals serves as a ruse displacing the reality of their own accommodation with academia.

While the notion of a symbolic capital of race is suggestive, it remains undeveloped in Nguyen's argument, which is hampered, I believe, by a somewhat reductive notion of interest. The foregoing account seems to suggest that Asian American intellectuals have some immediate self-interest and accrue material rewards by producing certain political representations of Asian Americans. This may be true in some ways, but if we understand the symbolic capital of race to be caught up in the economy of legitimacy, then we need a more nuanced argument that can factor in the intellectual field's complex exchanges of interest and disinterest, bias and objectivity. Intellectuals certainly do have interests, but these are, for the most part, not material ones, as Nguyen seems to imply. Rather, they are professional interests, or interests dictated by the academic field, that have to do with their position in the educational system and with the institutional structures and operations of that system.

How do we specify what constitutes the symbolic capital of race? What are the conditions of its production? Nguyen posits a fundamental identity between intellectuals, artists, and entrepreneurs. While they all may be seen as pursuing capital, each is concerned with a distinct kind of capital because the fields defining the kinds of capital at stake as well as the rules of competition are quite different. A larger problem is the confusion of commodification with the notion of symbolic capital. Nguyen begins by characterizing race and racial identity as "commodities," and although he also describes race as a form of symbolic capital, the two terms alternate at subsequent points in his text. This slippage of terms signals the lack of a clear conception of capital as well as of the relation between race and capital. Commodification derives from a Marxist theoretical language, whereas the concept of symbolic capital can be apprehended only within a mode of analysis employing Bourdieu's concepts of habitus and field, and it is opposed to the theory of commodification in several important respects.

The principal difference is that Bourdieu's conceptualization of the various forms of capital emphasizes those aspects of social life that revolve around forms of value that cannot be directly reduced to economic value. The Marxist notion of commodification refers to the transformation of social relations into market relations. Although symbolic capital is different from economic capital, it can be converted into economic capital under specific conditions. The concept of symbolic capital, moreover, highlights the relation of symbolic processes to economic processes, especially the specific forms of symbolic violence and domination that can operate independently of economic domination. The generalization of commodification from strictly economic processes to all aspects of social life contradicts Bourdieu's elaboration of modern society as a decentered structure composed of multiple, hierarchically organized, semiautonomous fields that cannot be reduced to the primacy of any one of them. Although he grants priority to the economic field—in that all other fields are still subject to the overall domination of economic forces—Bourdieu argues that the operations of other fields cannot simply be predicted from economic processes but that other fields respond to economic domination according to their own internal dynamics. The shift from commodification to symbolic capital enables a radical displacement of the binary of resistance and accommodation.

Bourdieu proposes that objective social relations are reproduced through the struggles of social agents who "play the game" of capital accumulation. This is not primarily a matter of consciousness or intentionality. One of his postulates is that all actions are motivated by interest, but his elaboration of the various forms of capital expands the notion of interest beyond that of a purely material and narrowly economic one. Indeed, one aim of all of Bourdieu's work is to produce a general theory of the economy of practices capable of articulating the basic principles underlying all the fields constituting the social totality.[4] This expanded notion of interest reflects Bourdieu's desire to break away from all forms of economism while at the same time retaining the capability to explain the forces that motivate social practices and to reject the opposition between interest and disinterest. The latter can thus be seen as the refusal or lack of a particular kind of interest (that is, economic) while being motivated by other sorts of interest. In certain contexts, for example, the refusal to accumulate economic capital can itself be part of the pursuit of symbolic capital, as in the more autonomous fields of cultural production, such as academia. To subscribe to this model of social dynamics requires a radical reformulation of what might constitute resistance.

Symbolic capital, then, can be understood as another name for ideology, which is the power to induce recognition. Louis Althusser's famous example of interpellation is that of the policeman hailing the subject: "Hey, you there!" By turning around, Althusser explains, "he becomes a *subject*. Why? Because he has recognized that the hail was 'really' addressed to him, and that 'it was *really him* who was hailed.'"[5] Interpellation consists first and foremost in the production of recognition and especially, as the emphases signal, in the recognition of what is understood to constitute the "real." Whereas Althusser removes ideology from the domain of consciousness in order to avoid the issue of false consciousness, Bourdieu's theory of capital enables a redefinition of ideology's relation to material interests. Althusser wants to see ideology as arising out of material practices. As he says, "ideas" or "representations" do not have a spiritual but a material existence, which is inscribed in practices governed by the rituals of the ideological apparatus or institution. The question is how one understands the nature of ritual practices and the ways that individuals participate in them. The conception of practice as ritual emphasizes the social or collective aspect of practices that transcend and oppose individual will or agency. Instead of ritual, Bourdieu conceives of ideology as an investment in the game. That is, every field defines a particular set of struggles over a specific capital, and in order to enter a field and join the game, one must subscribe to the implicit rules (or *doxa*) that define the specific capital in the field and so govern the struggles within it. Thus the subject is not simply an effect of ideology but (re)produces ideology by playing the game. In order to "win" the game, subjects must pursue strategies calculated to outmaneuver their competitors within the rules and parameters of the game. It is in negotiating the implicit structure and rules of the field that subjects give rise to ideology within their own "spontaneous" actions.

As I have argued, reflexivity in academic work must investigate the question of interest as the basis of practice. The recognition that representation, especially in the academy, operates in the domain of ideology should lead us to ask how the interests of representatives may or may not be aligned with the interests of those they represent. Political practice in fact constructs in many ways the interests that it represents, since one of the objects of political struggle among representatives is the definition of interests and how best to serve them. The "best" representation is the one that wins the consent of the represented or, we might say, the one that most effectively convinces them of what their interests "actually" are. In the academy, though, since representation is divorced from both consent and the question of practical action, the best representation is judged according to criteria of intellectual legitimacy. But what interests do those criteria serve? For Bourdieu, reflexivity is an essential component of sociological practice, enacted in the attempt to achieve a greater scientific objectivity by accounting for the distortions and errors produced by the methods of academic research itself. In the case of Asian American studies, I would argue, reflexivity must center on the attempt to specify the conditions of possibility for the acquisition and accumulation of the academic capital of representation.

One place for a reflexive cultural or literary studies to begin would be to chart the relationships among the various forms of interested and disinterested judgments made by scholars and critics. A reflexive social science aims at greater objectivity through the "objectification of objectification," an effort to grasp all the factors that may affect or distort the sociologist's construction and analysis of the object. Loïc Wacquant comments that "any adequate science of society must construct theories which contain within themselves a theory of the gap between theory and practice."[6] Inasmuch as Bourdieu's sociology aspires to the status of science, reflexivity tries to account for the distortions introduced by the tools and methods of analysis themselves. In the study of literature, though, reflexivity can mean only the attempt to objectify the position of the literary critic in the academic field in order to establish the difference between those interests impelled by a position in that field (as well as the academic field's structural relation to other fields, especially the political and the economic) and those positions taken in the political field. The question, in other words, is how one's political positions are related to, or inflected by, the strategic interests attached to one's position in the academic field. Thus any attempt to evaluate a politics of culture advocated by any literary or cultural studies must begin with an analysis of the literary field and its position in the larger academic field as well as in the entire structure of fields that constitute the field of power. Indeed, the fact that Asian American studies is engaged in struggles over cultural and political capital means that every political position must also be seen as a strategy of capital accumulation or, more precisely, as a specific strategy for the conversion of political into cultural capital, and vice versa.

One question that confronts us when looking at the history of the Asian American movement is why the accumulation of political capital was not sufficient to constitute the group. In other words, although the Asian American movement was first and foremost a political movement, it also encompassed many organizations that operated in domains other than politics. During the 1960s, racial identity politics took the form of cultural nationalism, or the attempt to create political unity by means of cultural identifications and practices. But as critics have noted, most cultural nationalist movements, including the Asian American movement, displayed a marked disregard for any of the conventional forms of political action.[7] To locate cultural nationalism in a framework of cultural capital would suggest that it engaged in a politics of culture so as to intervene in the production of cultural capital. This conclusion allows us to begin describing the mechanisms of conversion by which the power that is accumulated in one social domain might be translated into another.

It seems clear that the Asian American political project had to transcend the boundaries of the political field, since it was trying to realign symbolic divisions of race operating at the highest level of generality across all fields in the social structure. At the same time, the semiautonomous nature of these fields meant that no single political agenda could function effectively or uniformly in every field, thus requiring that the movement become a decentered conglomeration of varying projects unified by their shared interest in the construction of the Asian American category. If we think of this as the movement's central goal, it clarifies why political capital is insufficient by itself to achieve this end and why it must be supplemented by cultural capital. One way to approach the relation between political and cultural capital is to ask what kinds of cultural capital the movement has produced. Here I will discuss the example of Asian American literature and whether it now constitutes a new form of cultural capital.

Guillory's Cultural Capital *and the Crisis of Literature*

How can racial identity politics affect the system that reproduces the distribution of capital? What are the mechanisms and strategies of conversion that enable culture or cultural capital to affect the political field? I explore these questions in a book that seems to have become a touchstone on questions of identity politics and cultural capital in literature, namely, John Guillory's *Cultural Capital*, which also uses Bourdieu's conceptual tools to examine the "problem of canon formation." Prompted by the "canon wars" of the 1980s, Guillory shifts the terms of the debate from canon formation to literature's status as cultural capital. Guillory argues that both sides of the canon debate fail to recognize the real social conditions governing the crisis of the canon, which is the devaluation of the cultural capital of literature itself. Thus both the right and the left respond to this crisis in mystified fashion. The reactionary defense of Western civilization seeks to restore the value of the canon, while the radical call to dismantle the canon attempts to rescue literature from its outmoded past. Against what Guillory sees as the premise of the canon debates—that the canon is formed by its representative relation to particular social groups—he asserts that changes in the canon respond instead to transformations in class relations and the composition of cultural capital.

Guillory offers a provocative account of canon formation and provides a useful model for examining the development of literature's function as capital which, he asserts, exists as both linguistic capital and symbolic capital. There is a great deal in his wide-ranging discussions that opens up new terrain for further investigation, especially concerning the historical transformations of linguistic capital, but I will focus here on his response to the multicultural critique of the canon. Guillory begins by noting a certain impasse in the canon debates, one that becomes apparent "when the distinction between 'canonical' and 'noncanonical' works is institutionalized in two very different and even contradictory ways: as the canonization of formerly noncanonical works, and as the development of distinct and separate noncanonical programs of study."[8] These two approaches might be said to correspond to the integrationist and separatist strands of American racial politics. The question here is whether they are simply different or are in fact contradictory, as he insists.[9] While I agree with his assertion that both forms of politics derive from certain key assumptions of liberal pluralism and that they could be said to occupy the terrain of a politics of representation, I believe that not only are the integrationist and separatist strategies of curricular revision not contradictory but that they are in fact complementary and conjoined.

According to my analysis, we can, for example, recognize that the division between the canonical and the noncanonical is connected to the attempt to theorize Asian American studies' relation to the community as what I identified in the introduction as "nonrepresentative representation." The (non)canonical status of Asian American literature is tied to the (non)representative politics of Asian American studies as a field in that the former concerns strategies for the accumulation and conservation of cultural capital while the latter is concerned more with political capital. Although it may appear that integrationism and separatism contradict each other because no text can logically be both inside and outside the canon at the same time, I argue that this is not necessarily the case because it is not the same text that appears on the two sides of the divide. The conjunction of integrationist and separatist constructions of minority literature actually names two sides of a mechanism of exchange, between political capital and cultural capital, so that what appears on one side is the political text and what appears on the other side is the literary text.

Is Guillory's insistence on seeing the integrationist and separatist agendas as contradictory simply a logical error? Perhaps, although one might also describe it as ideological, that is, motivated by certain interests or desires. In order to understand what these are, we need to reconstruct the logic by which the book arrives at its conclusion. Guillory opens with the canon debates because they pose the question of the value of literature, and it is in relation to that issue that he situates the logical contradiction between integrationism and separatism. Although Guillory first characterizes them simply as "very different" ways of constructing the field of minority literature, that difference is reconfigured as contradiction by transposing integrationism and separatism into the "canonical" and the "noncanonical," appellations that subtly reinterpret and distort the two tendencies. It is important that they not simply be different but also contradictory because Guillory wants to split them apart so that he can retain the former while rejecting the latter. His primary interest, however, is not in maintaining the value of the canon, or if he strives to protect that value, it is not for the same reasons as those of the conservative defenders of the canon.

One consequence of literature's devaluation as cultural capital is that it exposes the absence of a credible rationale for literary study in the university. If the principal purpose of literary study is to accumulate cultural capital, then all the arguments regarding literature's humanizing or formative functions become suspect, to say the least. In Guillory's view, the canon debates only exacerbated this problem by calling into question the value of literary study. In one especially revealing aside, for example, he states that the multiculturalist critique of the canon means that

> it has become surprisingly difficult to define a progressive political rationale for the teaching of canonical texts. Leaving aside the option of not teaching them at all (an entirely logical alternative, if the teaching of canonical texts actually disseminates hegemonic values), progressively inclined teachers of these texts must reground the politics of their pedagogy on assumptions that are themselves theoretically weak.[10]

It is here that we begin to see why Guillory refuses both sides in the canon debates, although he is more concerned with the left than the right because he believes that the left has made a serious mistake in identifying itself with opposition to the canon, effectively ceding control over the canon to the right. His mission is thus to recuperate the canon for the left.

Why does Guillory simply dismiss the option of not teaching the canon at all, despite his admission that this would be an "entirely logical alternative." Although it would be highly instructive to pursue this line of thought, the reason that it must be left aside is that if the educational system did in fact decide not to teach canonical texts, then the teachers of those texts would simply be out of work. This is the ultimate consequence of the erosion of the rationale for literary study, and it makes clear that what is at stake in *Cultural Capital* is precisely the question of defining "a progressive political rationale for the teaching of canonical texts." Guillory positions himself between the two sides because he is caught in their cross fire as a member of the academic left who is invested in the canon. Beyond merely keeping their jobs, another issue is at stake here, which is that for left literary scholars, in Guillory's view, the canon is the only capital they possess that can be leveraged as a source of political power. In this regard, opponents of the canon are simply ensuring their own powerlessness.

These concerns become most apparent in Guillory's plan to rescue literary studies:

> Were the left/liberal academy to reappropriate the "humanities," that is, to take back the authority to define the cultural capital embodied in its curriculum of study, it would have to devise a rationale for an integrated curriculum of textual/historical study exceeding the laudable objective of affirming cultural diversity. A left rationale for an integrated curriculum would have to present all of the cultural works in that curriculum, whatever their provenance, as a species of cultural capital constitutively different from the capital embodied in technical and professional knowledge. This difference can be defined by the proposition that *everyone* has a right of access to cultural works, to the means of both their production and consumption.[11]

Because this is an academic-political program, it raises a number of intriguing questions, although it stands almost at the opposite end of the spectrum of left politics from the original project of Asian American studies. Guillory's suggestion here seems to be that the academic left should seize control of the means of production (in this case, the canon) in order to universalize the distribution of capital. This is, however, where the problems begin. In order to devise a politics based on the canon, Guillory draws on Antonio Gramsci's conception of the common school, in which the rationale for teaching the canon is not the transmission of "Western culture," a notion that Guillory rightly dismantles. Instead, the rationale pertains to fostering critical thought and democratic governance through a unified program of the reading of historical works.[12]

Although this is an old, and familiar, political rationale for liberal education and the teaching of the humanities, it only goes part of the way toward addressing the question of literary study. First, it would seem to have much less purchase given the ostensible decline of the nation-state in the global economy, but even if we were to grant the importance of political education, the question remains whether that goal would be best achieved (as Guillory clearly believes) by means of the literary canon rather than by some other means. If the canon is not in fact the repository of "Western civilization," then why would a liberal or humanistic education need to be tied to that particular set of texts? For Guillory, the issue has less to do with any specific content (although he continually refers to "canonical" and "noncanonical" texts as if this were a relatively stable distinction) than with the imperative that it must be the *same* set of texts taught in all schools or, in other words, a core curriculum, but one that is unified across all schools rather than simply in each school. Of course, the prospect of reaching anything resembling consensus on a core curriculum at a national level raises the prospect of political conflicts that would dwarf the culture wars, but I will leave this aside, as there are other issues to consider.

It seems more productive to approach the title *Cultural Capital* less as a declaration than as a question. The central issue in the book is not so much the argument that literature *is* cultural capital, which seems almost incontestable, but the question of what it *means* that literature is cultural capital. To those with progressive tendencies, literature's function as cultural capital should be a cause for alarm, given that cultural capital serves to naturalize the reproduction of social inequality by making it seem as if the dominant classes rule because of their superior intelligence or refinement rather than their possession of capital. It is this more thorny issue that troubles Guillory *in both the first and last chapters of his book, leading to his plan to disengage the study of literature from the perpetuation of social inequality. Herein lies the crux of the problem, however, for if literature no longer serves as cultural capital, then what rationale justifies the social expenditure to teach it? This apprehension is the reason, it seems to me, for the oddly contradictory attitude the book displays toward its main thesis, for if we look at the issue from this perspective, should we not welcome, rather than lament, literature's loss of value as cultural capital, since that means it is no longer part of the reproduction of domination?

The main contradiction in this agenda is Guillory's proposal that leftist politics can respond to the problem of cultural capital only by universalizing access to that capital, and he posits the educational system, through the specific instrument of the literary syllabus, as one means of providing that access. What Guillory does not acknowledge is that universalizing access to capital would effectively destroy its value. According to Bourdieu's analysis, almost anything can be capital but only if it is relatively scarce, that is, distributed unequally. The more unequal the distribution is, the greater its value. Guillory's program, then, really amounts to a plan for the destruction of literature as cultural capital, but it is puzzling that he presents it as a program to *conserve* the value of that capital. As he emphasizes several times, Guillory maintains that in order to sustain itself, any curricular intervention must "*reaffirm* the cultural capital" of literary works.[13]

If the canon appears to have nearly evaporated by the end of the first chapter of *Cultural Capital*, the last chapter of the book is devoted to restoring it through a complex and extended effort to recuperate the aesthetic as "aesthetic experience." This goal becomes clear only in the very last pages of the book, where Guillory asks the question that I have highlighted:

> If the status of cultural products as cultural capital is in certain historical circumstances overdetermined by limited access to certain works, or by limited access to the means of consumption, then one might hypothesize that a total democratization of access to cultural products would disarticulate the formation of cultural capital from the class structure and from the markets. In that event, what would constitute cultural capital?[14]

Guillory suggests that the answer to this question can be found in Marx, who posited that with the disappearance of the division of labor, there would no longer be artists but only people who engaged in art, among other activities.[15] Culture in a communist society would then come to approximate the field of restricted production, or production for producers rather than for the market, only universalized to society as a whole rather than restricted to a small sphere. Guillory asserts, however, that "such a condition does not . . . prophesy the disappearance of cultural capital. The universalization of restricted production would rather transform cultural capital into pure 'symbolic distinction.'"[16]

Even with complete equality of access to cultural production, Guillory maintains that cultural producers would still compete for recognition and "would still accumulate cultural capital in the form of 'prestige' or fame."[17] The question is whether pure symbolic distinction would still constitute cultural capital. It is difficult to see, for example, how it could be "capital," strictly speaking, without the structural inequality of the distribution of social resources. This is not merely a semantic question, because it concerns whether an aesthetic experience or judgment can exist independent of the structures of capital. Although I believe that it can, I would not call it capital, for the difference between "distinction" and "capital," we might say, is the difference between relative and universal judgment. It should be apparent that Guillory is a universalist in all things. His insistence that symbolic distinction would still be capital stems from a desire to establish aesthetic experience as a universal ground of judgment that would constitute an alternative source of value for the canon.[18] Aesthetic experience, in other words, would serve as the general equivalent in the cultural sphere in much the same way as money functions as the general equivalent in the economic sphere.

In contrast, it seems to me that aesthetic experience divorced from capital would still entail judgment, but in the absence of material domination those judgments would no longer be subject to a single, universal standard of value, meaning that many divergent criteria and standards would be possible. Although some definitions of literature might gain greater consent than others, this would simply reduce aesthetic value once again to taste or popularity, which would not provide an adequate rationale for literary study without its value as capital. Even if we were to grant the *political* utility of a humanities curriculum in the formation of the citizen-subject, this would offer no basis on which to assess the *aesthetic* qualities of any particular literary text. The singular "canon" can exist only when there is some presumed universal set of aesthetic criteria or standards that would legitimate the claim that canonical texts are manifestly superior to other texts. Is there an aesthetic experience or judgment independent of structures of capital? I would agree that there is, since one can identify numerous forms of cultural production and consumption that are highly developed and to which anyone has free access precisely because *they are not disseminated in the university or the school.*[19] The reason that they are not disseminated in the school is that they are not significant forms of capital.

I have engaged in this rather lengthy analysis because it is only when we perceive the political implications of Guillory's analysis that we can understand how and why he misconstrues the significance of the multicultural critique of the canon. For example, he charges that the politics of multiculturalism is essentially an imaginary politics—that is, a politics of the image—and that multiculturalists conflate aesthetic representation and political representation, which Guillory insists are simply discontinuous.[20] He further declares that multiculturalism ignores the institutional politics of canon formation, concerning itself only with representative images rather than substantive realities:

> Strategies such as the "opening of the canon," or the institution of non-canonical syllabi, repress the fact of reproduction through institutional forms in the belief that social relations are directly acted upon in the classroom. To insist again on what may now seem an obvious point,

the apparatus of stratification by which knowledge is socially distributed—the educational system itself, with its multiple levels of *access*
and procedures of *credentialization*—remains largely untouched by such
programs.[21]

Guillory never specifies the criteria by which he measures institutional
change, but it does not seem quite accurate to say that the educational
system remains "largely untouched" by faculty and programs dealing with
the study of race, gender, and sexuality. Certainly we might debate the
specific effect of such initiatives on the social structure as a whole, but
they definitely have had an impact on the institution, albeit varying across
locations. And they have had a significant effect on the humanities and
especially on literary study. Furthermore, by focusing narrowly on the
canon, Guillory himself decontextualizes the struggles over the canon
from the institutional history of minority efforts to gain entry into the
American university. But if political projects such as canon revision (or
its more notorious cousin, affirmative action) have not achieved the level
of success that some have hoped for in expanding *access* to higher education, my question is what effects the conflicts over the canon might have
had on processes of *credentialization*.

Astute readers of Bourdieu may notice Guillory's repeated emphasis on
the idea of "access" as the main function of the educational system. This
appears in the preceding quotation as well as elsewhere, as in the following passage:

> The system of educational institutions reproduces social relations by dis-
> tributing, and where necessary redistributing, knowledges. . . . The in-
> strumentality of the canon within this system is a function of its status
> as an objectification of the reproduction process, Benjamin's "cultural
> treasure," or Bennett's "legacy," which is inexhaustible because it appears
> to reproduce itself—it is wealth never consumed by consumption. The
> educational apparatus regulates, because it makes possible, access to this
> inheritable treasure.[22]

This gloss on the role of the educational system in social reproduction illustrates some of the ways in which Guillory has chosen to reinterpret key
aspects of Bourdieu's work. First is the characterization of cultural capital as a kind of treasure that is "inheritable" through access to education.

Second, Guillory continually links the notion of "access" to the function of "distribution," as in this pronouncement: "If the current educational institution does indeed . . . reproduce social inequities, it achieves this effect by the unequal distribution of cultural capital."[23]

The unequal distribution of cultural capital is indeed one of the effects of the educational system, but it is not the primary means by which the system reproduces inequality. What Guillory ignores through his emphasis on access and distribution is the process of credentialization as the institutionalization of cultural capital. That is, one of the most important ways that the educational system reproduces social relations is by ratifying or credentializing the cultural capital transmitted largely within the family.[24] Students from families with large amounts of capital progress further in the educational system, legitimating their inherited capital with more advanced degrees, while those with less capital to start with are expelled from the system at earlier stages. Hence the school reproduces the hierarchy of social relations but not principally by limiting or refusing access to cultural capital. Rather, credentialization masks the preexisting inequality of distribution of capital by converting economic capital into cultural capital. Guillory obscures this major aspect of the educational system by his narrow focus on objectified capital (the canon, literature, or knowledge) instead of embodied capital. The reason that Guillory wants to emphasize access over credentialization, I suggest, is that it promotes the illusion of greater agency on the part of the faculty, who now have some actual control over the capital of literature instead of being subordinate to the structures of capital in society as a whole.

The first thing that might be said about the politics of canon revision is that it is fundamentally a materialist politics in that what is included in the canon is taught in classes requiring instructors who generate research and scholarship and consequently attract more students to work on those texts. The struggle to include more works by minority writers in the canon is inseparable from the institutional foundation of classes, programs, and research centers devoted to those groups. It makes no sense, for example, to include in the canon works by writers that are not taught in any classes. While it may be true that the canon has relatively little effect on undergraduate education, the true force of the canon is felt at the graduate level where it plays perhaps the central role in the institutional reproduction of departments of English. After all, every graduate student of literature confronting the academic labor market feels pressure to be able to teach the standard required survey courses whose syllabi are determined most strongly by judgments of what is and is not canonical. Of course, these sorts of struggles over what should be included in the canon are not unique to minority literatures but are the basis of work in literary studies as a whole.

To begin to understand the material politics that motivates the multicultural critiques of the canon, we need to disengage from the discursive or ideological levels of the debates and look instead at the canon's function in credentialization, or the legitimation of inherited cultural capital. Briefly described, it is not the canon itself that serves this function but the relation between the literary text as objectified capital and the means of appropriation of this capital, which is "taste" or appreciation. The canon may not represent or express the values of "Western civilization," but it does constitute the objectified capital of the dominant culture, that is, the culture of the dominant classes. Why is it, for example, that some students simply seem to have an "innate" appreciation for canonical texts while others find them boring or baffling? This reason is the objective correlation between the cultural capital objectified in literary texts and the cultural capital embodied in the subject within the environment of the family. In the U.S. context, it is apparent that racial divisions structure the distribution of capital inequitably, which means that the cultural capital enabling the appropriation of canonical literature belongs overwhelmingly to upper-class whites. While Guillory is certainly right to declare that the canon does not in any straightforward manner express the values or ideology of the dominant classes, cultural capital (as objectified in the canon, among other things) is one of the primary means by which the dominant classes transmit their privilege from one generation to the next.

What happens in the multicultural literature classroom? Opponents of multiculturalism sometimes characterize ethnic studies or other minority studies classes as "feel-good experiences" rather than "rigorous scholarly inquiry." Such charges ironically echo the accusations leveled against the teaching of vernacular literature by those trying to defend the classics— and perhaps there is an analogous scenario of transition here in the history of the educational system. Those who teach multicultural literature are familiar with the way that students often approach it through the notion of "identification," in which their judgment of a literary work hinges primarily on whether or not they can identify with it. The first issue to recognize here is that identification as a mode of appropriation of culture is certainly not confined to minority students, although perhaps it is less apparent in classes treating dominant cultural texts, since students familiar with that literature will also understand that identification is not an acceptable mode of appropriating the text. But what really happens in that vague and mysterious moment that students can designate only by the term *identification*? Ethnic studies scholars often characterize their students' interactions with minority literature as the recognition of a reality that has never been represented aesthetically in the culture valued in the school. This justification, however, is susceptible to Guillory's argument that the culture presented in the texts of minority literature is not the culture of the students. He argues that the school does not reproduce any actually existing culture but that it reproduces only the culture of the school.[25]

This problem is compounded in the case of Asian American literature. What is the culture that these literatures reflect or reproduce? If it is already questionable, for example, the extent to which even a Chinese American literary work can be said to typify Chinese or Chinese American culture, students in Asian American literature classes usually read texts from a variety of Asian ethnic cultures. Indeed, the question that arises again is what constitutes the specificity of Asian American culture? Asian American studies practitioners will respond that the point of such classes is obviously not to validate students' culture or to instill "ethnic pride" but to help them understand American history, social structure, and racial dynamics. The purpose of Asian American studies, in other words, is to transform Asian ethnic students into Asian American subjects, who will, one hopes, become part of the Asian American body politic or "community." How does this happen? Asian American culture does not serve to confirm students' ethnic or cultural identity. Rather, it is the culture through which (through various processes) they "become Asian American," just as the acquisition of the cultural capital of canonical literature is part of the process by which one becomes "American" or "Western" or "white," depending on one's point of view.[26] In Asian American studies, this process is usually understood as one of politicization: to become Asian American is also to espouse a certain Asian American politics. Unfortunately, one of the central problems confronting the field is that the radical politics that was part of its origin is growing increasingly distant from the orientations of students shaped in a very different political climate. While Asian American studies classes still do sometimes produce a sense of pride or purpose, they less often manage to produce the radical politicization that is the implicit goal of much of the pedagogy in the field.

If the purpose of Asian American literary studies is not to transmit a culture but a politics, the problem is that politicization does not necessarily translate into any specific set of political positions. First, there is hardly a uniform politics even among scholars in the field, but when students do become politicized in Asian American studies classes, their politics can span a whole range of positions. The recognition of racial oppression in the history of Asian Americans, for example, does not automatically lead students to the radical politics that many think it should, inasmuch as a variety of possible political responses to racism, from the right to the left are possible.[27] Compounding this indeterminacy are the distinct patterns of racial inequality that affect ethnic groups differently according to their migration and settlement histories. To respond to the institutional conditions of its production, Asian American studies needs to reconceptualize how politicization works. I argue that politicization, or Asian American subject formation, entails not the transmission of any particular politics so much as the transmission of political capital—specifically, the political capital of representation. How else might we account for the sense of "pride" that identification with a symbolic category produces if not that this very action constitutes a transfer of value to the subject from the collective? This transfer operates through a kind of reciprocal recognition: in recognizing the Asian American category, the subject becomes one who is recognized (and who recognizes himself or herself) as a representative of that category.

The formation of a separatist field of Asian American literature derives from its function as the means of retaining and institutionalizing Asian American political capital. The literary canon serves as the primary means for credentializing linguistic capital (that is, the capacity to formulate and manipulate ideas in language or, more important, the ability to elicit consent or belief through speech). But Asian American literature obviously cannot constitute the same kind of capital as the canon; hence, there is no necessary contradiction between integrationist and separatist agendas. In fact, these can be seen as divergent but related strategies of capital accumulation. Given the relative disadvantage of Asian American students who lack the cultural capital of the dominant classes in American society, the formation of Asian American studies in the university is a strategy for accumulating and credentializing another kind of capital. Since credentialization involves converting economic capital into cultural capital, the same process operates in the case of Asian American studies except that it converts political instead of economic capital. Political capital, of course, cannot be directly accumulated in the university. The relation of integrationist to separatist strategies is the means by which the political capital accumulated in the "Asian American" category is converted into the cultural capital of academic credentials.

The establishment of separate minority studies programs and departments means, among other things, that they now constitute a distinct field in the academy, with their own forms of academic capital. Without the institutionalization of minority studies and its alternative capital, there would be little possibility of a critique of the canon arising from within the institution in the first place. Since Guillory does not recognize the possibility of multiple forms of capital circulating within the university, the canon wars must appear to him as contradictory in their very nature. At the same time, minority separatism cannot entirely separate itself from integrationism because new forms of cultural capital cannot be produced *ex nihilo* but can be *converted* only from some other form of capital. We may agree with Guillory that changing the syllabus does not change the institutional structures that reproduce inequality in the distribution of capital, but changing the forms of capital that circulate in the university may in fact have some effect on the reproduction of social structures, although what this might be remains to be established.

Social Space and Categorical Struggles

How are struggles over cultural or academic capital related to political issues in the "community"? From the subjects of representation—Asian American studies faculty—I turn now to the objects of representation by juxtaposing the theoretical paradigm proposed by Kandice Chuh with the model of relational analysis posed by Bourdieu. Citing the controversy over *Blu's Hanging* as her "point of departure because it brings into sharp relief the significant differences too easily elided by the rubric 'Asian American,'"[28] Chuh argues that Asian American studies should reconceive itself as a "subjectless discourse." In proposing a paradigm of "subjectlessness," she intends to "create the conceptual space to prioritize difference by foregrounding the discursive constructedness of subjectivity."[29] I will consider some of the implications of Chuh's proposal because it epitomizes certain conceptual and theoretical problems in recent Asian American literary theory, especially insofar as it uses what I have called the device of *nonrepresentative representation*. Elaborating on her arguments, Chuh declares that subjectlessness, as a conceptual tool, points to the need to manufacture "Asian American" situationally. It serves as the ethical grounds for the political practice of what I would describe as a strategic *anti*-essentialism— as, in other words, the common ethos underwriting the coherency of the field. If we accept a priori that Asian American studies is subjectless, then rather than looking to complete the category "Asian American," to actualize it by such methods as enumerating various components of differences (class, gender, sexuality, religion, and so on), we are positioned to critique the effects of the various configurations of power and knowledge through which the term comes to have meaning.[30]

According to this passage, Asian American studies can be understood as "subjectless" in two senses. First, it takes as its object a category, "Asian American," which is not defined by any normative subject or essential characteristic. Second, given the presumed indeterminacy of its object, Asian American studies itself can operate only in a negative or critical modality. Even though Chuh asserts that the indefinition of the Asian American category must be accepted a priori, her implicit insistence on retaining that category seems to contradict that assertion. What does it mean to define a category by the impossibility of its definition?

There are, of course, different kinds of categories, not all of which require strict definition. On a basic level, Asian American studies has devoted a great deal of attention to demonstrating that the racial category of the Asian (in its various incarnations as the Asiatic, the Oriental, the Malay, and the like) has no logical or empirical basis but serves political functions. From this perspective, Asian Americans exist only in a nominal sense, since they are grouped together according to arbitrary and externally imposed criteria, which are, generally speaking, those of the U.S. state. The invention of the term was part of the Asian American movement's political project to mobilize the group in order to transform it from an arbitrary collection of ethnonational communities into a collective united by common political goals and a common racial identity. In this sense, the Asian American category would be defined only in its "actualization," and it would comprise those individuals who "identify" as Asian American or who subscribe to a substantively defined political agenda. The central problem for Asian American politics, however, has been the large gap between these categories of nominal and self-identified Asian Americans.[31]

We can understand the disparity between those categories—in terms proposed by Bourdieu—as the distance between Asian Americans as a *theoretical* class, that is, a "fictitious regrouping existing only on paper," and a *real* class, "a group that is mobilized for common purposes":

> One moves from class-on-paper to the "real" class only at the price of a political work of mobilization. The "real" class, if it has ever "really" existed, is nothing but the realized class, a result of the struggle of classifications, which is a properly symbolic (and political) struggle to impose a vision of the social world, or, better, a way to construct that world, in perception and in reality, and to construct classes in accordance with which this social world can be divided. The very existence of classes, as everyone knows from his or her own experience, is a stake in a struggle.[32]

What the poststructuralist theorization of difference forgets is that the construction of the Asian American category is necessarily linked to the mobilization of the class of Asian Americans. Identity politics presumes the coincidence of the real class and the theoretical class, so that being Asian American automatically confers a specific consciousness and politics. This is, of course, a problematic assumption, and the demographic changes in the Asian American population have only made it more so. The difficulty arises from the effort to assert the congruence of the two categories. In the face of their disparity, the solution of cultural nationalism was to assert that those individuals who failed to adhere to the Asian American political agenda were not really Asian American; they were either Asian or assimilationists who had been brainwashed by white culture.

The history of Asian American studies as a field has been shaped by an extensive critique of cultural nationalism from a variety of angles: feminist, Marxist, queer, liberal, poststructuralist, and so forth (see chapter 4 for a more extensive discussion of Asian American cultural nationalism). Many of these critiques surprisingly reject identity politics and cultural nationalism even as they seek to retain the latter's conflation of the two categories. The rejection of identity politics meant that the field had to find a new definition of politics, as a result of which its main intellectual project became the effort to produce the theoretical grounds on which one might claim an equivalence between the group of mobilized or self-identified Asian Americans and the group of nominal Asian Americans. There are, however, two different conceptions of political organizing at

work here. One attempts to constitute a group first and then define a politics, while the other defines a politics and then seeks to enlist the group in
that politics. Identity politics, however, erased the irreversibility of these
two processes by insisting that constituting a group and defining a politics
were one and the same.

Although Chuh defines subjectlessness primarily in terms of the opposition of identity and difference, I would argue that the contradiction
expressed in the desire to construe the Asian American category as inde-
terminate responds to other imperatives as well. In the wake of the *Blu's
Hanging* incident, the "crisis of representation" concerns the legitimacy of
the AAAS's representation of Asian Americans. The notion of subjectlessness responds to this crisis not by examining the ways in which particular
instances of representation may fail to adequately reflect the needs and interests of the represented but by questioning the entire apparatus of representation. Despite the various deficiencies of the system of representation,
we need to ask what the theoretical paradigm of subjectlessness offers in
its place. If prioritizing difference is meant to free Asian Americans from
the restrictive limits of identity and subjectivity, it threatens to dissolve
the actual differences among Asian Americans, since it forestalls empirical
investigation in favor of an axiomatic theoretical presumption and thus
does not offer any basis for the comparison and evaluation of differences.
In this way, difference itself is produced as the locus of indeterminacy,
since there is no way to know what particular differences might exist. Not
only does subjectlessness evacuate Asian Americans as subjects with specific socially and historically produced differences, but it also obscures the
subjects who produce the discourse of Asian American studies, thus concealing the interests and motives of those with the authority to determine
the legitimate parameters of Asian American studies.

Chuh's account does not make immediately apparent why subjectlessness must be assumed a priori. If one of her main intentions is to contest
essentialized forms of identity and normative constructions of subjectivity, then I believe that subjectlessness does not go far enough. Casting it as
"the common ethos underwriting the coherency of the field," for example,
demonstrates that while Chuh claims to refuse identity and subjectivity as
such, her theoretical project actually seeks to locate the coherence of the
Asian American category and of Asian American studies in the *political
identity* (or "ethos") of subjectlessness and difference. That is, anti-identitarianism itself becomes the political identity of Asian Americans.[33] This
is the paradigmatic form of nonrepresentative representation, and it is the

gesture that Nguyen critiques when he argues that "Asian American critics have been concerned with the demographic heterogeneity of the Asian
American body politic and not with its *ideological* heterogeneity"[34] While
political identity seems to offer the possibility of an antiessentialist unifying principle, stipulating that a specific politics must be held a priori renders it essentialist because it becomes an ontological presupposition that
ignores the ideological heterogeneity of the Asian American population.[35]

Juxtaposing subjectlessness with Bourdieu's model of relational analysis reveals similarities but also significant discrepancies. A relational understanding of the social world, for example,

> affirms that every "reality" it designates resides in the *mutual exteriority*
> of its composite elements. Apparent, directly visible beings, whether indi-
> viduals or groups, exist and subsist in and through *difference*; that is, they
> occupy *relative positions* in a space of relations which, although invisible
> and always difficult to show empirically, is the most real reality . . . and
> the real principle of the behavior of individuals and groups.[36]

Although this account echoes the terms of Chuh's argument, the two are
opposed in certain fundamental respects. Chuh conceives of the Asian
American category as one that is characterized by "infinite heterogeneity
among its referents" and is "fatally unstable," meaning that any attempt
to construct Asian Americans as an object of knowledge will inevitably
distort and suppress differences.[37] For Bourdieu, in contrast, difference is
the place from which knowledge must begin, that is, in the relatively du-
rable structure of social relations constituted by capital. Bourdieu's project
begins with the precept that the real is relational. A relational mode of
analysis is posed against all forms of substantialist thought that see the
social world as composed of groups and individuals rather than sets of social relations.[38] Bourdieu emphasizes that identities come into being only
through the play of differences constituting the terrain of social space. No
stable or coherent Asian American identity can be defined through logical
abstraction, whether cultural, racial, or political, since identities always are
relational and contingent, defined only in relation to all the other identities or positions that make up the social structure at any given moment.

We can gain further insight into these issues by turning to another account of the politics of difference, that of Iris Marion Young, for whom
such a politics begins with the inability of distributive paradigms to
address certain important forms of injustice. Instead, the politics of

difference derives from a recognition of domination and oppression, terms that open up issues of democratic decision making, division of labor, and culture that are occluded by a distributive paradigm, and they allow for the incorporation of social group difference into discussions of justice. A politics of difference, as Young describes it,

> claims that hegemonic discourses, relations of power, role assignments, and the distribution of benefits assume a particular and restricted set of *ruling norms*, even though they usually present themselves as neutral and universal. The given economic, social, and political arrangements assume that social members and rights bearers either have or ought to have certain capabilities, desires, forms of reasoning, language, values and priorities, or plans of life.[39]

These unacknowledged norms mean that political and legal systems based on principles of formal equality and equal treatment will in fact produce hierarchical relations in which those who do not fit the assumptions are implicitly defined as deviant and thereby are placed at a disadvantage.

In laying out the general framework of her argument, Young emphasizes that it should not be construed as a *theory* of justice because theories attempt to derive principles by abstracting from the particularities of concrete instances. Theory thus "assumes a point of view outside the social context where issues of justice arise, in order to gain a comprehensive view."[40] This perspective, however, leads to a disjunction between theory and practice. That is, if a theory is truly universal and does not presuppose any particular situations, institutions, or practices, then it is too abstract a measure by which to evaluate any actual institutions or practices. In order to be useful in this way, a theory must contain substantive premises about the social context it is evaluating. Against universal theory, Young opposes the model of critical theory as a practice that "presumes that the normative ideals used to criticize a society are rooted in experience of and reflection on that very society, and that norms can come from nowhere else."[41] Accordingly, "difference" generates critical political potential only within and in relation to specific social and historical contexts.

More important to this discussion is Young's response to the paradox of identity and difference for subordinated groups. She reminds us that the affirmation of a positive identity by oppressed groups disrupts the embedded assumptions that universalize the perspectives and experiences of dominant groups. In this regard, the construction of "essentialist" identities can be seen as a response to the dominant culture's denial of difference in what Young calls the *assimilationist ideal*, which refers to "an ideal of justice that defines liberation as the transcendence of group difference."[42] The construction of minority group identities and cultures appears as antiessentialist in that it challenges the universalization of the dominant culture as the invisible norm by asserting the particularities of other cultures and experiences. When examined in terms of internal group differences, however, such group identities can themselves become essentializing by suppressing those differences. This apparent paradox, in which identities are simultaneously essentialist and antiessentialist (already demonstrated by Diana Fuss), can be attributed in a relational analysis to the fact that two different sets of relations are at work: those between the group as a whole and other groups and those among the various components of the group.

The attempt to establish difference itself as the basis of Asian American identity, as I have suggested, seeks to provide a theoretical solution to this paradox, but only by ignoring the relations of power within the group through the evacuation of concrete differences and their redefinition as pure negativity. That is, if everything is equally different from everything else, then no specific difference can be said to have priority. Oddly enough, this seems to mirror the assimilationist ideal in which equal social status means treating everyone as the same. In contrast to the principle of equal treatment, Young asserts that equality of participation and inclusion requires the recognition of group difference as well as, at times, differential treatment for certain groups. She asserts that "a democratic public should provide mechanisms for the effective recognition and representation of the distinct voices and perspectives of those of its constituent groups that are oppressed or disadvantaged."[43] In response to the question of how one might decide which groups warrant specific representation, Young replies,

> No program or set of principles can found a politics, because politics does not have a beginning, an original position. It is always a process in which we are already engaged. Normative principles . . . can serve as proposals in this ongoing political discussion, and means of envisioning alternative institutional forms, but they cannot found a polity.[44]

No theoretical formula or principle can resolve the paradox in which "Asian American" is simultaneously representative and antirepresentative,

identity and difference, because this is fundamentally a political problem. It can be described, analyzed, and evaluated, but it can be resolved
contingently only through public deliberation and, ultimately, political
action. A relational analysis requires giving up the last remnants of essentialism in the effort of constituting a political identity in theory or
a priori. Depending on which set of relations takes precedence at any
given moment, Asian American identity may appear as either identity
or difference, emancipatory or repressive, but both possibilities remain
implicit at every moment, or else disagreements over aims and methods of political action would never arise, as they would always be determined in advance. If the aim of theory is to ensure that Asian American
politics will always be resistant or oppositional (assuming that we even
know what these terms mean), we must heed the words of Stuart Hall
regarding the problem of ideology when he argues that relative openness or indeterminacy "is the only basis of a 'marxism without final
guarantees.' It establishes the *open horizon* of marxist theorizing—deter-
minancy without guaranteed closures."[45]

Identity and Difference in the Politics of Representation

We may get a better sense of what is at stake in linking questions of
identity and difference to representation by looking at a similar line of
argument proposed by Susan Koshy. In an essay examining the debates
in Asian American studies over whether the field should define itself in
national or transnational frames, Koshy concludes with a concise articulation of the questions of identity and difference that we just discussed,
noting that

> the boundary marking of the field is caught up in a perception of com-
> peting needs: the tension between the need for political identity and the
> need to represent the conflicted and heterogeneous formation we call
> "Asian American." These needs are antagonistic to each other only if we
> work from the assumption that there is a "real" Asian American identity
> to which our vocabulary and procedures can be adequated . . . . I would
> contend that "Asian American" offers us a rubric that we cannot not use.
> But our usage of the term should rehearse the catachrestic status of the
> formation. I use the term "catachresis" to indicate that there is no literal
> referent for the rubric "Asian American," and as such, the name is marked

by the limits of its signifying power. It then becomes our responsibility to articulate the inner contradictions of the term and to enunciate its representational inconsistencies and dilemmas.[46]

Koshy's terms raise a number of intriguing questions. What creates these needs, and whose needs are they? Why are they antagonistic, and how does the dissolution of the literal referent of Asian American resolve that antagonism? First, I assert that the need for identity and the need for representation of heterogeneity are not antagonistic but discontinuous. That is, if the need for identity derives from the necessity of political mobilization, the need to represent heterogeneity appears to arise more from intellectual than political concerns. The denial that "Asian American" has a literal referent recognizes that in the absence of its realization by political mobilization, it remains largely a theoretical class, which is indeed a purely fictitious classification characterized by "infinite heterogeneity." There is no real Asian American identity because Asian Americans do not exist as a real class. If this is the case, then "Asian Americans" can be said to exist as a coherent group only in representation.

One explicit goal of theories of difference is to produce strategies of mobilization not constrained by forms of identity, but as valuable as this effort may be, it is not apparent why it entails the denial of referentiality. I contend that this denial stems from the attempt to make the academic field continuous with the political field, especially because we are concerned here with the politics of culture. This is part of what underlies the effort to reconcile identity with difference. Since culture is preeminently the domain of representation, it can claim a political effect for itself most effectively by reducing the political to the domain of representation, which becomes the interface or mechanism of conversion between political and cultural capital. Continuity, however, does not necessarily imply cooperation, for the convertibility of political and cultural capital means that both fields now have a competitive stake in defining the means and rates of conversion. The antagonism of the political and cultural fields, moreover, derives from the opposing principles of legitimacy of their representations.

In the political field, representative legitimacy has largely come to be identified, at least in "democratic" states, with elections, so that legitimate representatives are those capable of mobilizing the group in order to win their votes, or consent.[47] In the academic field, however, the legitimate representation of a group is judged not by the represented themselves (at least in theory) but by the standards and procedures that govern academic research. These two standards of legitimacy contradict each other in that political legitimacy is said to derive from the consent of the people, whereas academic legitimacy is based on the autonomy of the university from popular or external influence. The denial of referentiality issues in part from the critique of political representation and the bases of its legitimacy in consent and accountability. If the group has no real existence, it cannot grant consent to "its" representatives and there is no one to whom the representative must be accountable. While the critique of political representation has a long history, that critique has tended to identify the problem as one of misrepresentation, whereas the denial of the referent rules out the very possibility of misrepresentation.

Without a referent, a representation can no longer be evaluated according to its fidelity or correspondence to an object. Instead, representative legitimacy must be assessed according to abstract ethical and political criteria. These are, however, the standards of the academic field, in which representations are not judged according to their immediate material and utilitarian ends, but to disinterested and objective ideals. In this manner, the critique of representation reaffirms orthodox standards of academic judgment even as it repudiates those standards at the level of explicit discourse. This contradiction becomes evident if we ask how it is possible to "articulate the inner contradictions of the term [Asian American] and to enunciate its representational inconsistencies and dilemmas" without any object or standard of evaluation. Similarly, what grounds the "ethos" of subjectlessness in the absence of the subject and the referent? How is politics possible outside concrete sociohistorical contexts? If it does appear to be possible, at least in theory, it is because politics unwittingly assumes a scholastic perspective toward the political field. This scholastic view, as Bourdieu describes it, "is a very particular point of view on the social world, on language, on any possible object of thought that is made possible by the situation of *skholè*, of leisure, of which the school . . . is a particular form, as an institutionalized situation of studious leisure."[48] It is, in other words, the institutionally produced distance from the object of study that enables scholars to assume an objective and disinterested stance toward the political field. The freedom from the practical imperatives of political mobilization resulting from this position expresses itself in the academic dismissal of group formation in the name of antiessentialism and anti-identitarianism, which is to project the politics and perspectives of the academic field onto others whose lives are shaped by vastly different circumstances.[49]

I believe that these antagonistic needs are not restricted to the academic field but belong to the domain of representation. The represented, after all, have only one need, the need for effective representation of their interests. Antagonism arises for representatives who must construct a more or less unified "identity" to represent the group out of the competing interests of its various factions. The elimination of the Asian American category reveals that what is at stake in this theoretical politics is less the realization of the group than its representation. That is, to constitute the group in representation requires legitimate representatives, and the competition to define legitimate representation structures the antagonistic relation between the political and academic fields. This is the political struggle in which theoretical formulations of "Asian American" as self-deconstructing or pure negativity are intended to be deployed and whose object is to define the form of legitimate representation as *nonrepresentation*. But exactly what does this mean?

Despite the rejection of representation, the retention of the Asian American category, as I have argued, indicates that something is being represented. One must, after all, represent something in order to even refer to any external reality; otherwise, one would have a purely idealist discourse. An obvious model of a completely nonreferential and nonrepresentational discourse is abstract art. By emptying the Asian American category of any substantive content, theories of difference reduce it to pure form, a formal identity. In this way, literary and cultural theory appears to repeat the rejection of representation as the founding gesture of modernist art, the gesture that leads to the autonomization of pure art. In the next chapter, I discuss at greater length the struggles over autonomy in the establishment of the first Asian American studies program at San Francisco State College. As an instance of the universalization of the ideology of the field of cultural production, I simply note that both Chuh and Koshy, following Gayatri Spivak, respond to the dilemmas of identity and representation by converting them into tropes (such as catechresis). Chuh even characterizes the term *Asian American* as "a *metaphor* for racism and resistance" and declares that there is a "literariness" to the term that renders it a kind of "poetry in itself."[50]

In the competition among fields, nonrepresentation resolves the dilemma of the theoretical class by replacing political representation with theoretical and cultural representation. Here, struggles over the political identity of the Asian American category are waged as confrontations among competing constructions of it, which are decided in large part by the capital resources that such constructions are able to mobilize. The question then becomes, what makes one representation more persuasive or effective than another? For example, what really separates a representation based in a putatively essentialist identity politics from one articulating an antiessentialist politics of difference? In the academy, these evaluations are made according to the intellectual legitimacy of categorical definitions, whereas in the political field they pertain to the extent to which a representation can mobilize a constituency. Ultimately, both are very different forms of symbolic capital produced in different fields and functioning in specific ways. While the theory of symbolic capital acknowledges the primacy of the economic by positing that all actions are driven by an interest in capital accumulation, it distinguishes between the material or economic capital that is produced by the economic sphere proper and the myriad forms of symbolic capital on which all other social spheres are based.

Bourdieu describes symbolic capital as "denied capital, recognized as legitimate" and therefore "misrecognized as capital."[51] It is, in other words, economic capital that denies itself as such and thereby converts itself into symbolic value, such as legitimacy, prestige, honor, or charisma. Although the concept of symbolic capital is one of the most complex in Bourdieu's conceptual scheme, I underscore the proposition that every form of legitimation depends on and requires particular forms of denial. We can understand on the most basic level that legitimacy is necessitated only by some fundamental condition of inequality; otherwise, there would be no need to justify any particular state of things. For Bourdieu, the symbolic capital of legitimacy derives from modes of symbolic domination, as in the contrast between a debt and a gift. The first produces "overtly economic obligations imposed by the usurer," while the latter creates "moral obligations and emotional attachments," or overt violence as opposed to symbolic violence.[52]

In the present context, the theory of symbolic capital enables an investigation of the modes of articulation constituting the relative autonomy of the university, somewhat analogous to the "invisible hand of the market." To conceive of legitimacy as symbolic capital is to acknowledge the university's dependence on the economic and political spheres, even as it requires us to think of that relation through the specific mechanism of denial. At stake in the Third World Strike was the question of how political power, or political capital, could convert itself into academic legitimacy in the context of the university. What makes one representation seem more legitimate than another, what enables it to command a certain belief or consent, is essentially the amount of symbolic capital deployed within a representation.[53]

The problem of representation is a problem of symbolic capital, and not of the relation between a representation and the reality that it represents. This shift of perspective also displaces the question of identity. Asian American representation cannot be evaluated in terms of its fidelity or responsibility to a prior "community"—which would be to assume as the preexisting ground of politics what Asian American politics seeks to bring into existence—or with "Asian Americans" but with the Asian American category. The fundamental precondition for anything to be considered Asian American is the very term itself, the category, which is constituted as a field. The Asian American category or field demarcates the space or terrain within which all the articulations or representations of Asian American identity struggle with one another for dominance or legitimacy. It is the construction of the category that transforms heterogeneous Asian subjects into "Asian Americans" proper.

We can now understand why it is necessary for even those critics most committed to an antiessentialist politics of difference to retain the Asian American category. It is precisely because the coherence of the category, its existence as a social fact, derives not from its realization in an Asian American "community" or collectivity but from its accumulated value as a sociopolitical category. The main achievement of the Asian American movement was to create the Asian American category and to turn it into a field. Of course, this process occurred within and against the state, but the category was produced as an object of struggle precisely because it had value, and that is what transformed it into a field. The Asian American field comprises all those who seek to represent Asian Americans, including politicians, bureaucrats, intellectuals, business people, members of various professions, cultural producers, community activists, students, and the like. This field perhaps is more complex than other fields because of its weak institutionalization and also because it encompasses people from so many other fields. Although the Asian American field is not part of those other fields, agents enter it with the specific capital from other fields, and so the Asian American field is the nexus of an enormous number of exchange ratios governing the conversion of different forms of capital into the symbolic capital of racial representation.

In this regard, Asian American studies is simply one subfield in the larger Asian American field, and it competes with agents from other subfields for representational authority over the field as a whole. To return to the "crisis" of Asian American studies, it seems quite clear that this crisis stems in large part from the sense that there now are significant alternative categorizations competing with the Asian American rubric for the same population. Although there have always been alternative categorical projects competing for the same racialized population, this competition appears to have intensified as a result of transformations in the American social structure as well as in the global economy. These alternative categorizations range from larger and more inclusive ones (such as transnational or diasporic identities) to more particular national or ethnic identities, as well as the ways that class, gender, and sexuality cut across those demarcations. In addition, the Asian American field must also compete with "sectarian" movements, such as those of mixed-race people, adoptees, and the secession of Pacific Islanders from the less widely recognized Asian Pacific American or Asian Pacific Islander terms. It seems clear that a major impetus behind Chuh's and others' efforts to account for the differences within the Asian American category is the desire to shore up the imperiled legitimacy of the designation (and thus of those who represent it) in order to ensure that other identities remain subordinated within it.

Theories of difference may engage in negotiations over the group's identity (that is, its needs and interests), but such negotiations take place as contestations among competing factions with alternative representations of the group. The conceptualization of difference not as other identities but as the negation of identity points us to its function within academic discourse, which is that it serves as a means to legitimate specifically academic criteria to evaluate the political. Both identity and difference are code words signaling problems of interest and power. The concept of difference is the means by which the interests driving political action are subsumed within theoretical discourse only to emerge as nonidentity and disinterest. This theoretical discourse is predicated on the opposition between "identity" as the sign of power and material interest, and identity's negation or denial, difference. The denial that constitutes academic knowledge and capital is a more specific version of the denial that is the basis of symbolic capital because the rules governing academic capital are much stricter in regard to the enforcement of objectivity and disinterest. Academic work thus either distances itself from, or tends to view with suspicion, all expressions of material interest, even when these are the overt goals of movements that political work supports. Although these interests may have legitimacy in the political sphere, they must be converted into some form of disinterest in order to acquire legitimacy in the academy.[54]

2

Contradictions in the Emergence of Ethnic Studies

This chapter returns to the founding of ethnic studies at San Francisco State College in order to investigate the competing ideas of autonomy expressed in students' demands and how they shaped the development of the field. My analysis centers on keywords in the student discourse of the time: *autonomy, self-determination, consciousness,* and *relevance.*[1] What did these terms mean to the various actors who used them? How did they function in the discursive framing of events and ideas? I am less interested here in the actual mechanics and history of these programs than in reexamining some of the questions and challenges that they posed to the institutional structures and norms of the American university. Although this history is well known in Asian American studies, I contend that a number of issues were either left unresolved or never explicitly identified in the first place and that returning to these questions may help us evaluate the current and future state of the field. In exploring how *autonomy* became one of the main concepts in students' demands for ethnic studies, I argue that what autonomy meant to the students was almost wholly opposed to what it meant in institutional discourse. It was, however, the openness and ambiguity of the term that made it a key point of articulation in material and ideological struggles over the shape and direction of ethnic studies. Since it could be defined in opposing and contradictory ways, it enabled the appearance of agreement even when there was substantial disagreement, but by the same token, once the Third World Strike was broken, it also facilitated the reversal of the original aims of ethnic studies by bringing it into line with institutional norms.

Besides the question of autonomy, this chapter also investigates the black studies curriculum that was developed in the Experimental College at SF State as an index of ethnic studies' relation to the traditional forms of higher education. Even though the black studies curriculum opposed the regular university curriculum as an instrument of institutionalized racial dominance, black studies courses in fact were nearly a mirror image of a traditional liberal arts curriculum, except that instead of defining itself in terms of "Western culture," it defined itself in terms of black culture. This should certainly provoke some reconsideration of what students were demanding in their slogan of a "relevant education." However students understood what a relevant education meant in theory, what it meant in practice was the transformation of blackness into a form of cultural capital because this was the only way that black studies could be institutionalized *in the university*. Accordingly, I propose a general model for the historical development of "Asian American" identity as a history of capital accumulation. That is, rather than casting it simply in political terms, I suggest that we can understand the emergence of an "Asian American" identity as a political solution necessitated by structural barriers to the accumulation not of material capital but of *cultural* capital.

When it entered the academy, Asian American studies had conflicting political and institutional agendas, which have largely been analyzed in terms promulgated by either cultural nationalism and identity politics or, more recently, theoretical discourses of antiessentialism and the politics of difference. These oppositions designate one's relation to the group, and as I have argued, the debates within these conceptual paradigms seem to have led to certain intellectual and political impasses. This chapter offers instead a different set of terms with which to revisit the struggles that shaped the origins of Asian American studies and ethnic studies as well as the future of these fields. I argue that in order to go beyond dichotomies of identity and difference, we must construct a new paradigm not defined by the boundaries of the group or category but by the relations and strategies of groups or agents with regard to the specific forms of capital and the fields in which they are produced. I identify in the formation of Asian American studies two somewhat discontinuous registers, which I call the *politics of mobilization* and the *politics of representation*. These are correlated with the categories of the real class and the theoretical class discussed in chapter 1, but they do not line up with dichotomies such as those of nationalism and assimilationism, integrationism and separatism, and identity and difference.

Rather than the politics of Asian American identity, mobilization and representation have differing relations to cultural capital as it is located in the university, and specifically to the various institutional mechanisms that sustain the autonomy of the research university. I have defined these terms only schematically because their meaning has less to do with specific agendas or goals than with the shifting, contingent relation between them. That is, although almost any political action might be considered a kind of mobilization—in the sense in which we speak, for example, of voter mobilization in the electoral system—representative politics generally substitutes for, and so displaces, mobilization, or the exercise of political power. One contradiction of representative politics is that it locates the source of its legitimacy in the representation of the people, which means that it must encourage acts that express consent. If mobilization were allowed to proceed too far, however, it would eliminate the need for representation altogether.[2] Thus the two terms do not necessarily define ranges of political positions or possibilities (for example, revolutionary versus reformist). We can see them, rather, as signifying different but related political strategies, necessitated to a certain extent by historical conditions. In other words, once the mass mobilization of the Asian American movement begins to dissipate, its politics must become a representative politics.

In order to develop a more complex and sociohistorically contextualized analysis of the aims and strategies of the Asian American movement, we need to see that the two modes of mobilization and representation do not merely describe separate factions or even moments of the movement. Instead, they are the two poles that defined at its origins the structure of the Asian American field itself and its relation to the university. Ethnic studies at SF State and the University of California at Berkeley did not simply challenge the racial composition of the campuses and the curricula. It also sought to construct institutional forms that were not only radically different from both schools' typical academic units but also were opposed to the academic and bureaucratic norms of the contemporary American university. The challenge posed by ethnic studies programs derived mostly from efforts to democratize the university by redistributing both its material resources and its institutional power. Ethnic studies thus became a dangerous site of heteronomy in the university, whose basis since its emergence as a research university in the late nineteenth century was the principle of faculty autonomy. Subsequently, the field was forced to adapt to the structures of institutional autonomy in order to become capable of exploiting such structures in some ways even as it still challenges them in other ways.

Ethnic Studies and the Struggle for Autonomy
at San Francisco State College

In their assessment of the current state of Asian American studies, Lane Hirabayashi and Marilyn Alquizola argue that "the evolution of the field, its principles and goals, is vitally contingent on safe-guarding its auton- omy."[3] Looking back to the origins of the field, Hirabayashi and Alquizola emphasize that

> the "administration" of the two earliest Asian American studies programs was original and radical, if not revolutionary, in intent and practice. In the late 1960s and early 1970s, a coalition of students, lecturers, and com- munity activists organized and ran the Asian American studies programs at San Francisco State and at the University of California at Berkeley. They collectively controlled all aspects of the studies, from the courses to the overall curriculum, to the hiring and firing of professors and even administrators.[4]

One of Asian American studies' most important and radical challenges to the university was its revolutionary institutional structure. It had an infor- mal, two-tiered system of governance, with a central planning council that oversaw the program and three area planning committees responsible for the curriculum in their areas: Chinese, Filipino, and Japanese American studies.[5] The most striking feature of this institutional arrangement was that it tied program governance to the actual ethnic communities that they were intended to serve. Perhaps most remarkably, both the SF State and UC Berkeley programs included students and community activists on their governing boards. In their analysis of the SF State program, Hira- bayashi and Alquizola observe that "it was precisely the principle of self- determination and self-governance that allowed Asian American studies to set up this arrangement, which *technically violated the standard hier- archical governing process of university departments*, as specified by Uni- versity faculty manuals."[6] Indeed, the principles of self-determination and self-governance—or in the words of another slogan of the times, "commu- nity autonomy"—meant that the program was set up to grant autonomy and control to the community rather than to the faculty.

The crucial point is that the autonomy of ethnic studies was diamet- rically opposed to the autonomy of the university, which is predicated on the ideology of research and faculty self-determination. The original institutional structure of Asian American studies sought to counter the autonomy of an institution that it perceived as participating in the subordination of Asian American communities by creating structures of community control over the first Asian American studies programs. The threat of these programs to the university was that they were essentially sites of heteronomy, that is, of external control over the institution and over the faculty. Clearly, this kind of organizational structure is antithetical in many ways to the norms and standards of the modern research university, but community mobilization enabled it to be set up in this manner and to survive as long as it did. Once this involvement began to evaporate or was distanced by the programs themselves, self-determination also eroded. Hirabayashi and Alquizola chart the shift from mobilization to representation at SF State:

> During the 1980s, a "pan-Asian" Asian American studies agenda emerged, diminishing the importance and role of the ethnic-specific planning groups and courses. Unfortunately, this shift also diminished the original mechanisms designed to insure relevance and accountability. Insofar as there is no specific ethnic community entailed in the concept "Asian American," Asian American faculty at State became both the source that develops and the "community" that evaluates Asian American studies.[7]

This analysis highlights the change from the actual communities directly involved in the academic program to a virtual community existing only in representation. This transformation took place literally as the actual community was removed from the program's governance and replaced by representatives of the community, who were, as Hirabayashi and Alquizola suggest, the faculty themselves. The program thus assumed a representative relation to the Asian American *category* rather than to communities, a transformation that occurred in part through the redefinition of categorical boundaries as the Asian ethnic community was subsumed under the larger panethnic Asian American coalition. While this shift may have been motivated in part by the imperative of institutional autonomy, representation also provided a means for resolving the conflicts between the institutionalizing and anti-institutionalizing tendencies inherent in the construction of Asian American studies.

The Asian American studies programs at SF State and UC Berkeley were formed on an organizational structure that opposed the division of labor presupposed by the structure of representation, a structure premised on the separation of representatives from those who are represented. Implicit in the first Asian American studies programs was an antirepresentational and anti-institutional model that resisted the academic production of pure research (or objective representations) and saw knowledge instead in terms of its immediate utility or applicability to concrete problems. Of course, these did not need to be mutually exclusive options, but it is quite clear that in the ideology of research, the latter is greatly devalued with respect to the former. The dissolution of the boundary between experts and amateurs presented a radical challenge to the strict hierarchies of the university, constructed as they are on principles of professional expertise, the unequal distribution of knowledge and power, and rigid classifications of category and rank. As Hirabayashi and Alquizola illustrate, one of the program's potentially most powerful innovations was its distribution of both material resources and institutional power to the community, a connection that was severed by the exclusion of community members, or nonacademics, from the program's governance. More important, this power was not distributed according to the primary criteria ensuring inequality of access, which is expertise, or the possession of academic credentials. Obviously, this distribution of power struck at the very heart of the academic institution itself, and the institution's response, we could say, was to compel a reconfiguration of power relations as relations of representation. In other words, the program was forced to redefine autonomy as autonomy from the community instead of autonomy from the institution.

As I have contended, mobilization turned to representation with the exclusion of community members (or any nonacademics) from the program's governance, but the simple inclusion of the community in the program was not sufficient to prevent the establishment of relations of representation. Community members on the program board certainly could take on a function of representation in relation to the community if, for example, the positions were elected or if they were chosen for their prominence or status. Other institutional measures would need to be taken in order to obstruct the relations of representation that the institution wanted to impose, if not through the direct exercise of force (as in administrative fiat), then through the gradual attrition of programmatic integrity by the pressure of bureaucratic routinization. Rather than acquiescing to the institutional structures excluding actual Asian Americans and substituting a figurative representation for them, I argue that in contrast, to bring Asian Americans into view, we must work against the relations of representation that keep the community out of the academy. In this way, the question of whether Asian Americans are the "subjects" or "objects" of Asian American studies discourse is obviated, since one of the field's goals might be to enable Asian Americans to become the subjects of their own discourse. The means of achieving this end, however, are not obvious, for it involves more than simply empowering those unable to produce what might be recognized as a discourse of their own.

The founding of Asian American studies is generally attributed to the Third World Liberation Front, but the Third World Strike was organized and led mainly by SF State's Black Students Union (BSU). Accordingly, a closer look at their actions can help clarify the comparatively less documented example of Asian American students. Although they appear to be fairly straightforward, I argue that the strategies used by the students at SF State were overdetermined in complex ways because they were based on abstract ideological concepts such as autonomy and relevance that could be interpreted differently by groups with competing interests and agendas. As many observers have remarked, SF State seemed like one of the least likely places for such an intense student protest, since it was one of the country's most progressive educational institutions. Not only did the student government control a large budget (more than $500,000 in 1967/1968), but they also funded and ran the Experimental College, where students created and taught their own classes. The strike was initially organized and called by the Black Students Union, who recruited other students of color to join them under the banner of the Third World Liberation Front (TWLF). As a prelude to the strike, the BSU submitted ten "nonnegotiable" demands to the university administration, and the TWLF subsequently appended five of its own.

The Ten BSU Demands

1. That all black studies courses being taught through various other departments be immediately made part of the black studies department and that all the instructors in this department receive full-time pay.
2. That Dr. Nathan Hare, chairman of the black studies department, receive a full professorship and a comparable salary according to his qualifications.
3. That there be a Department of Black Studies which will grant a bachelor's degree in black studies; that the black studies department,

the chairman, faculty, and staff have the sole power to hire faculty and control and determine the destiny of its department.

4. That all unused slots for black students from fall 1968 under the Special Admissions Program be filled in spring 1969.
5. That all black students wishing so be admitted in fall 1969.
6. That twenty (20) full-time teaching positions be allocated to the Department of Black Studies.
7. That Dr. Helen Bedesem be replaced from the position of financial aids officer and that a black person be hired to direct it; that Third World people have the power to determine how it will be administered.
8. That no disciplinary action will be administered in any way to any students, workers, teachers, or administrators during and after the strike as a consequence of their participation in the strike.
9. That the California State College trustees not be allowed to dissolve the black programs on or off the San Francisco State College campus.
10. That George Murray maintain his teaching position on campus for the 1968/1969 academic year.

The Five TWLF Demands

1. That a school of ethnic studies for the ethnic groups involved in the Third World be set up with the students in each particular ethnic organization having the authority and control of the hiring and retention of any faculty member, director, and administrator, as well as the curriculum in a specific area study.
2. That fifty (50) faculty positions be appropriated to the School of Ethnic studies, 20 of which would be for the black studies program.
3. That in the spring semester, the college fulfill its commitment to the nonwhite students in admitting those that apply.
4. That in the fall of 1969, all applications of nonwhite students be accepted.
5. That George Murray, and any other faculty person chosen by nonwhite people as their teacher, be retained in their positions.

What has not been fully appreciated, I think, is the astonishing phenomenon of the longest student strike in American history being waged in the name of faculty autonomy. Although the strike is often cited as the origin of black studies, many faculty and administrators at the time were puzzled by the BSU's demands because SF State already had a black studies program, which was approved in 1966 with Nathan Hare hired to be its first chair in 1968. During the entire period before and after the strike, successive administrations reiterated their support for black studies, including even the acting president, S. I. Hayakawa. For the students, though, the issue was less the existence of black studies than it was the state of the program. After his arrival on campus, Hare developed a proposal for a black studies department that was accepted in the spring of 1968 and was working its way through a six-step review process that ultimately required the approval of the trustees. The black studies program at the time existed largely in the Experimental College, along with courses in other departments that were cross listed. The students were frustrated that even though they had been demanding a black studies department since 1967, it still did not exist, and they felt that this was due to hostile elements on campus that were obstructing the approval of the department.

If we look again at the demands of the BSU and the TWLF, we can see a contradiction between them that highlights one of the most interesting elements of the students' demands. Whereas the BSU called for an autonomous black studies department controlled by the faculty, the TWLF's first demand was for a school of ethnic studies in which control would be vested with the *students*. One explanation for this discrepancy is that members of the BSU thought that *they* would constitute the faculty in the department, since they had been teaching the black studies classes in the Experimental College. Ordinarily, of course, student control would be antithetical to faculty control, but it seems that one of the underlying premises of both the BSU's and the TWLF's demands was the dissolution of the distinction between faculty and students, as had happened in the Experimental College. Despite the students' use of the term *autonomous* to describe their aims for both black studies and ethnic studies at SF State, what they intended were actually heteronomous units, in which institutional control would be granted to those outside the institution. Nevertheless, no matter how radical or innovative the educational model of black studies or ethnic studies might aspire to be, both were conceived and remained largely within the usual parameters governing a legitimate academic unit.

This concern with legitimacy is evident in the BSU's efforts to go through normal bureaucratic channels in order to have black studies approved. Jimmy Garrett, a Black Panther and member of the Student Nonviolent Coordinating Committee (SNCC) and the person most often credited with transforming the BSU into a militant organization, recalled that in the beginning, the students wanted to build black studies courses "into the institution of the [Experimental] College; we wanted to fit in with the institution. That is, that's the only way we thought it could live at the time."[8] Even later on, after the students had begun to see the institution itself as racist, the concept of the black studies department still largely reflected the structures and forms of "traditional" departments, even if the content was intended to be entirely different. For example, one of the demands regarding the department was that it be able to grant bachelor's degrees. In his examination of the emergence of black studies, Fabio Rojas argues that "Black Studies' institutionalization shows that movements test cultural boundaries; they do not mimic them, but expand them through hybridization. Social movements expand the 'institutional vocabulary' of a field such as higher education by questioning what is acceptable and extracting compromises between current behavioral norms and the movement's demands."[9] This hybridization can be seen at work in the BSU's articulations of such concepts as legitimacy, power, and autonomy. Its analysis of institutional racism led the group to understand that legitimacy was essentially a form of power.

Hannibal Williams, the only black minister on campus and a community organizer in the Western Addition in San Francisco, traced the roots of this analysis to the involvement of some BSU members in community struggles against urban renewal projects. After protesting through all the normal channels of political grievance, activists finally planted themselves in front of the bulldozers and succeeded not only in expanding lower-income housing but also in gaining commitments to hire more black workers on construction projects. Williams explains that these results were

> only achieved after we had exhausted the process of begging the white man and shining his shoes and kissing his butt and not getting anything for our trouble but political doubletalk. If there's any one single lesson that we learned from this process it is that there is only one alternate kind of power and that's the power of physical confrontation. The white man uses all the other kinds of power to deprive people of the legitimate goals that they are trying to achieve and until there is some exhibition of physical force, we get nowhere in our community because they make monkeys out of us when we have these verbal exchanges with them.[10]

Not only does this account encapsulate an understanding of the variety of forms that power can take, it also clearly identifies one of those forms as linguistic capital, identified here as "political doubletalk," or the capacity to make "monkeys" out of those without equal rhetorical fluency or political savvy.

As evident from the strikers' demands, one of the figures most responsible for the growing political awareness among the black students was George Murray, the Black Panther Party Minister of Education and a graduate student instructor in the English department at SF State whose firing was one of the precipitating causes of the strike. In a speech at Fresno State College, Murray declared: "We maintain that political power comes through the barrel of a gun. And if you want campus autonomy, if the students want to run the college, if the cracker administration don't go for it, then you control it with the gun."[11] According to this account, autonomy rests on the exercise of power—political power to be more precise. If black studies could not be established through ordinary bureaucratic channels, then the BSU would use extraordinary means to achieve that end. This effectively meant, however, that it was attempting to institute a legitimate academic unit by illegitimate means. Although the strike did succeed in founding black studies, the subsequent history of the department illustrates the way in which the reduction of legitimacy to power fails to recognize autonomy as an institutional structure.

The notion of hybridization may illustrate how disparate discourses become intertwined or transformed by political struggles over definition, but it does not tell us much about what happens in specific interactions. In this respect, the model of symbolic capital provides a more powerful analytical tool. In his personal reflections on the strike as a faculty member in the English department, Leo Litwak offers an analysis of the denials underlying the symbolic economy of academic legitimacy, writing that the BSU

> wanted full autonomy for a Black Studies Department, including "the sole power to hire faculty and determine the destiny of its department." They were, in fact, demanding power that no other department on campus possessed. I sympathized with their indictment of the curriculum, which I, too, believed had no inherent logic but merely reflected the aggrandizement over decades of established academic empires. Great efforts had been made to accommodate student needs without sacrificing established power. And these efforts were bound to fall short. . . . The strikers meant

to end this hypocrisy. They intended to impose unity by force. That's one consequence I saw to the call for relevance. Logic and coherence could be achieved by dissolving the vested interests of the separate departments. That would take a revolution.[12]

Litwak regarded relevance as the forceful imposition of unity, logic, and coherence in the university; it was in large part the many conflicting intentions and commitments emanating from different parts of the institution that the students perceived as evidence of its hypocrisy and duplicity. Although they recognized that academic legitimacy was a form of power, their actions seemed to be predicated on the reversibility of that relation, that is, that legitimacy could be instituted through force. In attempting to produce legitimacy by illegitimate means, the protests exposed the denials constituting it, but insofar as they regarded denial as mere hypocrisy, they failed to heed the necessity of denial as the mechanism by which power could convert itself into legitimacy. Autonomy, then, can be described in a basic sense as a function of denial.

Of course, the students did not seek to recreate wholesale the forms of academic legitimacy characteristic of the "traditional" disciplines. But they did seek to have black studies recognized as a legitimate academic subject, because otherwise any degree in the field would be meaningless. One of the limits of political struggle in the university, then, is the necessity of conserving academic legitimacy, since that is the only value specific to it. The students tried to create "unity" in the institution by demolishing the barriers between the university and the community, as well as between the various sectors of the university itself, but in doing so they undermined the very structures that upheld the autonomy they wanted for black studies. As I have argued, power cannot sustain autonomy, only capital can. In this regard, one of the intriguing aspects of the BSU's and TWLF's demands is that for whatever reason, they do not actually state the precondition for the autonomy of either black studies or ethnic studies, which is simply guaranteed and irrevocable funding. Because this was necessary for the autonomy of either unit, one wonders why it was not made explicit. Overtly demanding funding, of course, might have shown how unlikely the demand was to be fulfilled.

As Litwak pointed out, this was power that no other department possessed—at SF State or any other college or university in the United States. It was not simply that SF State's administration did not want to give the students guaranteed funding, as the students thought, or even that the state legislature or Governor Ronald Reagan did not want to give it to them, although this undoubtedly was the case. In fact, permanent funding is something that no *political* entity can guarantee, since the political process is, by its nature, impermanent and contingent. Essentially, what the students wanted was their own independent, endowed college. Somewhat ironically, as radical as this demand may have been, it also harks back to the very origins of higher education in the American colonies.

Although the first colonial colleges were modeled on Oxford and Cambridge, there were some differences between the American colleges and their English prototypes.[13] Oxford and Cambridge consist of a number of privately endowed, relatively autonomous colleges. While the colleges perform teaching and residential functions, it is the "university," or the overarching entity, that has a royal charter to conduct examinations and award degrees. No American institution, in contrast, has ever included more than a single undergraduate college, and they combine instruction with certification. More important, the governing structures of American colleges did not emulate the Oxbridge model but the Scottish and Continental universities, because the American colonists were opposed to the aristocratic insularity and disdain for research and scholarship bred by the autonomy of colleges at Oxford. Rather than faculty control, all the colonial colleges instituted external boards to ensure accountability, a form of governance that has subsequently been copied at nearly every American college and university.[14]

The only institution that possessed anything like the kind of autonomy being demanded for black studies and ethnic studies was the Oxbridge college. One of the reasons that no similar college was ever established in the United States was that there were no patrons with sufficient wealth to provide a large enough endowment until well after the institutional forms of American colleges had already been defined. Without the requisite capital for black studies, the only source of funding was SF State itself. In *College in Crisis: A Report to the National Commission on the Causes and Prevention of Violence*, the San Francisco State Study Team identifies the lack of institutional autonomy as one of the primary factors in the escalation of conflicts leading up to the Third World Strike.[15] The college administration lacked the authority to implement the students' demands and was subject to the power of the trustees and the California state legislature.[16] John Summerskill, president of SF State from 1966 through 1968, complained in his resignation statement about the "political interference and financial starvation" of the state college system, which he attributed to the Reagan administration, and he declared that the "whole system is going to break down if the trustees and politicians are going to hire and fire professors."[17] As the BSU demands make clear, the autonomy of the black studies department was seen as necessary to guarantee the department's freedom from the power of the trustees.

Despite the apparent congruence between the BSU's and the college's demands for autonomy, the two also were opposed because the BSU sought autonomy not simply from the trustees and legislature but also from the college itself. In formulating their demands, the students appropriated legitimate institutional discourse but reversed it so that it signified the opposite, that is, student/community control rather than faculty control. Nevertheless, "autonomy" was used to mean either of these two opposing conceptions, depending on the context in which it was articulated. While this use of autonomy may have been an example of the successful hybridization of discourse, it also joined two antithetical goals with two radically different political agendas. If the aim was in fact to establish an autonomous black studies department based on academic legitimacy, then the best way to accomplish this would have been to strengthen the autonomy of the school itself. But since the students saw themselves and black studies as opposed to the school, the strike ended up eroding the school's autonomy. As a consequence of the strike, the student government lost control of its budget, and a significant amount of power was transferred from SF State's president and administration to the chancellor of the state college system and the board of trustees.

In fact, a large part of the reason why the strike could be so successful in the first place was that the university did not possess much institutional autonomy and was thus subject to political pressure, as much from the chancellor, trustees, and the state legislature as from the students. The Experimental College itself was perhaps the greatest site of heteronomy on campus, which is why it was the incubator for the students' demands. Both Summerskill and his successor, Robert Smith, were sympathetic to the BSU's demands, and both struggled to gain more autonomy in order to implement these demands. The largest obstacles were actually the trustees, state legislators, and Governor Reagan. Summerskill and Smith did resist the students' demands, however, insofar as they sought to institute policies and procedures that were detrimental to campus and faculty autonomy, and in this regard, they were unable to resolve the strike precisely because it was directed, consciously or not, at campus autonomy. Since this was the goal most important to the school administration, it became the immediate target of the students' actions. In contrast, the next president, S. I. Hayakawa, was able to break the strike precisely because he did not care about campus or faculty autonomy. It was not simply that Hayakawa marshaled public opinion on his side or that he was willing to carry out the directives of the chancellor and trustees. It was that he had no qualms about politicizing the campus even more than the students had done. If Summerskill and Smith responded to the students by trying to prevent the intrusion of external political intervention on campus so as to preserve faculty control, Hayakawa's strategy was to deploy even more political power than the students.

In their demands, the students seemed to equate autonomy with control and self-determination, but they failed to grasp the limits imposed on faculty autonomy, which is that they have control over only their own professional activity. I argue that the spontaneous adoption of the concept of autonomy created certain (largely unrecognized) impediments to the future development of ethnic studies and shaped its evolution in ways that need more thorough consideration, a project that this book only begins. In the case of Asian American studies, we can observe that the lack of critical attention to the problematic of autonomy led to certain difficulties, according to the assessment offered by Hirabayashi and Alquizola, who assert that "practitioners of Asian American studies should do everything in their power to win autonomy and self-determination as a basis for reconceptualizing the field."[18] The question that they address is what autonomy and self-determination might mean in the rather different circumstances of the 1990s, as opposed to the 1960s.

Looking back over the history of the field, Hirabayashi and Alquizola attribute the decline of its original counterhegemonic aims primarily to the contradictions of cultural nationalism:

> We propose that the political autonomy that the TWLF demanded was in fact an expression of a theoretical position known as "cultural nationalism." Cultural nationalism entails an "ethnic nationalist ideology" . . . which highlights "unique" cultural traits based on language, history, and values. Ethnic-specificity is thus the hallmark of cultural nationalism, requiring the militant promotion of a unique ethnic identity . . . as well as the prioritization of cultural preservation and "community control."[19]

In particular, Hirabayashi and Alquizola charge cultural nationalism with the turn to service-oriented general education courses in SF State's Asian

American studies program and with the weakening of relevance and accountability as program administrators became increasingly caught up in bureaucratic politics on campus. Although cultural nationalism certainly is implicated in these developments, it seems highly debatable whether it was the main factor in the difficulties confronting the field when, for example, the hostility of many administrators and faculty toward ethnic studies seemed to many to play a much larger part.

In their recommendations for revitalizing the field in accordance with changing historical circumstances, Hirabayashi and Alquizola contend that

> if we do not take the initiative to redefine what Asian American Studies, as an integral part of Ethnic Studies, is and what it involves—if even on a working and provisional basis—universities and their schools, departments and faculties will define these for us. The pursuit and evaluation of what constitutes Asian American Studies should be self-determined by a collective body of Asian American scholars, committed to a range of theoretically informed practices, rather than by distanced practitioners of traditional disciplines.[20]

This passage seems to suggest that the problem with cultural nationalism is not its demand for autonomy but the kind of autonomy it wanted: political autonomy. In contrast, what Hirabayashi and Alquizola advocate is academic autonomy, since what they describe are the basic institutional features of an academic *discipline*. The question of why ethnic studies has refused to define itself as a discipline is one that the next chapter will take up; the issue here concerns what constitutes "self-determination." Although it is not explicitly stated as such, the implication is that the only way for the field to attain autonomy now is by means of academic legitimacy. This necessity appears to underlie the critique of cultural nationalism, but it is curious that they insist on seeing academic autonomy as continuous with "the original vision, curricular focus, and radical organization of Asian American studies" which they believe "are well worth reconsidering today."[21]

One of this book's central questions is whether faculty autonomy is or can be made congruent with the original purposes of the field. Hirabayashi and Alquizola do not explain why it is possible now for Asian American studies to achieve its original aims by means of academic autonomy, since as their own analysis demonstrates, the first programs were set up in opposition to the norms of academic legitimacy. Although the field has largely had to adapt to the forms of faculty autonomy, my question is whether that choice is inevitable or whether it is possible to change the structures of autonomy. In the case of black studies, Rojas remarks that it "achieved a degree of stability by abandoning cultural nationalism and community education. The academic system, for the most part, is not organized around notions of community service. Some academic disciplines, such as public policy, do have public service missions; most do not."[22] Academic disciplines have two basic functions: the production and transmission of knowledge and the certification of expertise. Ethnic studies began with rather different purposes, and Rojas concludes that in the confrontation between political and academic objectives, "community-education abandonment resulted in the embrace of these two principles: black studies programs were pulled toward research and elite training."[23] Or, in other words, the waning of political capital meant that the field was increasingly forced to rely on the accumulation of academic capital.

Culture and Consciousness in the Formation of Black Studies

From the contradictions of autonomy, I turn now to the question of "relevance." One of the most pervasive terms in the discourse of student activism, the demand for relevant education was a constant refrain in the 1960s. But what exactly is a relevant education, and to what is it relevant? The short answer is that it is relevant to the community. As the Reverend A. Cecil Williams described it, the black students wanted

> a program that . . . would be relevant in regards to the educational process by which they could go back to the ghettoes and work with people. . . . They had tried everything that the white man taught them, and we had tried it, and it didn't work. And we were now saying in fact that there are new moods and new tempos and new vibrations that we understand which are not understood in the academic community, and if they're going to be workable they must become a part of the educational process.[24]

Williams encapsulates here the basic narrative in the discourse of relevance and black consciousness. One of the sources of this story, insofar as it concerns the educational system, was Carter G. Woodson's influential book *The Mis-Education of the Negro*. Woodson's argument that the American school system neglected black history and culture and thus taught blacks to accept their inferiority was repeatedly echoed by black activists. The answer to this indoctrination into whiteness was black consciousness.

The first point that must be made about "relevant education" was that it was not "practical" education but that at the same time, it did not seek simply to replicate the "traditional" liberal arts curriculum. In this way, I believe, "relevance" signaled a new strategy regarding black higher education. The first black colleges were established during Reconstruction by northern white benevolent societies and denominational organizations, and black religious groups soon followed, although they had fewer resources and thus could support a smaller number of schools.[25] The common ideology of both groups was that of "racial uplift," whose aim was to produce black leaders capable of guiding their people into full participation in American society. These leaders would essentially mirror their white counterparts, which meant that they would need the same classical liberal education as white elites received. This is the educational program perhaps most closely associated with W. E. B. Du Bois and his call for a Talented Tenth. In the latter decades of the nineteenth century, a competing educational agenda emerged that was spurred by Northern industrial philanthropy and that became identified with the Hampton-Tuskegee program of industrial education. The Northern philanthropic foundations that promoted industrial education had the capital that the religious organizations lacked, but they also tried to impose a much more conservative racial ideology and were opposed to liberal education for blacks because they felt that they needed practical training that would suit the kinds of occupations appropriate to their place in American society.

Relevance thus marks a new direction in black education beyond the debates between liberal culture and industrial education. Black studies emerged in the wake of disillusionment with the limitations of the civil rights movement and the turn to cultural nationalism and black power. The point that I want to emphasize here is that even though it opposed the Eurocentric ideal of liberal culture, black studies as it emerged at SF State was essentially a mirror image of a liberal arts education, especially insofar as cultural nationalism was centered on the construction of a positive black *culture*. The nascent black studies courses developed in the Experimental College began with the Black Arts and Culture Series in 1966 and eventually expanded to cover history, the social sciences, and the humanities. In 1968, the black studies curriculum included "Sociology of Black Oppression," "Modern African Thought and Literature," "Recurrent

Themes in Twentieth Century Afroamerican Thought," three semesters of composition taught by George Murray, psychology classes, and several on the arts.[26]

Black culture opposed liberal culture as its mirror image, identical except reversed, as in a photographic negative. If a liberal education appeared irrelevant to the concerns of the new black students, it was, of course, never intended to be. While relevance was defined in relation to the needs and concerns of the community, liberal culture was intended to distance one from the community in order to mark one's status as a member of the (white) elite. Black cultural nationalism thus redefined distinction as assimilation as explained, for instance, by Hannibal Williams:

> The traditional Uncle Tom, Sam, shoe-shining type Negro that we have had in the past has rushed to the university to get himself a white education. Then he has rushed pellmell from the black community in the same manner that white people have been fleeing to the suburbs, and we think this is the most reprehensible of creatures because he denies his own birthright. It's his brothers and sisters and mothers and fathers from whom he is running.[27]

As much as this may be a critique of the failure of the black middle class to assume responsibility for the problems of poor black communities, it also reflects the frustration over the lack of immediate tangible benefits from the victories of the civil rights movement. The failure of legal equality to produce substantial material equality called into question the integrationist project to accumulate the cultural capital of liberal education. Cultural nationalism provided an alternative project, to construct a new capital of blackness derived from black culture rather than white culture or, in other words, to credentialize blackness as cultural capital. As Williams noted, the new vibes in the community had to become part of the educational process.

The purpose of black studies was to produce community leaders with a black consciousness, and it did so by instilling in them black culture, in very much the same way that liberal education sought to produce an elite by endowing them with classical Western culture. Blackness, then, must be understood as designating a black cultural capital, or a capital of black identity, and authenticity in this context becomes the object of struggles over the authority to define legitimate blackness. This is true primarily, however, of black cultural nationalism as it attempted to institutionalize black culture and identity in black studies programs in the university, and it also helps explain why, as Rojas points out in his survey of black studies programs across the United States, despite the field's origins in teaching colleges such as SF State or Merritt College in Oakland, California, "the degree-granting black studies program is most commonly found in research-intensive institutions" or the ones at the top of the educational hierarchy.[28] As I have argued, black studies exhibited the contradiction of establishing a program with complete autonomy that was also part of the university. Unlike the Black Panthers, who founded their own elementary school in Oakland, or the Nation of Islam, which went even further in constructing an entirely separate, self-contained black community, the black student movement in higher education had to confront the problem of pursuing its political aims in an environment that was hostile to (at the very least) external political influence.

If the logical conclusion of the demand for complete autonomy was to set up a completely separate school, the lack of capital was one reason for the failure to do so. Another reason for insisting on establishing black studies as an autonomous department, however, would be to create in the university a locus for the conversion of political capital into cultural capital, as I argued in the last chapter. That is, blackness in the separatist cultural economy cannot be cultural capital, first because everyone within that economy is black, so it cannot be, by definition, capital unless it concerns incremental degrees of blackness. Second, blackness can become cultural capital only when it enters into circulation with, and is convertible to, other forms of capital. The vicissitudes of the struggle for black studies at SF State illustrate the somewhat circuitous process by which this conversion was effected. It could hardly have been straightforward, since it was not simply a matter of converting one capital into another, but of creating the social and institutional conditions by which the legitimacy of the cultural capital of blackness would be recognized as such, and this was a much more involved and protracted process.

We can see some of the contradictions inherent in this process in a statement made by Ben Stewart, chair of the BSU from 1968 to 1969:

> We see ourselves being basically servants of the community. That is to say, we go to a college campus and we learn academic skills and we see ourselves as returning back to that community to enhance the progress of that community rather than to exploit or misuse it as the traditional Third World lackey, Uncle Tom bootlicker students have done in the past.

Also another thing: we see ourselves as educating our communities to the fact that education is not going to make them free.[29]

There are two competing interpretations of education at work here, signaled most clearly in the final declaration that the black students see themselves as "educating" their community "to the fact that education is not going to make them free." Stewart is apparently referring here to two different kinds of education, black studies as opposed to liberal arts, an opposition echoed in the assertion that the students can bring their academic skills back to the community, even though these skills were evidently imparted by the same education that will not "make them free." The fact that Stewart must use the same term to talk about these two opposing forms of education reveals the contradictory perspectives inscribed in the foundation of black studies and ethnic studies in general.

Since relevant education was opposed to the kinds of "practical" (which usually meant technical or vocational) education that was meant to help the lower classes better themselves, we have to ask how black studies actually prepared students to help the community. The *Black Liberator*, for example, a black radical newspaper in Chicago, published a series of debates on the methods and purposes of black education. In one article, Phil Hardimon responded to the appointments of the first African American presidents in the Chicago city colleges:

The mere fact that these two colleges are now headed by Black men does not at all guarantee immediate relevance in education. Nor does it mean that a new day has dawned for Blacks in Chicago's junior college system. . . . For now, the Presidents and the Black students at Crane and Wilson, by establishing a curriculum which will prepare them to provide technical assistance to the Black community for its development, have the opportunity to delve into the real meaning of Blackness. Only then will the colleges be meaningful to the Black community.[30]

"Technical assistance" to the black community was not in fact what black studies was set up to provide. While activists did address concrete problems in the community, it seems fairly clear that despite the rhetoric, the purpose of black studies was not to train students to provide practical, technical solutions but to impart a particular consciousness ("the real meaning of blackness"). Or perhaps it would be better to say that the two were not in fact separate, meaning that "technical assistance" was in many ways a function of the cultural capital that students could bring to the community.

We can observe this process in one of the first community projects with which the BSU became involved, which was a tutoring program for black children in the Fillmore district in San Francisco. The program was originally created by five SF State students, four white and one black, but the BSU became involved because "they were concerned about what was happening between the tutors and the kids. . . . There were some very destructive things going on—like kids becoming very dependent on white tutors, and they [the tutors] reinforced this, and then when the whites had to leave, they left, and there the kid was, hanging."[31] But when the BSU tried to recruit more black students to tutor, they discovered that "the orientation of the black tutors we were sending was no different from that of the whites."[32] They then began using the Black Arts and Culture Series to develop the black students' consciousness: "Through the experimental college we hoped to reeducate black students who were identifying with the white community. . . . We would then talk about the needs of the black community."[33] Jimmy Garrett later recalled of the tutorial program that

> we had the only solid, concrete program, cultural program, on the campus. . . . What we had done, we had not only taught children how to read, we had . . . given them such a base of understanding that when they went back they had enough confidence to read what they wanted to read. . . . None of the programs were revolutionary programs, although they were designed to build black consciousness.[34]

Literacy in itself is of little value without the consciousness—that is, the knowledge and the conceptual frameworks—that enables one to understand the significance of what one is reading, as well as the confidence to use these skills. In this context, though, of a radically uneven distribution of knowledge, it inevitably becomes a form of capital. There is no purely "technical assistance" apart from the cultural capital, or the "meaning," of blackness.

Juxtaposing Garrett's comments with a statement from an anonymous participant in the Third World Strike makes these contradictions more concrete. When asked what he thought the ideal educational system would be, he replied,

Let me take that in the perspective of a Latin American. It would have in it the realities of how they came to exist in this society. That is it would include in it the realities of the condition of our people."

For example, if we had a course in the economics of the Mission District, if we wanted to talk about the 42-year-old, we would get a 42-year-old Puerto Rican or Mexican to teach that, because he knows it. He lives it. It is his life. We are not talking about getting someone who studied a book which is an abstract of that book, so you are twice removed from reality.

What we are talking about in essence is really revolutionizing the whole concept of education. By that I mean that we are talking about dealing with reality, by living reality, by being in contact with reality, rather than by studying it.[35]

These remarks reveal a fascinating theory of education that speaks to certain popular (mis)conceptions about the function of education and the significance of the diploma. This is, we might say, the degree zero of relevance. These comments collapse not only the physical distance between the school and community but also the conceptual distance that enables scholarly reflection. What would education look like, after all, if it consisted simply of "living reality"? Why would anyone need to go to school? As this statement demonstrates, "relevant" education tends to destroy autonomy in that it seeks to eliminate the separation between the academy and society. But at the same time, in seeking to establish black studies in the university, the student movement worked to sustain the university, if only because the existence of black studies came to depend on the existence of the university. These two tendencies correlate to heteronomy and autonomy, and as I have demonstrated, the students' demand for departmental autonomy for black studies could be interpreted to mean either one. The main issue was who would wield power in the department: students and community members or faculty?

In its most expansive definition, Bourdieu's conception of cultural capital encompasses all forms of knowledge or information; it is not limited to aesthetic production but also includes scientific or technical knowledge.[36] The question is what relation autonomy bears to the production of knowledge as cultural capital. The activists' attempt to redistribute knowledge back to the community outside normal institutional processes tended to erode the value of any knowledge as capital. At the same time, the movement for ethnic studies also emerged as a response to the disparity in the cultural capital that minority students had in comparison with whites. The establishment of ethnic studies would provide an alternative to the accumulation of Euro-American cultural capital by credentializing the culture of minority students instead. The objective contradiction in the student movements lay in the opposing tendencies to either "democratize" education and engage in the redistribution of knowledge and skills, or to institutionalize ethnic studies in the university, which required establishing it as a site for accumulating cultural capital. These two strategies, however, seem to correspond to the amount and kind of capital that students possessed. That is, democratization as a strategy for the destruction of cultural capital would appeal to students who lacked inherited capital and so would always remain at a disadvantage in the university, whereas those who already possessed some capital would try to enhance their competitive advantage by maximizing their strategies of accumulation.

Revising the History of "Asian America": Strategies of Capital Accumulation

We can elaborate on the foregoing analysis of cultural capital by returning to the Third World Strike in order to rethink what it sought to achieve as a political-institutional project. Specifically, why was the university the principal target of political activism? If the Asian American movement was not concerned with formal politics, it was concerned with the educational institution, since the establishment of Asian American studies is often cited as one of the movement's major accomplishments. Partly this was a matter of historical circumstance, since the Third World Strike was led by black activists, not Asian Americans.[37] Recognizing this fact, however, only pushes the question back, requiring us to situate the Third World Strike in the evolution of racial struggles during the twentieth century. To answer this question, we first need to ask what the goal of institutional transformation in the educational system was. One frequently given answer was to expand access, but this raises certain questions about what it meant for minority students to gain access for other minority students. The logic of the market, after all, dictates that expanding access to higher education results in a general devaluation of degrees. How do we understand the impulse to increase the numbers of students of color in the university? This is not to say that student activists' political commitments can be entirely reduced to economic interests, even in a symbolic sense. It is, however, to ask whether a purely voluntarist account can adequately capture the complex determinations motivating those impulses.

Bourdieu's analysis of the crises of 1968 in the French university is relevant here, despite major differences of social and institutional context, because it points to the general structural contradictions produced in educational systems at the time by related processes of social and economic transformation.[38] Specifically, access to public education in many industrialized nations expanded exponentially owing to the sustained economic growth after World War II, but the entry of new populations into the educational system also resulted in the general devaluation of educational credentials because more workers in the labor market now had formerly scarce credentials and also because those credentials were attached to workers who had less inherited capital. In the American university in the 1960s, these factors were compounded by the fact that students of color who earned a university degree would have discovered the relatively lower value of their degrees in a social context in which they lacked the dominant cultural capital of Western culture. What strategies did these students use to contest their marginalization within the institution? In this context, the rhetoric of inclusion and access recasts in more general terms the struggle waged against the institution for the greater inclusion—that is, the equal value of credentials—of the minority students already in the university.

The establishment of Asian American studies was in many ways the project of an emergent native generation who entered college as part of the group's struggle to acquire educational credentials. Believing in the ideological representation of the educational system as based on merit and hard work, they soon discovered that inequality was structured into the game in mysterious and invisible ways. The name that they gave to this phenomenon was *institutional racism*, but many of its effects can be attributed to the processes that Bourdieu describes as producing the credentialization of inherited cultural capital. These students were forced to seek strategies outside or against the system in order to achieve the same conversion rates for their capital as had the traditional clients of the system from the dominant classes. We might say that they were caught between an older and a newer mode of reproduction of the system, between the reproduction of the older dominant classes and the production of new sectors of the labor force. The project of institutional transformation, then, reflects an understanding that discrepancies of outcome were not simply the result of overt discrimination or unequal treatment but were also inscribed in the neutral, bureaucratic norms of the institution and hence could not be overturned without destroying significant parts of the institution. Needless to say, this was not a goal that could be attained.

I have argued that one way to understand the formation of Asian American studies is as an attempt to establish an institutional mechanism to convert political capital into cultural capital. This cultural capital, while not exclusive to Asian Americans, tended to be restricted to Asian Americans by the logic of race, hence the investment in racial identity. One implication of this argument is that the construction of the Asian American category itself is part of a larger collective project aimed at accumulating cultural capital. This thesis may seem somewhat surprising, given the explicitly political orientation of the Asian American movement. Why would the primary goal not be political capital? As I have already noted, the movement's relative neglect of formal politics indicates that the acquisition of *political* capital per se does not appear to have been the most immediate goal. Or to put it another way, the movement's strategies might have been dictated by the realization that the acquisition of political capital was not a goal that could be pursued directly, given the numerous disadvantages Asian Americans confronted in the American political system.

The relation between culture and politics has typically been understood as flowing largely in one direction; that is, the goal of Asian American cultural production was to produce a collective identity that would foster political unity. Debates about the role of culture in the Asian American movement consequently have tended to revolve around how culture might best serve the movement, with opposing sides advocating either an autonomous culture or a politicized culture. The underlying assumption has always been the subordination of culture to politics. My analysis overturns the hierarchy of this relation. That is, I have already argued that political stances need to be seen as particular strategies of conversion for political and cultural capital. Since these both are forms of symbolic capital, the crucial question has to do with the structure of relations between them that defines a particular mode of reproduction of inequality. Neither form of capital can be assigned priority in advance, since the very nature of identity politics consists essentially in the specific strategies for converting material and symbolic capital engaged in by different fractions of the Asian American movement in concrete sociohistorical conjunctures.

In their theory of racial formation, Omi and Winant suggest that racialization in the United States underwent a dramatic shift in the 1950s from a structure of racial domination to one of racial hegemony as a result of the civil rights movement and its achievement of formal political and legal equality. I contend that one effect of this transition was that the balance of the means of reproduction of social inequality swung from the public sphere to the private sphere. Although racial inequality was no longer enforced by state institutions that determined more or less directly the distribution of material capital, the mechanisms of reproduction of inequality that operated outside the political domain were left largely intact. Indeed, they came to assume a greater prominence in the reproduction of inequality, which henceforth operated more and more in the domain of culture through the unequal distribution of symbolic capital. The "new social movements" can be seen as marking this transition as they responded to the new configurations of domination resulting from the displacement of the center of social reproduction.

The movement from the "old left" to the "new left" follows a trajectory from the politics of material capital and the domains most closely associated with it, politics and economics, to a politics of symbolic capital and the forms of inequality located in the realms of social life that fall in the domain of culture. In this new dispensation, for example, instead of exclusion from politics, minorities remain subordinated in politics, as they had no representative legitimacy. Similarly, their marginalization in the educational system is no longer ascribed to inherent failings of race but to cultural defects often attributed to environmental factors. Both these explanations simultaneously point to and mask the underlying problem, which is the lack of symbolic capital. Moreover, we must recall that the power to constitute the group is the exemplary form of symbolic power, which suggests that group formation requires a certain minimal amount of capital.

If we see the history of Asian American politics as a history of capital accumulation, then we may postulate that the Asian American category itself was formed when a certain threshold of capital in the group (although it had not yet been constituted as one) was reached. During the period of racial domination, members of the minority group had little access to material capital, although a few managed to acquire a significant amount. The achievement of formal equality and the shift to racial hegemony opened avenues to material capital for a relatively larger proportion of the minority population. Even with the accumulation of some material capital, however, minorities discovered that they still were at a disadvantage in the struggle to retain their resources and transmit them to subsequent generations. This problem derived from the lack of established mechanisms to convert material capital into symbolic capital, which is the basis of the power to change the symbolic divisions of the social order affecting the structure of distribution of capital. One essential function of cultural capital, according to Bourdieu, is to enable the disguised transmission of capital in situations in which it cannot be easily transferred in its material form. When minority holders of capital seek to employ the mechanisms of that transmission, they find that the ratios of conversion of their cultural capital are much lower than for members of the dominant culture, thus devaluing their capital holdings and imposing a penalty that effectively is a hidden tax that redistributes their capital back to the dominant classes.

The establishment of ethnic studies in the university can be understood as an attempt by the holders of capital to equalize the conversion ratios of material to cultural capital and to remedy the disparities in the credentialization of inherited capital. The school system functions to credentialize the cultural capital of the dominant class, or the dominant culture, which means that those who lack this capital and culture enter the educational system already at varying degrees of disadvantage. What kinds of strategies can be used to contest this hidden inequality? The dominant culture seeks to impose assimilation on minorities because it consigns them to competing for a dominant cultural capital they will never fully command. Assimilation reaches its limit in the disparity between cultural capital that is inherited and cultural capital that is acquired in the school. The former has a greater value than the latter, and these two forms of capital can be distinguished by those who have the means of recognition, a discrimination that is socially reinforced by the racial essentialization of culture (that is, cultural capital is the inheritance of those belonging to the dominant culture, or Europeans). Moreover, assimilation exposes the contradictions in the dominant ideology of individualism. For minorities, assimilation can be only an individual strategy, as it compels the renunciation of any nondominant cultures or identities (meaning the rejection of ethnic community). Minorities who compete as individuals, however, are at an inherent disadvantage, since the construction of a dominant culture in the racialized social structure of the United States constitutes a *collective strategy* for the production and accumulation of cultural capital that disproportionately benefits whites. Guillory's plan for the democratization of the school offers a sophisticated rationale for an assimilationist curriculum, but one that also reveals its deficiencies.

In response to the collective nature of cultural capital as a structure of domination, minority cultural nationalism is a collective effort to produce an alternative culture and cultural capital. Ethnic studies and other minority studies programs are the concrete institutional results of these efforts. Asian American studies credentializes the capital of representation, which exists in two interconnected forms, political and cultural. Since the school credentializes the cultural capital inherited by members of the dominant class, one way to contest this process is to find ways to credentialize the culture that minority students do possess. As one might expect, though, this seems much easier than it actually is, given that the separatist dream of an entirely autonomous ethnic economy is basically unfeasible. In other words, one cannot simply produce an alternative symbolic economy out of good political intentions. Nevertheless, this is the goal to which cultural nationalism aspires. Among other things, the credentialization of a minority cultural capital means producing a "culture" that can be assimilated to the needs and demands of an academic curriculum, which means that it must be largely formalized and abstracted from the actual concrete cultures of various segments of the minority group. Since Asian Americans, for example, are a racial group that has no cultural identity, Asian American culture results from an act of invention. Thus it would seem that the corresponding embodied cultural capital is only now, after one or two generations, taking shape in a transmissible form.

In the absence of a more or less coherent mass movement, what endows the Asian American category with a socially recognized reality is not an identity, culture, or politics but capital. It is this capital that enables the creation of an identity, culture, or politics, not the reverse, and it derives from those who claim membership in the group. Bourdieu observes that "the profits which accrue from membership in a group are the basis of the solidarity which makes them possible."[39] Indeed, claiming membership in the group is the principal investment because it implies a commitment of one's individual capital and labor to the group's goals and interests. Depending on the size and nature of the group, membership also has a multiplier effect on the value of each member's capital. If assimilation restricts minorities to individual strategies of capital accumulation and limits the convertibility of material to symbolic capital, the formation of a group answers both problems. Even though the Asian American category contains both material and symbolic capital, its existence is predicated on symbolic capital. While purely material capital commands social labor power, it has only a limited effect on symbolic struggles and is confined largely to the individual level. Because a group requires symbolic power, the denial of this power is a means of obstructing group formation.

When asking how symbolic capital is retained or perpetuated, we can see that identity, culture, and politics are the embodied forms of Asian American symbolic capital, the symbolic structures that shape perceptions of social reality and produce the forms of recognition that legitimate the Asian American category and its capital. The effort to contest the disparity of convertibility from material to symbolic capital leads individual agents to separatist strategies of group formation. The group or collectivity thus serves as the primary mechanism for producing an oppositional symbolic capital in both its political and cultural forms. That is, the group becomes the means by which individuals can remedy some of their deficiencies in the competition to retain their social position and capital holdings. Because it is formed from its capital, the group is defined by certain parameters and categorical boundaries that produce the structure of a field. But how does the group or field become a space of capital accumulation? The main precondition of capital accumulation obviously is that the capital not be dispersed. This was the source of the conflicts in the first Asian American studies programs, as we saw in the last chapter. Capital is accumulated when more of it comes in than goes out, which means that access to it must be limited. The primary function of an Asian American identity, then, is to enable capital accumulation by restricting the number of members of the group who have access to the capital that the field contains.[40] Earlier I described the specific capital of the Asian American field as the capital of representation, whose embodied form is the capability to recognize someone or something as Asian American and, perhaps more important, to perform the reverse operation, that is, to recognize someone or something as *not* Asian American. Of course, this recognition is not actually based on the object's qualities or features but is the recognition of the object's Asian American cultural capital. Put another way, a particular feature is defined as Asian American *not* because of some essential quality it contains but whether it has been qualified as Asian American by those with the power to legitimate those designations. Thus an object that is "really" Asian American under one schema of legitimation may not be so under another.

The theory that the current crisis of representation stems from the heterogeneity of the Asian American population is based on the notion that the Asian American category cannot be represented as a unified group. There is, in other words, no single interest or political agenda capable of uniting the diversity of Asian Americans, which would certainly seem to be the case given the large deviation between nominal Asian Americans and self-identified Asian Americans. I have argued that what unites all Asian Americans is an interest in the capital contained in the Asian American field, but this is true only of those who identify—that is, seek membership in—the group. What accounts for the disparity between the two groups? We might speculate that one major difference is class. Since the capital at stake in the Asian American field is predominantly the symbolic capital of representation, a minimum level of capital resources are required to enter the competition to become a legitimate representative of the Asian American category. We must constantly keep in mind that the foregoing analysis applies mostly to Asian Americans who have some capital and are thus in a position to play the game of representation. This suggests that for Asian Americans, class division also is expressed in the opposition between material capital and symbolic capital, which allows us to explain one of the differences between self-identified and nominal Asian Americans. Although they both are concerned with material capital (albeit with differing interests and priorities, as in, for example, struggles over the minimum wage versus the glass ceiling), it is mainly those who already have material capital and are looking for ways to retain it or new avenues of profit who have an interest in struggles over symbolic capital.

Representation and Resistance

The difference between self-identified Asian Americans and nominal Asian Americans, I suggest, corresponds to the division between representatives and the represented. To identify as Asian American is to want to be recognized as a legitimate representative of the Asian American group and to thus gain access to its symbolic capital of representation. But without official mechanisms of delegation, such as elections, how does one become a representative? What might constitute consent to representation? Elections simply ratify the unequal distribution of capital and power, legitimating the rule of the dominant classes, but they at least provide a means for selecting representatives and enforcing a minimal degree of accountability. Without any institutionalized means for choosing representatives or expressing consent, the question of who is a legitimate representative of Asian Americans becomes a struggle among the various competing constituents of the category, as well as those construed as outside the category but who also seek to represent the group in various capacities. These struggles are complicated by the negotiations and transactions between those representatives who are anointed by the institutions of the dominant culture and those who have or claim to have some actual constituency in an Asian American community.

The question of identification is extremely difficult to quantify, since identity is contextual and shifting. Although I have described the discontinuity between the two groups of nominal and self-identified Asian Americans as more or less clearly defined, the division between them is obviously more amorphous and fluid than that. Nevertheless, statistics offer some insight into the degrees and kinds of identification of the Asian American population. Lien, Conway, and Wong offer a complex analysis of the various factors that might be presumed to contribute to identity formation for Asian Americans.[41] I am not concerned here with the details of their analysis but with one of the general findings of their study. In seeking answers to how Asian Americans identify themselves, the survey asked the respondents three questions. When asked to identify themselves as American, Asian American, Asian, ethnic American or by their Asian ethnicity, about a third chose to identify either as ethnic American or by ethnicity alone, whereas only one-sixth of the respondents chose the Asian American identity. This rather small percentage may actually be even lower, since a subsequent question asked the respondents to rate how often they thought of themselves as Asian American, with four in ten replying either not often or not sure.

What is intriguing but difficult to determine from the survey is what accounts for the difference between identifying oneself first as Asian American *before* one's national or ethnic identity, as opposed to only secondarily or occasionally. The small numbers of the former underscore just how artificial, or unnaturalized, Asian American identity is. As opposed to the highly institutionalized but also highly diversified mechanisms that inculcate national or ethnic identities, the institutions that produce Asian American identity are narrow, informal, and irregular. In fact, those who do identify as Asian American first very likely work in some occupation that requires them to continually think of themselves in that way, such as in certain professions, branches of government, the nonprofit or social services sector, or academia. These occupations require a continuing consciousness of one's relation to the Asian American category because they typically involve interacting with Asian American clients or acting on behalf of Asian Americans as a representative. In contrast, the larger proportion of the population who only sometimes or secondarily think of themselves as Asian American could be construed as those who have "given their consent" to representation in the abstract, while the remaining portion are those who have not consented.

For Asian Americans, it is not the represented who choose the representatives but the representatives who choose one another and themselves, through a process of mutual recognition and contestation. In other words, anyone can declare himself or herself to be an Asian American and thus a representative, but that person becomes a representative only when recognized as such. This recognition typically takes the form of identifying someone as either an ally or an opponent in the struggle over representative legitimacy, for disputing one's claim as a representative also implies recognition that one is in the game and must be taken seriously. The indeterminacy of this situation is compounded for those outside the game who lack the means of recognition and are therefore incapable of distinguishing among various claims to representative status. They are thus reduced to accepting all claims unless they are contradicted by someone else whom they perceive as more legitimate. In fact, almost the only way that one can be refused as a representative is to be ignored altogether. Those who seek to represent Asian Americans in the political field, even if only informally, at least confront the possibility that those they represent may protest or otherwise voice dissatisfaction with their representations. This is much less likely to happen in regard to representations in the cultural field, such as aesthetic or academic representations, since the autonomy of those fields is institutionally secured, hence the interest and importance of political protests in the cultural arena.

Autonomy in the cultural arena creates a relatively protected space for critique and opposition, but it also sustains culture's function as capital in facilitating the reproduction of social inequality. Since minority culture does not benefit from the protective apparatuses of the dominant culture, the political and ideological dimensions of cultural production are more visible, and the denial of autonomy is one of the means by which the dominant culture keeps minority cultural production subordinate, although that very subordination provokes resistance and a tendency to identify with the dominated. Moreover, once identity is constituted as cultural capital, it becomes self-perpetuating because representatives will now have a vested interest in retaining and expanding the capital of the field. The fact that it is capital, however, also means that there will be an opposing interest, to exclude those who do not belong in the field in order to restrict the number of claims to a share in its profits.

In the debates over race and class among certain segments of the academic left and, to some extent, in the public sphere more generally in American society, there are no doubt those who will see my analysis as further proof that racial politics does not pose any challenge to capitalism, in contrast to a truly oppositional class-based politics. While certain aspects of my argument may seem to support such a contention, I would emphasize that in most cases, the question of what a true "class politics" might actually be remains more a theoretical rather than a practical notion. Moreover, such a class critique (like Guillory's) would have to contend with Bourdieu's attempt to elaborate a general economy of practices. Bourdieu seeks to explicate the many forms of "interested" economic activity that cannot be subsumed by the structures and mechanisms of the capitalist market. His interest in culture stems from the ways in which culture has been conceived as outside or opposed to the market, even though it is marked by all sorts of calculations and strategic maneuvers, hence the generalized notion of capital. In examining the "economic" calculations that motivate all human activity, Bourdieu elaborates a general economy that sees the specific economics of capitalism simply as one instance of a larger and older economy of human societies. Those who see the kind of racial politics that I have described here as evidence of complicity with capitalism must confront this larger question of the general economy, since it can also be said that some forms of calculation and interest are opposed to the kinds of economic activity specific to capitalism. This is the basis of the antagonism between the holders of cultural capital and the owners of material capital. For example, just as those who have educational credentials but little inherited cultural capital struggle to increase the value of the former, they also tend to expand the autonomy of the educational system at the expense of the dominant class's control over it. Whether such activities can properly be said to "resist" or "subvert" capitalism is a question that I will leave for another occasion.

Bourdieu is frequently criticized for the way that he conceives of resistance and domination. In his critique of minority separatism, Guillory introduces Bourdieu's skepticism of those strategies of the dominated that seek to reclaim the very identities and qualities by which they have been dominated, as exemplified by the slogan "Black Is Beautiful." Bourdieu does not deny that there is always some measure of resistance among the dominated, but he often cites working-class opposition to the school system manifested by truancy and delinquency as an example of how resistance often means simply that one excludes oneself from the system, thereby confirming its operation and producing the intended result nevertheless.[42] At the same time, Bourdieu acknowledges that "to accept assimilation by adopting school culture amounts to being coopted by the institution. The dominated are very often condemned to such dilemmas, to choices between two solutions which, each from a certain standpoint, are equally bad ones."[43] This is perhaps the greatest contrast between Bourdieu's work and the tradition of British cultural studies, since there are otherwise a number of resonances and connections between them.[44]

Bourdieu seems to me to suggest not that those with no capital are incapable of resistance but that the effectiveness of political action increases with the amount of the actors' capital, including technical and organizational skills. In this respect, he tends to privilege the institutional and organizational aspects of political movements, whereas theorists of subaltern politics have argued that it is precisely the recalcitrance of popular movements to rational and bureaucratic forms of organization that make them effective in opposing the expansion of capitalist modernity.[45] Bourdieu has always espoused the creation of autonomous institutions as one of the most valuable legacies of the modern world, and his vision of the most effective role that intellectuals can play in political movements is the expansion of the autonomy afforded to them by the educational system. In his keynote address to the 1999 Modern Language Association convention, for example, Bourdieu called for the formation of a collective intellectual that would be constituted as a transnational scientific field using the combined intellectual capital accumulated by its members. This collective intellectual, he declared, would be capable of contesting a neoliberal discourse that increasingly relies on scientific authority by subjecting it to a rigorous critique that exposes its ideological presuppositions. The collective intellectual, moreover, could participate in the "collective work of political invention," or the theorization of new modes of social organization and political mobilization.[46]

This vision of an intellectual politics is based on the autonomy of the educational system in liberal democratic societies, an autonomy that also serves to maintain the school system as one of the primary sites for the reproduction of social inequality. The notion of the collective intellectual would thus seem to reflect the recognition that the transformation of the educational system will not be led by those who are most invested in it.

Bourdieu would undoubtedly be the first to admit that his own academic trajectory, which led him to the apex of the French academic field, meant that he was one of the most invested, especially since it was academic capital that he was able to use in the political field. At the same time, the conception of the collective intellectual as necessarily occupying an external relation to any political movement it would aid reveals the limits of the effectiveness of intellectual capital, circumscribing its actions within the boundaries of the sphere of culture and the academy. When Bourdieu asserts that "we must . . . work to *universalize in reality the conditions of access* to what the present offers us that is most universal," it is important to realize that he is conceiving of universality as the historically contingent product of the development of autonomous fields.[47] That is, universal or disinterested gestures are produced only in fields that can create an interest in disinterest or, to put it another way, the conversion of material into symbolic capital. The question I pose here is what relation does Asian American studies have to this process?

3

Disciplinarity and the Political
Identity of Asian American Studies

In 1996, the journal *Social Text* published physicist Alan Sokal's article on the "transformative hermeneutics of quantum gravity," which ignited a public debate over the place of theory in the academy until Sokal's hoax was revealed. Shortly afterward, in 1998 the long-standing discontent with the work of Lois-Ann Yamanaka finally erupted into the open with the award that she received from the Association for Asian American Studies (AAAS) for *Blu's Hanging*. Although these two events provoked crises of somewhat different orders of magnitude and may appear entirely unrelated, I suggest that they mark the two poles between which the field of Asian American studies has been stretched in the past several decades. If the Sokal hoax highlighted the intellectual and political struggles between the humanities and the sciences in the academy, the *Blu's Hanging* controversy revealed the tensions between Asian American studies and various segments of the Asian American population that it claimed to represent. Both conflicts are refracted in Asian American studies in the question of what unites the field either academically or politically.

After its early struggles simply to establish itself in the university, Asian American studies began a period of growth in the 1980s with the founding of new programs and an influx of new graduate students in the field. This growing institutionalization, however, also brought new issues with which the field had to grapple. One such issue that emerged in the late 1980s and early 1990s was the impact of poststructuralist and postmodern theory on the political-intellectual project that had defined the field since its inception. This project translated the political aims of the Asian American movement into academic work centered on historical and sociological research, work that sought to recover a "buried past" and to produce accurate and authentic representations of Asian Americans, their identities, and their culture. The "cultural turn" brought about by the introduction of literary theory into a number of academic fields also affected Asian American studies and partially displaced this original vision and its disciplinary bases, thereby provoking new debates over the relation of literary studies and theory to the political goals of the field.

The Sokal and *Blu's Hanging* incidents are connected by the questions of legitimacy that became central to the debates around them. The Sokal case, for example, took what was essentially a disciplinary struggle within the university and turned it into a public issue. The strategy of producing a fraudulent essay was obviously geared toward this end and could not be dismissed in the way that a conventional scholarly article about postmodernism written by a physicist could be. Nevertheless, the issue at the center of the entire affair was the academic legitimacy of theory. In contrast, in the *Blu's Hanging* episode, academic legitimacy was never really the main issue, although some participants tried to make it so. Instead, the primary point of contention was the political legitimacy of the fiction award given to Yamanaka and, by implication, the political legitimacy of the AAAS and of Asian American studies as a whole. Somewhat ironically, this actually mirrored the debates within the field over the status of theory, since whatever intellectual issues scholars might have had with theory, in the end their judgments hinged almost entirely on what they perceived to be its political implications. In much of the discussion about these topics, though, the relation between the political and the academic was never clearly delineated, and the two were often collapsed together as if they were or should be continuous.

Using the debates over theory as its starting point, this chapter investigates questions of disciplinarity in Asian American studies. Why is this an interdisciplinary field, and more important, how does the field understand the meaning of disciplinarity? The theory debate offers perhaps a good opportunity to examine such questions because it brings together discussions about academic legitimacy, what research is, what the field's responsibility is to the community, what the field's political objectives are, and how it might engage in political work in the academy. Although the discussions about theory range across the entire field and are continuing, the special issue of the journal *Amerasia* entitled *Thinking Theory in Asian American Studies*, published in 1995, provides a condensed schematic of these debates. For this issue, a number of scholars in the field were asked to assess the impact of theory (postmodernism in particular, as in the Sokal case) on the project of Asian American studies as it was originally understood.

In their introduction, the editors, Michael Omi and Dana Takagi, suggested that the influence of postmodern theory on almost every aspect of the field had produced an intellectual divide: "On the one hand are historians and social scientists who vigorously defend concepts of 'social structure,' and on the other are literary and cultural studies intellectuals who, heavily influenced by postmodern thought, privilege 'discursive practices.'"[1] Actually, one of the striking features of the various pieces in this issue is that almost all the scholars identified with "discursive practices" argue that this is a false opposition, whereas those on the side of "social structure" insist on the incompatibility of the two approaches.[2] Evidently, the crisis provoked by theory did not appear equally pressing on both sides of the disciplinary divide. For example, it seems significant that both editors of the *Amerasia* issue were sociologists. I do not want to rehearse the debates over theory's value or utility to the political-intellectual project of the field. Instead, I want to examine how the various essays are situated in relation to theory within academic discourse. How do these positions correspond to their location in Asian American studies or other disciplines/fields? By tracing some of these lines of demarcation, we can begin to construct a map of the multiple vectors of force and objects of struggle for Asian American studies as an academic field.

Although the explicit topic of the *Amerasia* issue is the impact of theory on Asian American studies, it quickly becomes clear that first, what is at stake in the debates is the boundary of Asian American studies and its relation to other disciplines or fields and that, second, the writers' stances toward theory reveal the delineations and classifications implicit in the particular strategies they employ in their struggles over academic capital. Much of the debate over theory centered on how the field conceived of identity, community, and politics, but one curious feature of this discussion was the way that disagreements over political strategy (identity politics or anti-identitarian politics?) came to be superimposed on the divisions between the disciplines. Although the issue's editors commented on this disciplinary-political alignment, and it formed the background for many of the essays, there was almost no theoretical reflection on why this alignment existed. The debate over theory, then, concerns not just its general intellectual and political ramifications but, more important, the identity of Asian American studies as an academic field and a political project.

Although the university is the most immediate context of work in Asian American studies, the interests of academics themselves are the object of intense denials—which is, after all, how academic work becomes "disinterested—but these denials lead to certain persistent aporias regarding the political implications of academic work and its relation to the community."[3] In this regard, the disciplinary-political alignment reveals the structure of the field of Asian American studies as made up of two principles of legitimacy that are somewhat at odds with each other: the academic and the political. The former derives from the overall structure of the academic field of Asian American studies. The political discourse of the field, in contrast, expresses the legitimacy that is specific to it, which is the political capital of representation. This does not mean that the political discourse is not actually political; rather, this discourse is the product of a number of disjunctive political dynamics and is, in the strongest sense of the word, overdetermined. The first half of this chapter examines the debate over theory, and the second half looks in greater detail at how the interdisciplinary relation between history and literature was transformed by the paradigm shift in Asian American cultural studies that occurred over Theresa Cha's text *Dictée*.

Mapping the Space of Asian American Studies

If theory in the Sokal controversy was the front line in the battle between the humanities and sciences, it entered Asian American studies rather belatedly and in a specific context, that of the critique of racial identity politics (or its frequent avatar, cultural nationalism). The Asian American feminist challenge to the male domination of racial politics was articulated through poststructuralist and postmodern theory and expanded into a critique not just of identity politics but of identity in general. Subsequently, the theoretical elaboration of difference and the defects of identity (politics) have become fundamental to most of the critical work in Asian American literary and cultural studies. The opposition of identity and difference pertains not, however, to merely those two areas of study but has been connected to almost all the major debates that have structured the field of Asian American studies. The binary of identity and difference has thus been enlarged to include the permutations of practice and theory, the community and the academy, nationalism and transnationalism, and agency and structuralism.

In an illuminating analysis of the Sokal case, John Guillory argued that the publication of Sokal's essay, entitled "Science Wars," resulted from "the literary academy's desire to annex science studies to a theoretical program internal to its own discipline (roughly indicated by the name of postmodernism), as well as its desire to conscript science studies into the culture wars."[4] The appeal of theory for literary studies derives from a problem inherent in its origins as an academic discipline. The field as we now know it did not emerge, at least in the American academy, until the latter half of the nineteenth century, through the transformation of the classical curriculum from one emphasizing grammar, philology, and rhetoric to one engaging in cultural criticism and the interpretation and analysis of vernacular literature.[5] This shift was motivated by the decline of interest in the classical curriculum, a decline that can be attributed (among other reasons) to the rise in the prestige of science. Even though the new ideas about research were brought back by Americans who studied at German universities, research in the emerging American university became more strongly identified with scientific experimentation rather than German philosophical idealism, owing in large part to the efforts of educational reformers for more practical and utilitarian education. Classical education, in contrast, was associated with snobbish elites and effete gentlemen.

The origins of literary studies and cultural criticism were (de)formed by the triumph of the scientific paradigm and its monopoly on the definition of truth. Theory offered a discourse that provided new intellectual weapons against the tyranny of scientific positivism and empiricism and also derived from the highest traditions of Western philosophy (hence its efflorescence in France, where philosophy still reigns supreme). In this latest phase of the struggle between the humanities and the sciences in the American academy, which was marked by the Sokal affair, the most contested terrain was that of the social sciences, in which can be found the outlines of the larger disciplinary struggles. Thus while the humanities in general can unite in opposition to science, this division is internalized within the social sciences, as, for example, in the internecine rivalries between those committed to quantitative versus qualitative research. Broadly speaking, the crisis of theory is not a crisis for the humanities, since they have nothing to lose, whereas the intrusion of a literary postmodernism into the social sciences can only exacerbate the tensions that already have fragmented them internally.[6]

Despite the apparent morphological similarities between the rhetorics of the larger disciplinary debates in the academy and those in Asian American studies, the two do not overlap. That is, whereas the debates over theory in Asian American studies are clearly driven by the dynamics of the broader conflicts, they cannot be reduced to localized instances of them but are refracted through the particular history and configuration of Asian American studies as an academic field. Thus what is at stake in each debate is somewhat different: in the academic struggle, the central object is academic legitimacy and the definition of knowledge, while in Asian American studies the main object of contention is the principle of unity of the field. My argument is that it is impossible to assess the impact of theory on the politics of academic work in Asian American studies without a clearer sense of the larger institutional agendas and motivations that theory brought with it.

In the special issue of *Amerasia*, the historian Gordon Chang offers one of the strongest indictments of theory, contending that postmodernism is of "limited use" in historical investigations because Asian American history is primarily social history, "the effort to describe and explain the lived and felt experiences of Asian American communities."[7] Ethnic studies, according to Chang, has sought to "help build minority identity by giving prominent place to the lives, ideas, perspectives, and experiences of minority peoples. It has helped legitimize, no, even more, it has helped establish these experiences in the historical record and required at least lip-service to what is called 'multi-culturalism.'"[8] Chang objects to postmodernism for two reasons, one "philosophic/intellectual" and the other "social and political." The first has to do with the commitment to understanding and reconstructing a knowable past, and the second concerns the "connection between intellectual activity and the social responsibility of an intellectual."[9] These two rationales, academic and political, reflect the legitimacy of the two fields of history and Asian American studies, and they are, for Chang, perfectly congruent with each other. The disciplinary commitment to the historical representation of the past is aligned with the political commitment to the representation of Asian Americans as an integral part of American history and society.

Although Chang's statement lays claim to an originary status as a recapitulation of the field's founding ethos, the equivalence of academic and political rationales seems perhaps a bit too neat and raises certain questions about how easily the aims of the Asian American movement could be translated into the priorities of academic research. First, Chang suggests that while the exclusion of Asian Americans from historical research was due to racism, the disciplinary methods of historiography are themselves sound. He affirms, for example, the value of historical work that is "by most standards rather traditional and narrative," implying that the political struggle to include Asian Americans in history can be fought within the discipline itself and requires no external (that is, political) intervention.[10] If this is the case, then postmodern skepticism has nothing to add to this project and only threatens it. It is in this vein that Chang concludes:

> A fundamental tension exists between those persuaded by the skepticism of postmodernism and those who have a desire, some may call it a pretension, to know and to reconstruct the past. It is doubtful there can be any serious reconciliation of the two, and perhaps there should not be any effort to do so, for the conflicts between them may simply reflect the tensions inherent in the different ways we try to live socially conscious lives.[11]

Even allowing for the polemical tone of Chang's argument, this assessment may seem needlessly antagonistic, especially given the professed willingness of those on the other side to overcome their differences in order to join forces. Lisa Lowe, for example (along with almost all the other cultural studies critics in the issue), questioned the way that the issue opposes "Asian American studies" to "theory": "It is history and historical necessity that have affected the shape of current Asian American projects, not the theoretical products of poststructuralism, Anglo-American feminism, or postcolonial theory."[12] The stridency of this denial may give one pause, though, since Lowe's own work depends in many ways on precisely those theoretical products that she enumerates. Even the terms of her own argument for historical necessity raise questions, since in the very next paragraph, she declares that we must "take seriously that we are subjects produced by history." How is history being defined so that it excludes the determinations of the academic institution? Isn't "theory" part of history, and isn't the university one, and arguably the primary, context of Asian American studies?

What becomes evident in juxtaposing Lowe's arguments with Chang's is that beneath the debates over theory and practice, or realism and skepticism, lie more fundamental questions about the boundaries of Asian American studies as a field and its relation to other disciplines. When Chang suggests not only that there is no possible reconciliation between postmodern theory and history but also that we should not even make the effort, he is talking less about "the tensions inherent in the different ways we try to live socially conscious lives" than he is about the tensions among disciplines in the perpetual competition over academic legitimacy. On the other side of this coin, though, Lowe's efforts to bridge the disciplinary divides express more than an expansive interdisciplinarity. If political legitimacy for Chang aligns with disciplinary legitimacy, resulting in the desire to enforce disciplinary boundaries, Lowe's desire to erase those boundaries reflects the way in which the political legitimacy of realist representation in Asian American studies conflicted with the disciplinary legitimacy of theory in literary studies. It is not mere historical coincidence that ethnic studies entered the American academy just before the eruption of theory in literary studies because they both responded to the pressures and transformations of the 1960s, albeit in opposing ways. That is, theory, we might say, produced a heteronomous discourse in order to bolster the autonomy of literary studies, while ethnic studies led to a discourse of autonomy in order to create heteronomy in the university.

Continuing his analysis of the Sokal controversy, Guillory offers an account of the emergence of cultural studies in the American academy that helps explain the force of Lowe's denial. Guillory writes that "what literary critics did under the sign of cultural studies . . . was to extend techniques developed for analyzing literary texts to other cultural objects and practices." What enabled this expansion was

> a tacit analogy between the obvious constructedness of the literary artifact and the constructedness of normative (usually this meant repressive) identity categories. Because the concept of construction was tacitly identified with the notion of *representation*, the relegation of literature in cultural studies amounted to its unwitting universalization. If social construction was the Archimedean lever by which the world itself—the world as culture—was to be dislodged from its normative complacency, the effectiveness of this lever was largely dependent on the strength of the analogy between literary representation and social construction.[13]

Guillory's argument is that literary theory was able to claim a political effect basically by disavowing any separation of the academy from society. In order to make this claim, however, literary theory had to repudiate the study of literature as an object belonging to an aesthetic domain separate from the social domain. This did not mean, however, that literary theorists ceased to study literature but that they made *everything* into literature. The world, in other words, became a *text*, or an artificially constructed object that was then subject to ideological critique. Lowe's denial exemplifies this analysis, since it can bring theory into Asian American studies only by providing it with a political rationale, but this requires the denial of theory as an *academic* discourse.

Lowe's assertion could be interpreted as indicating that theory is inside history, not outside it. That is, we might believe that Lowe is refuting the terms of a debate that opposes theory to history (as Chang does) by arguing that theory itself cannot be understood as determining, since it already is part of history. Unfortunately, this reading seems to be contradicted by her own assertion that we should conceive of "various theories as 'tools' for situated materialist critiques."[14] The notion of theory as a "tool" seems to suggest that theoretical concepts and methods can be abstracted from their historical contexts of production and reception. I argue that Lowe is trying to have it both ways. In other words, it is only by abstracting theory from history that it becomes possible for it to circulate in the world as materialist critique. In order for cultural studies to claim political effectiveness, it had to universalize literary studies. This also meant, however, that cultural studies had to refute the separation of the academy from society, for only by making the academic field continuous with the social field could one claim a political effect in the latter for "theoretical interventions" in the former. If Guillory is right to say that the expansion of cultural studies depended on a tacit "analogy between literary representation and social construction," then the theoretical discourse of difference operates by the implicit reduction of the domain of politics to cultural politics, or, more precisely, a politics of the cultural field.[15] The purpose of this reduction was not to eliminate the political; on the contrary, it was to make it possible to assert material, social effects for antirealist and antiessentialist philosophical discourses that were skeptical of the materiality of the social world.

Although the realism/antirealism binary may initially appear to map neatly onto the disciplinary division of the field between historians and social scientists, on the one hand, and literary and cultural studies scholars, on the other, this characterization tends to obscure the fact that Asian American studies has always been oriented mainly toward the humanities. Indeed, until recently, most of the social scientists in the field did not engage in quantitative research. Thus the realism of the field is not aligned with the scientific realism that defines the dominant discourse of truth. Rather, realism in Asian American studies is derived from the field's activist origins in opposition to the false and distorted images of minorities prevalent in the academic discourse of the time. In other words, this was a political rather than a philosophical or methodological realism, and instead of upholding the autonomy of academic work, it opposed the idea of "research." Nevertheless, over time, as the field began to be absorbed into the educational institution, this original antiacademic realism gradually began to be redefined as its opposite, as an epistemological realism.

As a matter of intellectual responsibility to a reality external to the academy, realism is a corollary to political responsibility to those people or communities outside the academy. Thus, Chang can confidently espouse this realism as the basis of historical research in large part because of its congruence with the general intellectual orientation of history as a discipline. The same might be said for the social sciences. Omi and Takagi expressed a widely shared perception that

> interestingly enough, the broadening of the domain of theory has impacted the disciplines within Asian American studies in unequal ways, privileging some and disadvantaging others. In contrast to an earlier period, it is the humanities, especially literature and comparative literature, and not the social sciences, that mostly define the tone and range of theoretical discussions.[16]

One of the effects of theory's expansion was the elevation of literary and cultural studies above history and the social sciences, which had previously been the central disciplines in the field, especially given its political realism. To many scholars, this appeared to be a turn away from the original political aims of the field, hence the defensiveness of the responses of the literary and cultural critics. We might say, moreover, that the turn to theory in Asian American literary studies, while obviously influenced by the direction of literary studies in general, was prescribed by the political realism of the field, which—if it were capable of being recast in history and the social sciences as its opposite, as a realist epistemology—set Asian American literary studies at a distinct disadvantage in its own discipline, since the prevalent antirealism of the latter would make the work of a realist Asian American literary criticism appear to be academically illegitimate or unsophisticated.[17]

This was the context, I argue, for the emergence of the theoretical critique of identity in Asian American studies. One of the effects of this critique was to revise the field's original definitions of political legitimacy, a necessity if Asian American literary studies were to become legitimate in its own discipline in the same way that history and social science had. The problem, of course, was that in order for literary studies to do this, it had to redefine political legitimacy in the field in antirealist and antirepresentational terms that then undermined the original basis for the legitimacy of history and social science. I locate the historical emergence of this critique with the publication in 1991 of Lisa Lowe's seminal article "Heterogeneity, Hybridity, Multiplicity: Marking Asian American Differences," whose title not only contains the term *difference*, but also three variations of it. This article marked a watershed in Asian American literary studies, if not the field as a whole.

Although Lowe's critique of identity politics has by now become foundational to the field, I would like to revisit the essay's repeated anxious insistence that identity politics and difference are not in fact irreconcilable and that they are actually complementary. Lowe ends her essay with these assertions:

> I am not suggesting that we can or should do away with the notion of Asian American identity, for to stress only our differences would jeopardize the hard-earned unity that has been achieved in the last two decades of Asian American politics. . . . In fact, I would submit that the very freedom, in the 1990s, to explore the hybridities concealed beneath the desire of identity is permitted by the context of a strongly articulated essentialist politics. Just as the articulation of the desire for identity depends upon the existence of a fundamental horizon of differences, the articulation of differences dialectically depends upon a socially constructed and practiced notion of identity. I want simply to remark that in the 1990s, we can afford to rethink the notion of ethnic identity in terms of cultural, class, and gender differences, rather than presuming similarities and making the erasure of particularity the basis of unity.[18]

The language here is straining to bring together two things that the essay's own theoretical framework construes as opposed. In fact, the passage does not so much reconcile identity with difference as it simply asserts that each is important and has its own place. Identity and difference can be made to coexist only because each has been assigned its own domain, and those domains have been carefully fenced off from each other. This compartmentalization is subtly inscribed in the passage in the way that the articulation of differences is said to depend on a "*socially* constructed and practiced notion of identity" or that the desire for identity depends on a "*horizon* of differences." In other words, the practice of identity belongs to the social domain, while the theory of difference belongs to the horizon, which is, I would suggest, a trope for the academy. The separation created between these two terms is most obvious in the assertion that identity "conceals" hybridity. Despite the rhetoric of connection, these phrases reinsert forms of disjunction that serve to insulate difference from identity.[19]

We can gain a larger perspective on the contradictions of identity and difference by turning to someone whose work has defined these issues in decisive ways, Judith Butler. In the anthology she coedited with Joan Scott, *Feminists Theorize the Political*, Butler addresses the same concerns as the *Amerasia* issue in her introduction entitled "Contingent Foundations: Feminism and the Question of 'Postmodernism.'" I shall consider Butler's arguments in some detail here, since they offer one template for the anti-identitarian discourse of difference in Asian American studies. Toward the end of her essay, Butler concedes that

> within feminism, it seems as if there is some political necessity to speak as and for *women*, and I would not contest that necessity. Surely, that is the way in which representational politics operates, and in this country, lobbying efforts are virtually impossible without recourse to identity politics. So we agree that demonstrations and legislative efforts and radical movements need to make claims in the name of women. But this necessity needs to be reconciled with another. The minute that the category of women is invoked as *describing* the constituency for which feminism speaks, an internal debate invariably begins over what the descriptive content of that term will be.[20]

Noting that claims for the ontological specificity of women as childbearers or in the social relations of maternity or ways of knowing all create divisions within the category of women, Butler argues that "every time that specificity is articulated, there is resistance and factionalization within the very constituency that is supposed to be *unified* by the articulation of its common element."[21]

Despite admitting the necessity of identity politics, Butler nevertheless tries to qualify that concession as much as possible by asserting that

> any effort to give universal or specific content to the category of women . . . will necessarily produce factionalization, and that "identity" as a point of departure can never hold as the solidifying ground of a

feminist political movement. Identity categories are never merely descriptive, but always normative, and as such, exclusionary. This is not to say that the term "women" ought not to be used, or that we ought to announce the death of the category. On the contrary, if feminism presupposes that "women" designates an undesignatable field of differences, one that cannot be totalized or summarized by a descriptive identity category, then the very term becomes a site of permanent openness and resignifiability. I would argue that the rifts among women over the content of the term ought to be safeguarded and prized, indeed, that this constant rifting ought to be affirmed as the ungrounded ground of feminist theory.[22]

Butler never explains why the category of women should be retained but concedes only that "it seems" as if there is some political necessity for the term. The apparent motive for the evacuation of identity here is the desire to avoid the "painful" factionalization that it provokes, in place of which Butler substitutes the affirmation of "constant rifting" among women. It is not clear, though, why constant rifting would be less painful than factionalization, apart from its being "prized" in some way. In fact, the very notion of "constant rifting" suggests an odd ontology, as if difference inevitably gives rise to dissension and conflict, and therefore the only way to deal with it is to make the recognition and negotiation of conflict itself the purpose for the group's existence. The circularity of this reasoning, however, would not seem to leave much room to do anything else. If the group were perpetually occupied with internal rifts and conflicts, how could it muster enough unanimity to take any action at all? Of course, we might say the same thing about identity, but here we come to the crux of the matter.

If any group large enough to exert a social impact is characterized by infinite heterogeneity, then only a few of those differences will become significant enough to create the factionalization that Butler is so anxious to avoid. Otherwise, no group would ever be able to overcome its internal differences in order to constitute itself as a group. What transforms some differences into the source of factional conflicts is, of course, interest; that is, there must be something of value at stake in the construction of a particular difference in order for it to become the object of conflict and contestation. Insofar as the identity of the group implies specific political priorities, struggles over identity also are negotiations over the political agenda and objectives of the group's actions. But if identity itself is not the source of these conflicts, then seeking to remove it would seem to be misguided at best. In this context, Butler's argument seems to imply that the difference between factionalization and rifting is less the refusal of identity than of *interest*. The notion that we should refuse identity echoes ideologies of color blindness or gender blindness (albeit directed toward opposite political ends), but I believe that it is not so much a matter of ignoring identity here as of disregarding the interests that motivate identies. In other words, the logic here seems to be that if we could learn to discount the conflicts of interest that lead to factionalization, then the differences would be neutralized and become simply symbolic disagreements.[23]

Stated bluntly in this manner, such a proposal may seem unlikely, but the logic nevertheless should be quite familiar, for the capacity to ignore interest is the mechanism that produces the disinterest of academic work. The only way that Butler can resolve the persistent contradictions between the theoretical critique of identity and the political necessity of retaining identity in some way is by universalizing the scholastic point of view, or the habitus of the academic field that imposes the denial of interest on all its members. If theory could claim to be a political discourse only by erasing the division between the academy and society, the obverse of such a move would be the blindness created by the scholastic fallacy, or the failure to recognize the distinct forms of subjectivity or habitus produced only in the academic field, a failure that is hardly unique to Butler. This blindness leads to a politics that envisions the answer to the ills of (post) modernity or global capitalism to be the renunciation of material consumption and capital accumulation—a world, in other words, in which everyone was an academic, or at least thought and acted like one.

My point, however, is not that it is difficult to make identity and difference both opposed and complementary at the same time. Rather, I want to ask what is at stake in attempts at either resolution or division. Although a number of contradictions arise in the attempt to do both simultaneously, we must first identify what it means to do either. On the most basic level, as I have already argued, difference connotes theory and academic legitimacy, whereas identity clearly is associated with political legitimacy. Along the axis of opposition, the valuation of difference over identity corresponds to the prioritization of academic criteria over political criteria, and vice versa. Given Butler's perfunctory nod to the necessity of identity, her discourse leans heavily toward the pole of academic legitimacy. At the same time, though, we might ask why she does not simply reject identity altogether. This would surely simplify the issue. As I have suggested, insofar as identity politics was retained in fields that were marginalized with regard to a purely academic legitimacy (women's and gender studies, ethnic studies, LGBT and queer studies, and so forth), it reflects the necessity of supplementing academic legitimacy with political legitimacy, which takes the specific form of the political capital of representation. Political legitimacy, or political capital, is antithetical to academic legitimacy, however, so the attempt to resolve identity politics with difference expresses a specific means of conversion in which political capital can be exchanged for academic capital through the denial of interest enabled by its negation in antiessentialist theory. In this regard, Butler's theoretical dissolution of the materiality of the body could be read allegorically as an effort to rid gender and sexual politics of the material interests that they threaten to introduce into the space of the university.[24]

Ethnic Studies as an Interdisciplinary Field

I now return to the question that I posed at the beginning of the chapter: Why didn't ethnic studies define itself as a discipline? Although ethnic studies and its components have always been interdisciplinary fields, the possibility of redefining the field as a discipline does reemerge periodically. In posing this question, I am less interested in the possibility of disciplinarity for Asian American studies than in what an analysis of this question might reveal about the tensions and forces defining the space of the field. In his survey of black studies programs at three urban research universities—the University of Illinois at Chicago, the University of Chicago, and Harvard University—Rojas observes that each program evolved in a different way that had a major impact on its ability to survive. Generally speaking, black studies and ethnic studies programs were pulled in two directions, toward either what Rojas calls "community education" (as in the original demands for black studies and ethnic studies at SF State) or "academic black studies."[25] These are not mutually exclusive alternatives, and most programs incorporated at least some elements of each, but ultimately academic black studies prevailed.

When looking across the field, Rojas found that "black studies has many of the features one would expect of an established academic discipline."[26] The demographic profiles of faculty in the field are similar to those in other fields in the humanities and social sciences. Black studies has its own journals, conferences, and professional organizations, and many of its practitioners believe that the field has its own distinct objects and methods of inquiry. At the same time, however, the field has extremely porous boundaries compared with those of more established disciplines. Black studies is not nearly as self-contained as English or mathematics, for example, since many of its faculty are trained in other disciplines and also tend to hold joint appointments with other departments. In this respect, Rojas suggests, black studies, along with the other components of ethnic studies, can be regarded as a permanent "interdiscipline." Moreover, remember that the original demand at SF State was for a department of black studies located within a school of ethnic studies. We now have departments of black studies or African American studies, as well as Asian American studies, so having achieved departmental status in at least a few universities, why hasn't there been a greater effort to redefine the field as a discipline? In fact, ethnic studies actually appears to be moving in the opposite direction, toward even greater interdisciplinarity.

Proponents of interdisciplinarity often understand it in terms of the opposition between nationalism and transnationalism, suggesting that the older disciplines have become outmoded "academic empires" (or perhaps nation-states) and that interdisciplinarity offers the possibility of new forms of knowledge production not constrained by struggles over disciplinary boundaries. Such Foucauldian arguments exploit the pun by figuratively associating interdisciplinarity with the liberation of knowledge from the punitive discipline of entrenched departments, so that interdisciplinarity itself is cast as the political-intellectual project of ethnic studies.[27] In this manner, interdisciplinarity is touted as the future of the field, reinvigorating it while also sustaining its essential core. If these polemics have become widespread in the discourse of theory (itself fundamentally interdisciplinary), they must still contend with deeply ingrained disciplinary allegiances sustained by departmental power. Accordingly, advocates of interdisciplinarity identify it with ethnic studies as a political project opposed to the university, which they tacitly equate with the department. As a counterpoint to this view, we could look back to the history of black studies at the University of Illinois at Chicago and the University of Chicago. Black studies at the former was able to survive a period of retrenchment precisely because it was a department as opposed to the interdisciplinary program at the latter, which eventually collapsed.

The *Thinking Theory* issue, however, makes clear that not even all Asian American studies faculty agree with this perspective on interdisciplinarity. We have already seen that Chang's criticism of postmodern theory is bound up with his opposition to interdisciplinarity. The question is what this means to Asian American studies. The lead article in the *Amerasia* issue is by Sau-ling Wong, entitled "Denationalization Reconsidered: Asian American Cultural Criticism at a Theoretical Crossroads." Wong's article achieved a certain notoriety in the field not only because it expressed reservations about recasting Asian Americans as transnational or diasporic subjects but also because it dared to recuperate identity politics and cultural nationalism. When comparing the articles by Chang and Wong, we find that while they both invoke the original vision of Asian American studies as their guiding principles, Chang is able to do so in ways that are nearly congruent with the disciplinary parameters of history. Wong, in contrast, couches her critique of transnationalism almost entirely in terms of the history of Asian American studies, with little consideration of its implications for the discipline of literary studies. These differences were no doubt due in part to their institutional locations, since Chang at that time was a member of the history department at Stanford University, and Wong was in ethnic studies at the University of California at Berkeley. While they both display a political commitment to nationalism and identity, they may seem opposed in terms of their allegiance to either Asian American studies or more established disciplines.

This opposition, however, becomes more complicated when we recall the contradictions of autonomy examined in the last chapter. If nationalism is not inherently opposed to disciplinarity, it does require a heteronomous conception of academic work antagonistic to the faculty autonomy that is the basis of departmental power. I argued in chapter 2 that ethnic studies was forced to reject nationalism in order to accommodate itself to the university. This did not mean, of course, that the field abandoned nationalism altogether but that nationalist ideologies came to occupy specific locations in the educational system. In a survey of black studies faculty, Rojas found a high level of agreement with the proposition that black studies is a distinct field with its own core ideas and research methodologies. The one significant variable in the responses concerned whether the faculty member taught at a public or private university, with those at public universities being more likely to agree than those at private universities. Rojas conjectures that this difference was based on the greater power wielded by established departments in private universities, as well as their commitment to the ideology of research and academic legitimacy, whereas the missions of public universities are teaching and service, especially to minority students, which make them more amenable to academic work having those priorities. The black studies programs with the largest student enrollments are at schools like California State University at

Long Beach and campuses in the City University of New York system, and these also happen to be programs with faculty like Maulana Karenga and Leonard Jeffries who espouse Afrocentric or nationalist doctrines.

Not only do Wong's and Chang's different perspectives fall along this axis of public and private, but one article in the *Amerasia* issue also proposes an "Asiacentric" paradigm for Asian American studies. Written by Paul Wong, Meera Manvi, and Takeo Hirota Wong (the first two are identified as faculty at Washington State University, and the third as an ethnic studies major at the University of California at San Diego), the article explicitly draws on the work of Molefi Asante and other Afrocentric scholars to argue that theory is a product of European thought and culture and that Asiacentrism can provide an "alternative to the dominance of Eurocentric epistemology, theories and methods in Asian American studies."[28] If we see this article as marking one end of a spectrum in the issue defined by the two poles of autonomy and heteronomy with respect to Asian American studies (that is, most specific and least specific to Asian American studies), then we could situate the articles by David Palumbo-Liu and Dorinne Kondo at the opposite end.

In his article, entitled "Theory and the Subject of Asian American Studies," Palumbo-Liu contends that opposing theory to Asian American studies "offers the scholar of ethnic studies a dubiously circumscribed space of his/her own," whereas Kondo advances perhaps the most strident apology for theory in her article, entitled "Postmodern Theory as Political Necessity." Both writers affirm the political import of theory, but they do so with little or no reference to the history of the Asian American movement or Asian American studies as a field. The point is not that their perspectives are illegitimate or irrelevant to the field but that they occupy positions outside it and so have little investment in establishing its distinctiveness. To the contrary, as new entrants to the field, Palumbo-Liu and Kondo would be excluded by any narrow or rigid boundaries, so they are located at the pole of interdisciplinarity.[29] Thus Asiacentrism and postmodernism define the two poles of disciplinarity and interdisciplinarity, or ethnic studies-specific and extradisciplinary orientations, with this opposition intersected by the binary of academic legitimacy and political legitimacy. That is, in terms of the former, someone like Chang is opposed to the protheory contingent, but in terms of the latter, he is actually aligned with them. Despite his invocation of responsibility to the community, Chang is careful to identify that responsibility as academic rather than political.

If we attempt to factor in institutional location to this polarity of orientations toward either Asian American studies or other disciplines, we observe that one's position on this spectrum correlates with one's academic capital. The more prestigious the department and university are, the less likely it will be to need or value Asian American studies capital, and vice versa. When Rojas analyzed responses to the question of whether black studies had its own research methodology, he found no split between public and private. Instead, he found a disciplinary split between the social sciences and humanities, with the former less likely to agree.[30] Although the reasons for this are unclear, Rojas surmises that the study of race has been central to social science for decades and that its graduate programs are more effective at instilling belief in the widespread applicability of its methods. In contrast, the humanities has ignored race as an important aspect of culture until quite recently, and its methods have derived largely from the study of European culture, which may have given rise to a sense that the study of other cultures requires different approaches.

My analysis suggests another explanation, which is that the notion of "core ideas" in black studies may connote "nationalism," whereas "research methodologies," at least in literary studies, may be associated with "theory" (as particular methods of reading). If this is the case, then the disciplinary division that Rojas observes may correlate with the opposition regarding theory, since most of the literary and cultural studies scholars were eager to claim a provenance for theory in minority history and culture in order to refute its indictment as a Western discourse. But at the same time, they also are the most opposed to nationalism (or at least those oriented toward research). In any event, it does seem as if the two oppositions regarding core ideas and research methods intersect in certain ways. The belief in core ideas, for example, appears to be inversely correlated with academic legitimacy, but the issue of research methods seems less concerned with the legitimacy of ethnic studies as a field than with the question of how legitimate research is defined. In other words, academic legitimacy is conceived in various ways depending on which side of the epistemological divide one falls. Generally, disciplines or fields that pursue realist and positivist approaches, and thus align with the overall dominance of scientific knowledge, take an orthodox stance toward academic legitimacy. Those whose methods are perceived as unscientific tend to assume a heterodox orientation, which regards itself as political precisely because it is forced to contest the order of things by which it is delegitimated.

Thus the conflict between realists and antirealists, which is couched as a conflict over identity politics and cultural nationalism, owes at least as much to the relation of forces in the academic field as it does to anything having to do with the community or the Asian American population. Those who belong to illegitimate disciplines tend to pursue interdisciplinary strategies because they have less to gain from conformity to their disciplinary paradigms. We can now begin to see the factors that make unlikely a move toward disciplinarity for ethnic studies. First, disciplinary status is associated too closely with nationalism, which produces an inherent tension between the service and community orientations of ethnic studies and the aspiration to academic legitimacy that disciplinarity implies. Second, for ethnic studies to become a discipline, it would have to resolve the dispute between realists and antirealists, but it would have little reason to define itself as a realist discipline, since it seems that methodologically it would only end up replicating history and social science. Constructing itself along antirealist lines, however, would only compound the illegitimacy it already suffers while also calling into question its political claims to represent minority groups. This issue points to a larger obstacle to disciplinary status, which is that the field needs to achieve some degree of unanimity regarding its objects, purposes, and methods. As a collocation of faculty from disparate (and ever expanding) sectors of the university, the field has never been able to define a coherent intellectual project capable of providing equal standing to all its various branches.

The special issue of *Amerasia* offers a pertinent example of this dilemma because it illustrates how the interdisciplinary nature of Asian American studies can lead to all sorts of conflicts regarding the norms and purposes of academic work. Without the divisions provided by disciplinary boundaries, Asian American studies is especially susceptible to such professional antagonisms. Professions, after all, are characterized by the inherent tension between the impulse to unify based on common interests and the fragmentation resulting from competition among members. Without any coherent disciplinary identity grounded in autonomous institutional units, the question is what holds the field together. The answer is capital, but at the level of intellectual discourse, I argue that political identity unifies the field, which is why academic debates (such as those over the question of theory) can be elaborated only through recourse to a political rhetoric and to the ideological/symbolic motifs of the "community" or identity. This may seem counterintuitive, given the intense political conflicts that occupied the field in its first years, but here we perceive the relation between academic legitimacy and political legitimacy. Since the imposition of academic norms drove out those with political agendas that were antagonistic to the university, these norms actually produced a high degree of *political* conformity, but with the concomitant effect of substituting intellectual disagreements for ideological disagreements. That is, the principal conflicts in the field became academic rather than political.

Responding to the protests of the 1960s, Martin Trow noted that the American university has always been divided between two main functions, the autonomous and the popular (or what I have referred to as autonomous and heteronomous).[31] The three main autonomous functions are the transmission of high culture, the production of knowledge, and the certification of social elites. The popular function consists primarily of teaching but also of utility, or the belief that universities provide knowledge and skills that will benefit various sectors of society, such as industry, agriculture, the military, health professions, and social services. In answer to how the university has been able to fulfill both these functions given the inherent conflicts between them, Trow cites the division of labor in higher education as the primary mechanism for insulating the autonomous functions from the popular functions. In accordance with the hierarchical structures of the educational system, many schools are largely geared toward only research or teaching. For instance, the elite private universities subordinate almost every other function to research, and the top liberal arts colleges are basically preparatory schools for graduate and professional training. In contrast, a much greater number of schools are essentially service institutions, such as teaching colleges, small liberal arts colleges, normal schools, junior and community colleges, and vocational and technical schools. In between these two classes are the big state universities, which have both autonomous and popular functions. These universities offer a variety of mechanisms that insulate the autonomous functions from popular and service duties, beginning with the division of labor at almost every level, from the separation of schools and colleges within the university, to the division between graduate and undergraduate education, to the organization into departments and disciplines and the various ranks of faculty, lecturers, and adjuncts.

At its roots, black studies in the Experimental College at SF State gathered together courses from several different departments partly as a matter of expediency but also, as I argued, because it was trying to reproduce the standard liberal arts curriculum in the separate sphere of black culture. Its structure as an interdiscipline, I contend, has thus reproduced within the field the divisions of labor operating at the level of the department outside it. In a loosely defined and somewhat amorphous field such as Asian American studies, which is subject to a variety of competing definitions, interdisciplinarity itself is one of the mechanisms for defusing conflicts and managing disputes over the academic priorities of the field. Therefore, it becomes apparent that the discourse of difference may have less to do with the Asian American category or population than with Asian American studies as a field and with the difficulties of uniting it under any singular definition of academic work. As I have suggested, the implicit political agenda of cultural nationalism in the university was to credentialize minority culture in order to produce it as cultural capital. This cultural capital would identify and certify "leaders," or the elites empowered to speak for and to represent the community in politics, business, social services, academia, culture, and the like. Historically, this capital was embodied in the acquisition of liberal culture, and while Asian American cultural capital is produced across the entire field, I contend that Asian American literary and cultural studies in particular (though by no means exclusively) has taken on the task of formulating a discourse capable of unifying the field. Put another way, this is the task of producing the specific capital of the field.

Even though this project operates in the domain of culture, to call it cultural capital may be misleading because it is not primarily a capital of culture; it is, rather, the specific form of cultural (or symbolic) capital that I have identified as the political capital of representation. More concretely, political capital is manifested less in its adherence to a political orthodoxy than to the rules of political discourse in the field. Thus one need not be either for or against identity politics (most likely the latter), as long as one has a position on it and recognizes that the question of identity and its political ramifications is central to the field. In this way, both the most formalistic kinds of literary analysis and the most rigorously quantitative social science research can occupy the same intellectual space because they both agree that identity is important, even if they investigate the topic within completely different (and even antithetical) conceptual paradigms. Of course, despite the intense disagreements over some of the central political issues in the field, acceptance of the boundaries of discourse is intended to produce a certain degree of uniformity.

The *Amerasia* issue amply illustrates the extent to which there is a common set of references and assumptions in the political discourse of the field. We might also look to other evidence such as Glenn Omatsu's essay "The 'Four Prisons' and the Movements of Liberation: Asian American Activism from the 1960s to the 1990s," which has been reprinted a number of times and is included in several introductory Asian American studies anthologies. This essay has become an almost canonical statement of a certain political orthodoxy in Asian American studies, but I want to ask how it came to occupy this position. Despite any postmodern skepticism of historical narratives, Omatsu's essay is most often cited as a self-evident description of the historical reality of the period, one that requires no commentary because its facticity is beyond doubt.[32] What is of interest here is less the historical veracity of his account than some of the ways in which it consolidates its rhetorical credibility. Omatsu begins the essay by recounting a lecture that he heard in an Asian American studies class at UCLA in which the professor interpreted the rise of the Asian American movement within the context of civil rights. As Omatsu comments, "The lecture was cogent, tightly organized, and well-received. . . . There was only one problem: the reinterpretation was wrong on every aspect."[33] Omatsu then presents his own, more radical interpretation of the movement, one that is not an interpretation (much less a *re*interpretation) but simply the *correct* account.

The issue is not whether Omatsu's account of movement politics is right but whether those politics, as the essay clearly implies, were the movement activists' *only* politics. It seems rather peremptory to declare that no one involved in the Asian American movement may have subscribed to a civil rights agenda. In fact, most accounts suggest that the movement succeeded precisely because it was able to mobilize people across an entire range of political positions with heterogeneous agendas and interests. Retracing the history of the movement through the 1990s, Omatsu contends that its success created a new breed of Asian Americans, young professionals who claim an Asian American identity and oppose racism in American society but do so in terms of a neoconservative politics that opposes affirmative action and other government programs for "special-interest groups." In this way, the essay depicts Asian American neoconservatives and the "activists" who carry on the radical politics of the movement as engaged in a political struggle for hegemony over the community. Omatsu declares that

 ideologically and politically, activists confront a new and interesting paradox in the Asian American community of the 1990s. On the one hand, there is a great upsurge of interest in the community and all things Asian

American. Almost daily, we hear about new groups forming across the country. In contrast to 25 years ago, when interest in the community was minimal and when only progressive activists joined Asian American organizations, we now find a situation where many different groups—including conservatives and neo-conservatives, bankers and business executives, and young professionals in all fields—have taken up the banner of Asian American identity. On the other hand, we have not seen a corresponding growth in consciousness—of what it means to be Asian American as we approach the twenty-first century.[34]

As much as this passage concerns the ideological heterogeneity in contemporary Asian American communities, it clearly reveals an anxiety over the activists' loss of political hegemony in the community (as debatable as it may be whether such hegemony ever actually existed). But who are the activists that this passage mentions? While Omatsu specifies the demographic characteristics of every other political ideology, the "activists" remain curiously indistinct and rather shadowy. It is this very lack of location and definition that signals their universalization as the normative subject of the community; that is, they represent the "real" community. In fact, I believe that in Omatsu's essay, "activism" is a code word for "Asian American studies" and that the essay is referring to the "crisis of representation" precipitated by the conflict between the "old" activists in the field and the "new" professionals who are taking over (and misrepresenting) the community. Readers of Bourdieu, however, may be struck by the extent to which the contrast that Omatsu depicts corresponds to the dichotomy between the holders of material capital and the holders of cultural capital anatomized in *Distinction* and elsewhere. In this regard, another question I would pose is whether academia itself is not a profession.

Again, the point is not that Omatsu's account is wrong or that I disagree with his version of activist politics (in fact, quite the contrary). Rather, my analysis demonstrates how the community and identity are constructed as objects by competing groups in struggles over representative legitimacy. Moreover, the essay (and the politics it espouses) can become orthodox in Asian American studies because it universalizes the perspective of the academic field (or at least certain particular sectors of it) in order to construct an image of the community (through the surrogate of the activist) that legitimates the academy's representations of it. Membership in the field of Asian American studies is predicated on the consent to the "activist" politics that Omatsu describes. This does not mean that one must become an activist but that one agrees to play the game of politics in the field, which means recognizing the stakes of the field as political stakes and engaging in struggles over the legitimate definition of the community and of Asian American identity.

What becomes evident is that political discourse in Asian American studies serves a similar function as academic jargon; that is, it demarcates the boundaries of the field and distinguishes insiders from outsiders. Rather than the intellectual debates that define most academic fields, the specificity of Asian American studies inheres in its political debates. Somewhat paradoxically, political discourse becomes the principal means by which the field maintains its autonomy, since it excludes those who cannot translate concepts and arguments from other disciplines into the specific political discourse of the field. The more institutionalized the field becomes, though, the less effective these mechanisms will be, because the more capital the field offers, the more attractive it will be to those who were not trained in it and therefore are not familiar with the political discourse. These new entrants, however, bring capital from other disciplines into the field and so raise the general amount of capital while diluting the specific capital of those whose primary membership is in Asian American studies, thus further propelling them toward interdisciplinary strategies of capital accumulation.

I conclude this section with one other example of how intellectual disputes become coded as political conflicts. As I have argued, one of the major factors impeding a disciplinary identity for Asian American studies is the impossibility of defining a coherent methodology that would be equally legitimate in all its various fields and disciplines. In chapter 2 I discussed an essay by Hirabayashi and Alquizola on the origins of Asian American studies at SF State. Here I consider a later essay of theirs in which they examine the current state of the field with regard to the general topic of this chapter, that is, theory and its relation to the political and intellectual identity of the field. Responding to the challenges that theories of "difference" have raised about the possibility of unifying Asian American studies, Hirabayashi and Alquizola maintain that

> despite the complex controversies and polemical debates between subject areas and interest groups within the field . . . there is actually a fair amount of continuity between the issues and methods of [Asian American studies], from the 1970s until now. A discussion of this continuity demonstrates that [Asian American studies] is indeed a field rather than

a mere conglomeration of focal areas with an "Asian American" subject matter.[35]

By "field," it seems to me, they mean something close to what I call *disciplinarity*, but I want to highlight the consequences of their efforts to reassert the original identity of the field.

One section of their essay provides an overview of contemporary work in Asian American studies that they deem to "unite past concerns with present concerns,"[36] a list mainly of historians and sociologists. Perhaps more pointedly, the list does not include any scholars in literary or cultural studies. Hirabayashi and Alquizola do refer to the value of literary works, but the only cultural works they cite are a few literary/critical anthologies, such as *Making Waves, Breathless—Erotica*, and *Our Feet Walk the Sky*.[37] It is their rationale for the value of literary work (as opposed to literary studies) that is most pertinent here, for they give two reasons why literary works are important:

> On the one hand, it is clear that authors often engage in extensive substantive research, collecting oral histories and generally digging up the buried past, to seek perspectives and factual grounding for their writing. On the other hand, once produced, poetry, plays, novels, and short stories have also been used in Asian American studies courses to generate discussion on subjectivities—perhaps because the passage of time blocks direct access to those who came before us.[38]

These are, of course, the very sorts of reductionism that literary studies is anxious to defend against, and in Hirabayashi and Alquizola's accounting, literature is valuable only if it either is written as history or can be read as history.

My intention here is not to defend literary studies from these charges but simply to point out that an analysis that appears on the surface to involve primarily the political aims of the field actually concerns just as much, if not more, the disciplinary divisions within the academy as a whole. How should we understand the relation between the politics of the political field and the politics of the academic field? It would be too easy (and equally reductive) to accuse Hirabayashi and Alquizola of criticizing literary studies merely in the name of their own disciplinary self-interest. At the same time, even though I agree with much of their critique of theory, it is apparent that their construction of the field's intellectual identity devalues not only an entire arena of scholarship but, it would seem, a large part of the domain of culture as well. Disciplinarity in this case ends up functioning as a kind of limit, constraining what it is possible to think or ask, and restricting the political domain so as to exclude most of the field of cultural production. Although the principal intellectual purpose of a discipline is to define legitimate objects and methods of study, the conflation of disciplinary struggles with political struggles means that disciplinary boundaries also come to define how we conceptualize political problems.

In other words, there are two separate registers of political and intellectual discourse that have an essentially arbitrary relation to each other, in that they can be linked in a variety of ways. It is, then, the question of articulating the two discourses that is the primary object of struggle in Asian American studies because this articulation is the means by which the specific capital of the field can be converted into the capital of other academic fields, and vice versa. As in the *Amerasia* issue, we see here that Hirabayashi and Alquizola use political criteria to adjudicate intellectual arguments; that is, they judge disciplinary practices not mainly in academic terms but in terms of their political implications. Their basic argument is that historical and social scientific research is political, whereas literary studies is not only not political but actually undermines the political efforts of the former. Viewing this from the opposing perspective, we might say that the politics of (literary and cultural) theory consists of the effort to deconstruct a realist identity politics. Given the two sides' mutually exclusive premises, we need to ask how we should decide who is right. After all, we are weighing the political effects that each side *claims* for itself, even though these claims cannot be gauged in any meaningful way. If political evaluation is indeed impossible, then what does it mean to use political criteria to assess academic practices?

I am not arguing that academic work should be evaluated only according to academic criteria; rather, the salient question is the relation of political strategies to intellectual practices. If the main object of struggle in the field is to produce the most compelling argument for the political effect of a particular intellectual discourse, without any concrete measure of its effectiveness, the credibility of the argument would seem to derive only from the accumulated capital behind it. What is really at stake in such debates: the needs and interests of the community or the needs and interests of those who seek to represent it? My point here is not to assert either the impossibility or undesirability of interdisciplinary work. Instead, to begin disentangling the politics of the political field from those of the academic field, we must situate Asian American studies within the institutional dynamics of disciplinary struggles over academic legitimacy. The persistent conflation of political and intellectual discourses only reinforces the denial of the most immediate contexts that motivate them, which are those of the university.

Antirealism and Historical Representation

We can grasp some sense of the complex agendas of interdisciplinary endeavors by examining more closely one particularly fraught site of disciplinary crossings, which I have already mentioned, and that is the interface of history and literature. These two disciplines are obviously closely related, and perhaps their very proximity, as well as the history of their formation as distinct disciplines with a common origin, may help explain the antipathy of some historians to any attempts by literary scholars to poach on their territory. At the same time, the vexed tradition of historicism in literary criticism (of which the New Historicism is only the latest instance) exemplifies an equal and opposite reaction by literary studies to the reduction of literature to mere historical evidence. In this context, I look at Laura Kang's *Compositional Subjects: Enfiguring Asian/American Women* in order to delineate some of the issues regarding interdisciplinary work in Asian American studies. I then trace a certain trajectory of theoretical dilemmas through the work of Lisa Lowe and end with what is arguably the central event in the history of Asian American literary studies, the critical transformation enacted around Theresa Cha's *Dictée*.

In her book, Kang provides a meticulous and valuable survey of the ways in which Asian and Asian American women have been constituted as epistemological objects by regimes of representation in several different disciplines. Her detailed analyses of the construction of particular objects of representation provide a complementary perspective to this study in that both projects attend to representations based not on their empirical referents but on the interests that motivate them. As she explains, her project "is directed less at an unveiling of some truth that has been misrepresented than a foregrounding of the particular historical circumstances, ideological suppositions, and methodological tactics that enable and constrain" each representation.[39] Despite this declaration, however, Kang never explicitly confronts the problem of evaluation, which is how one critiques any representation without an external point of reference.

That is, given a commitment to epistemological skepticism and relativism, on what basis can we judge a representation to be lacking, inaccurate, or distorted? All these terms would seem to require normative or objective criteria as a standard of comparison, and without them, the only possible assessment is to compare one representation with another. Although Kang's aim is to investigate the contexts of production of those representations and not to gauge the adequacy of any representation, her analyses in fact rely on normative and realist evaluative criteria in that they seek to elucidate how academic disciplines consolidate "disciplinary regimes" of power/knowledge from the perspective of what she terms a "trenchant interdisciplinarity."[40]

One of the places where the realism of Kang's critique surfaces is in regard to the question of history when, midway through her book, she declares, "Although I have thus far attempted to interrogate the figurations and interpretations of Asian/American women through literature and cinema, often criticizing their displacement and erasure of significant historical realities . . . I now focus my critical lens on 'history' as yet another vexed compositional terrain."[41] The question that arises, of course, is the status of the historical reality that she tenders with one hand while withdrawing it with the other. Being forced to confront this question precipitates a rhetorical crisis as she concedes:

> I now stand to compromise the trustworthiness of the "evidence" that I have referenced in my counternarrative. For while I have tried to (re)narrate Asian American women as an integral definitional other to a normative, legal "American" citizenship, I must do so with the awareness of the figurative and intertextual nature of this construction.[42]

As Kang somewhat elliptically acknowledges, the status of historical knowledge seems contradictory only because her critique is political, which inevitably is normative and entails realist claims. History thus furnishes the ground for her judgments, as in the preceding "significant historical realities" or when she concludes that critical debates over Maxine Hong Kingston's *The Woman Warrior* are "symptomatic of the problem of delineating what counts as 'Asian American literature,' how 'Asian American literature' always fails to stand for 'Asian Americans.'"[43] This conclusion depends of course on knowing who "Asian Americans" are.

Despite her rejection of referentiality, Kang's critical method seems to repeatedly fall back on it. The other problem here is whether a recognition of the limits of historical evidence actually constitutes a critique of history as a discipline or whether it is in fact already part of the disciplinary methods of history. To fault the representation of Asian/American women in particular works of historiography is not the same as saying that history as a discipline is responsible for those misrepresentations. This whole quandary could be easily avoided simply by dropping the claim to a disciplinary critique, so the question is why Kang feels she must sustain that claim even if she struggles to specify the critique. I would argue that her commitment to antirealism and antirepresentationalism derives from her position in the academic field and is a strategy of legitimation in the primary institutional locations of her project: literary/cultural studies, Asian American studies, and women's studies. In practice, she is able to prevent the conflict from surfacing elsewhere in the book by dividing "history" from the discipline of "History," implying the prior existence of one before its inscription as the other, even though she explicitly disavows this possibility. As it turns out, Kang has borrowed her critique of history from Lisa Lowe's analysis of realist representation in historiography, but as I will show, she also has borrowed from Lowe the device of splitting history in two.

Lowe's work has been highly influential in defining an interdisciplinary model of culture as the basis for an Asian American politics. Instead of securing it in an essentialized racial or cultural identity, Lowe proposes a complex model of Asian American culture as the product of the historical contradictions of liberal capitalist democracy. In her analysis, the Asian American subject is formed in relation to citizenship as the site of contradiction between the state's production of the national subject and the capitalist production of abstract labor power. History, then, constitutes the antiessentialist ground that enables us to theorize the basis for unifying the Asian American collectivity and culture. This is where questions immediately begin to arise, and although Lowe is cognizant of the problems, she is unable to resolve them completely. For example, Kang cites the contrast that Lowe draws between two different kinds of historiographical projects: the first is a representational project "motivated by a desire . . . to make visible the erased and evacuated histories in realist and naturalist modes," whereas other projects "offer alternatives to realist narratives of resolution to the nation . . . in order to generate conceptions of collectivity that are neither regulated by notions of identity nor prescribed by aesthetic, psychoanalytic, and political modes of identification."[44] Are the latter an alternative to realism, or are they opposed to realism? Lowe explains that in the first project, "the immigrant is fixed and taken as the *symbol* of Asian Americans," but in the second, "the immigrant is at once both *symbol* and *allegory* for Asian Americans," where allegory is understood as signifying the opacity of social and historical processes that take place through "correspondences" rather than "figures that represent or reflect a given totality."[45]

Despite this carefully nuanced articulation of antirealist and antirepresentational forms of history, it is striking that Lowe characterizes the counterhistorical project as *both* symbol and allegory, since the former is characterized by a "persistent belief in a knowable social totality" while the latter signals the "impossibility of totality."[46] She tries to resolve this epistemological impasse between history and literature by displacing this disciplinary division into a political opposition in which certain forms of history and literature are aligned as oppositional while other forms are hegemonic. What enables this reconfiguration is the deployment of a chiastic relation between literature and history so that state ideology is said to operate through certain cultural forms, such as literary realism, on the one hand, while requiring the exclusion of a recalcitrant history, on the other:

> For Asians within the history of the United States . . . "political emancipation" through citizenship is never an operation confined to the negation of individual "private" particulars; it requires the negation of a history of social relations that publicly racialized groups. . . . For Asian immigrants from Vietnam, Korea, or the Philippines, this negation involves "forgetting" the history of war in Asia and adopting the national historical narrative that disavows the existence of an American imperial project. It requires acceding to a political fiction of equal rights that is generated through the denial of history, a denial that reproduces the omission of history as the ontology of the nation.[47]

This passage uses a highly nuanced rhetorical strategy in which the reversal of historical realism into antirealism is concomitant with the revision of a realist literary politics into an antirealist one. That is, state or hegemonic ideology is construed as a fiction of history, one that is naturalized by literary realism. Against this realist historical fiction, Lowe opposes another kind of history, but one, as it turns out, that belongs to the domain of culture: "the 'past' that is grasped as memory is, however, not a naturalized, factual past, for the relation to that past is always broken by war, occupation, and displacement. Asian American culture 're-members' the past in and through the fragmentation, loss, and dispersal that constitutes that past."[48] State ideology masks itself as realist history, whereas historical reality, which is excluded from the fictions of the state, is manifested most prominently in antirealist or antirepresentational forms of culture. To put it most bluntly, American history is fiction, but Asian American fiction is history.

As neat as this account may appear, it retains traces of its own irresolution. The circuitousness of Lowe's formulations signals her intense efforts to avert the various pitfalls inherent in her attempt to dismantle the disciplinary firewalls between literature and history. On the most basic level, any reconciliation between the two must negotiate the threat that each discipline poses to the other, which are the corresponding reductions of history to mere story(telling) or of literature to mere history (or facticity). Securing literary and cultural studies in history threatens to reduce the literary or cultural text to a mere conduit for historical evidence or experience. This threat is especially apparent in the history of Asian American literature, since before the establishment of Asian American studies, an Asian American literary work would almost certainly have been found in the university only outside of literature departments. The few Asian American literary texts found in the curriculum were taught as history or sociology or anthropology, not literature; hence there has always been a certain anxiety around literature's relation to history in Asian American literary studies. Perhaps of greater concern is that predicating the evaluation of culture on its congruence with some external reality or history (the problematic of representation) leads directly back to the whole discourse of authenticity and cultural nationalism. It is these concerns that seem to lay behind the claim that Asian American culture is the "material trace" of Asian American history while simultaneously trying to disclaim the notion that culture offers any immediate access to that history. The paradoxical presence or absence of history in culture (which is the structure of representation itself) means that the postulate that "the contradictory history of Asian Americans produces cultural forms that are materially and aesthetically at odds with the resolution of the citizen to the nation" can only be axiomatic.[49] Because Asian American history can be understood only in uncertain and fragmented ways, it is impossible to demonstrate the hypothesis that it is this history that produces Asian American cultural forms and not some other influence, such as the literary field.

This paradoxical relation between history and literature becomes most apparent in the chapter of Lowe's *Immigrant Acts* entitled "Decolonization,

Displacement, Disidentification: Writing and the Question of History." This chapter is particularly relevant to my analysis here, for if we ask how Asian American literature is derived from history, we will find that "it is the kind and degree of contradiction" between the "historical specificities of racialization, ghettoization, violence, and labor exploitation" and "the national narratives served by the cultural institution of the novel" that "generates formal deviations whose significances are misread if simply assimilated as modernist or postmodernist aesthetic modes."[50] Lowe illustrates this argument with readings of three Asian American texts, but I will focus here on her discussion of *Dictée*, in which she comments on a passage alluding to the student revolt of April 19, 1960, and its suppression by the South Korean government. For Lowe, this passage exemplifies

> a conception of history that treats the "historical" not as a continuous narrative of progress, maturity, and increasing rationality . . . but as a surplus of materiality that exceeds textualization, that renders inoperable the vocabularies and grammars of nineteenth-century, post-Enlightenment narrative. . . . The materiality of history is, in this passage, what will not be ordered, what does not coagulate and cohere. This materiality does not become accessible with a mere change of perspective or even a shift to another narrative; it is not exclusively a question of creating more "accurate" narratives. Rather, "history" becomes "visible" not in its narrative representation but in its defiance of the dominant regimes of representability.[51]

Despite the finely calibrated rhetoric of Lowe's argument, there is a crucial slippage here between realist narrative and narrative as such. Are there not forms of narrative that are neither linear nor developmental? This is a question that is never asked. In any event, this passage argues that subaltern histories cannot be depicted in narrative but appear only as the surplus that disrupts narrative, as what cannot be narrated or represented.

Behind this account is a different kind of historical narrative, one signaled in the nineteenth-century periodization of realist narrative, as it was the emergence of modernism in the late nineteenth century that led to the erosion of literary realism. Lowe asserts that *Dictée* did not emerge from the same historical conditions as either modernism or postmodernism and that Asian American culture in general is "unassimilable to modern institutions" and cannot be construed as high art that "resides in an autonomous domain outside of mass society and popular practices."[52]

I will return to the question of *Dictée*'s location in the field of cultural production, but at this point I note only that Lowe's desire to pose Asian American culture in opposition to the legacy of modernism concerns how modernism constituted itself through the rejection of a realist representation that it associated with history and referentiality. Lowe's argument, in contrast, is that the formal features of a text like *Dictée* are instead an expression of the recalcitrance of Asian American history to its narration by dominant cultural forms.

Despite its attribution as the material trace of history, Asian American culture seems actually to be the locus of the *unrepresentability* of history, and it is this absence of history that is the generative principle of *form* in Asian American literature. That is, because history cannot be represented at the level of content (since it contradicts modes of realist representation), it can manifest itself in Asian American literature only at the level of form (as a deviation). By regarding the narrative and representational content of the literary work as a misrepresentation of history, which can truly emerge only through form (albeit negatively), Lowe is able to effect a rapprochement between history and literature by means of the split between form and content. In this way, her model constructs the basis for an interdisciplinary paradigm of Asian American studies by reaffirming the separation of history from literature and installing them in two discontinuous domains. Interdisciplinarity ends up operating again through the displacement of disciplinary divisions, this time by relocating that division within the literary text itself. Moreover, by protecting form from its reduction to content, this partition allows historical realism to reenter as the "surplus of materiality" that exists before its narrativization because it has now been safely consigned to a sphere essentially outside the text proper, which is also the space of criticism. That is, if it is possible to discuss the question of history in *Dictée* at all, it is because history is supplied to us not by the text itself (since it cannot be) but by the critic.

At this point we may have identified the particular structure of articulation between history and literature, but the question of what motivates this effort remains. We can begin to answer this question by detailing how Lowe's model revises the critical orthodoxy that has defined Asian American literary studies since its inception. The guiding assumptions of this critical perspective are exemplified by Elaine Kim's pioneering study *Asian American Literature: An Introduction to the Writings and Their Social Context* (1982), in which she notes the bifurcation of critical responses into "literary" and "content" analyses. Although she affirms the importance of both approaches, Kim declares that she has chosen to "emphasize how the literature elucidates the social history of Asians in the United States."[53] Lowe's book revises Kim's work in several important ways. One is that she attempts to reconcile Kim's historicist approach with formal analysis, rather than opposing it. By recasting history in an anti-realist conceptual frame, Lowe's model deflects the tendency to evaluate literary texts according to how accurately they reflect the reality of Asian American experiences. Although I have suggested that the desire to circumvent historical reflectionism comes from the effort to evade a cultural nationalist aesthetics, this does not necessarily lead to the conclusion that a historical formalism is what is warranted. The necessity of the latter, I would argue, cannot be derived simply from the exigencies of the former, although why one would want to introduce formalist criticism into Asian American studies is hardly a mystery. It is not simply that formal analysis remains the basis of most academic literary criticism but that the dearth of this kind of analysis was one of the main factors in the impression that Asian American literature and literary studies were "underdeveloped" and thus lacking complexity and sophistication.

If antiessentialism was the conceptual linchpin allowing theory to claim for academic work a political effect by labeling social constructionist critique as political intervention, the theory of form as the product of historical absence would give a political rationale to the literature valued in the autonomous field (and in the academy). *Immigrant Acts*, in other words, is concerned with questions of legitimacy. To understand struggles over legitimacy as confrontations between divergent strategies of capital formation and accumulation can help demonstrate some of the basic issues of interdisciplinarity and academic politics. For example, one of the main difficulties that Lowe's theoretical model confronts is reconciling the aesthetic value of Asian American literature with its political value. In the case of literature, the antithesis of aesthetic and political value has to do partly with how identity politics and cultural nationalism (according to the prevailing account in the field) construed the political value of the Asian American literary text according to its representational content in an evaluative framework of accurate or authentic images and false or stereotypical images. These political criteria, though, resulted in the acclamation of literary texts with the least legitimacy in the autonomous field (since those criteria devalue realism and other kinds of representational content) and also required a critical practice perceived as illegitimate in the academy (content analysis rather than formal analysis). The rejection of realist representation, then, opens a space for the revaluation of more formally complex literary texts as well as more "sophisticated" critical modes, but this revaluation necessarily requires a political rationale in order not to be seen as simply capitulating to institutional demands (among other reasons).

Although Lowe is generally careful to avoid normative or evaluative judgments, the question of legitimacy becomes evident when she asserts that Asian American literature is characterized by "formal deviations whose significances are misread if simply assimilated as modernist or postmodernist aesthetic modes. Asian American work is not properly or adequately explained by the notion of postmodernism as an aesthetic critique of high modernism, for Asian American work emerges out of very different contradictions of modernity."[54] As compelling a theoretical formulation as this may be, when forced to identify what sustains the argument that Asian American culture emerges outside the aesthetic domain, the rhetoric reverts to a language of legitimation in such terms as *misread*, *properly*, and *adequately*. The judgment of what might be a proper or adequate reading is entirely contingent, and as the invocation of propriety discloses, what is at stake here is the question of property or ownership, namely, the ownership of Asian American literature by Asian American literary studies. Whatever else we might say about this argument, we must recognize that in the institutional struggles over academic capital, Lowe's argument functions first and foremost as a claim that Asian American literature is most properly read by Asian Americanist critics. This is one reason for the effort to relocate the interpretive horizon of an Asian Americanist hermeneutics from literary tradition (the property of traditional literary studies) to Asian American history (the property of Asian American studies).

Historical Transformations of Political and Cultural Capital

In what way are questions of property tied to debates over representation? Even as critics argue that Asian American literature can not or should not represent Asian Americans, they are simultaneously engaged in struggles over who can properly or legitimately read Asian American literature and what the appropriate critical or theoretical frameworks are for representing that literature. Accordingly, the effort to resolve Asian American culture's contradictory relation to history as both realist and antirealist can be read as the production of a mechanism of exchange between the political capital of Asian American identity and the cultural capital of Asian

American literature. In this context we return to the extraordinary transformation of Asian American literary studies that was mobilized around readings of *Dictée* in order to ask why representation came to be seen as something that had to be rejected. In her influential reading, Shelley Wong posits the demographic changes in the Asian American population as rendering identity politics increasingly untenable, but her account leaves out the more immediate institutional and disciplinary contexts that seem evident in this revisionist impulse. As much as the rereading of *Dictée* may have been motivated by a crisis of identity politics, I suggest that it also was motivated by a crisis of legitimacy, a crisis that required new strategies of capital accumulation which then subsequently restructured the entire field of Asian American literary studies.

The outbreak of the "canon wars" may have been provoked by efforts to intervene in the structures of reproduction of embodied cultural capital by disrupting the stability of its objectified correlatives—by displacing the particular texts in which that capital was embedded and also by attacking the forms of legitimation that upheld the universality and disinterestedness of those texts—but what happens to those minority texts that are successfully integrated into the curriculum? Do they become canonical in the same way, as Guillory asserts, or is canonicity itself modified? Here I shall use *Dictée* as a case study not of canonization but the countercanonization of an Asian American text. If Asian American literary studies began as a nationalist project for the credentialization of Asian American culture, then the critical watershed provoked by *Dictée* can be seen as the turn to an alternative strategy, which is the reappropriation of legitimate culture as Asian American. In other words, the first task is to legitimize an Asian American culture that has no legitimacy in the university, while the second task is to extract legitimacy from cultural works produced by artists who can be "reclaimed" as Asian Americans. This reclamation, as we shall see, turns on its head the cultural nationalist dictum that real Asian American literature can be produced only by authentic Asian Americans.

Shelley Wong begins her essay on *Dictée* by declaring that it is "not a representative work."[55] It was this refusal of representation, according to Wong, that was responsible for its neglect, since Asian American cultural politics before the 1990s espoused a cultural nationalist paradigm in which representativeness and authenticity were the key indices of a text's value. It was in this context that *Dictée* was excluded from the Asian American literary field because it rejected the core values of the aesthetic realism that defined the field: "correspondence, mimesis and equivalence," according to Lowe.[56] What accounts for the sudden critical revaluation in which *Dictée* is not only included in the field but also elevated to a position of prominence? Wong asserts that this turn of critical fortunes had less to do with the text's aesthetic or avant-garde qualities as with

> the changing frameworks of reception within the Asian American community, changes that are the result not of transitory literary fashions, but, rather, the conjunction of several historical developments in the 1970s and 1980s: major demographic changes within the Asian American community from 1965–1985; the growing strength and influence of the women's movement; the postmodernist concern with fragmentation and multiple positionalities; and the emergence of new social movements that necessitated the rethinking of oppositional strategies.[57]

The story, in essence, is that the Asian American community was once relatively homogeneous and unified, conditions that fostered the emergence of identity politics with its corollary aesthetics of realist representation and developmental narrative. Because of various historical shifts within the Asian American community, though, identity politics subsequently became so heterogeneous and internally divided that no singular representation of the category was possible any longer.

This attribution of the theoretical turn that was consolidated around *Dictée* and led to historical transformations of the Asian American community has attained the status of orthodoxy in Asian American cultural studies., but some questions remain. Although this has been taken to mean at times that identity politics is now outmoded for Asian Americans, neither Wong nor Lowe makes this argument. In fact, Lowe ends her analysis of *Dictée* with the following reflection on identity politics:

> Resistances to domination based on identity have been essential, and it seems inconceivable that they will diminish while the material conditions which produce them—racism, colonialism, capitalism and sexism—not only continue, but, in particular regions and spheres, seem to have refortified. At the same time, the urgent concerns of a politics of difference, rather than identity, demand attention and dialogue. . . . These interrogations of heterogeneity, intersection, and multiplicity do not, and should not, supplant the earlier mode of identity politics, as struggles continue and extend their modes, sites, and forms of contestation . . . the two

differing political modes must engage, conflict, and necessarily shift one another's strategies and priorities.[58]

As a characterization of the relation of the politics of identity to the politics of difference, this passage is incisive and nuanced. The question is how this account of the political sphere can be applied to the cultural sphere. The political and cultural fields seem to be discontinuous, for even if we grant that identity and difference are dialectically related in the political field, it is less evident how their corresponding aesthetic modes engage each other. Is it possible, for example, to say that *Dictée* is representative in some way if it also refuses representation or that it is both realist and nonrealist? Lowe argues that *Dictée* disrupts the conventions of the realist novel, but if realism is conceived as the production of verisimilitude, then any text that disrupts verisimilitude would seem, by definition, to no longer be realist.

Anne Cheng asks another version of this question: "What does it mean to read this increasingly prominent text as a 'multicultural, feminist, postcolonial and ethnic memoir' when its process of recollection continually stalls and refuses identification even on the simplest level?"[59] Similarly, Sue Kim points to the tension between readings that ascribe the political significance of *Dictée* to its recovery of marginalized histories and experiences, as opposed to those that valorize its formal disruptions. If we privilege its aesthetic strategies, for example, then what distinguishes *Dictée* from other forms of avant-garde or postmodern art? If the difference lies in her identity as a Korean American woman, this would seem to revert to identity politics. Kim's essay offers a corrective to the overemphasis on *Dictée*'s formal politics by historicizing the text in relation to the debates about aesthetic politics encapsulated in *Apparatus*, the anthology of film theory edited by Cha herself, as well as in relation to the suppressed histories of Korea and Korean Americans. Kim concludes that

> placing Cha's work in the histories of form indicated in *Apparatus* leads us, ironically, to the argument that the political intervention of *Dictée* stems less from its formal experimentation than from its emphasis on those suppressed histories. That is, the particular innovation of the novel comes from its coupling of the formal strategies, which always self-reflexively insist upon skepticism of signification, with the particular histories and contexts dealt with in the novel.[60]

Although I do not disagree with this assessment, I do want to qual-ify one aspect of Kim's argument, which is that the inclusion of Korean/American history is a political intervention only *in the dominant aesthetic field*, the primary context of the "histories of form" in *Apparatus*. In con-trast, in the Asian American cultural field, it is the formal aspects of the text that register as innovative or unorthodox. Given Cha's previous work in film history and theory, the argument that *Dictée*'s effect derives from its inclusion of Cha's own history in that field seems compelling. What is less so is the contrasting implication: that her references to Korean history and immigration somehow mark the text as a work of Asian American lit-erature. I suggest that many of the disagreements about *Dictée* and its ap-propriate interpretive contexts are based on the least visible precondition of the entire discourse around it, which is the claim that *Dictée* belongs to the Asian American literary field. For example, despite Wong's assertion that *Dictée* is not a representative text, she refers to it repeatedly as a text by a "Korean American immigrant woman writer." Although she is refer-ring to *Dictée*'s refusal to represent *Asian American* identity, the relation of the category of "Korean American immigrant woman writer" to the text is unclear. How can *Dictée* be characterized as a Korean American immigrant woman's text if it does not have a representative or exemplary relation to that category? If *Dictée* does not reflect a significant aspect of Korean American immigrant women's experiences, then what is the pur-pose of classifying it in those terms?

Let us, for instance, take the argument that *Dictée* critiques Asian American identity by refusing to represent it. What happens to this argu-ment if we no longer consider *Dictée* to be an Asian American text? In that case, the absence of any representation of Asian American identity would not appear to be a critique; Asian American identity would simply be one of many things *not* represented in the book. The lack of repre-sentation appears intentional only when the text is located *in the Asian American literary field*. Many of the political claims made for *Dictée* may appear in a different light when we consider that there is little indication that Cha saw herself as part of either the Asian American political or lit-erary field. Regardless of her own self-conception, the more important is-sue is that those who belonged to the Asian American literary field did not view her as operating within it. This is not to say that *Dictée* should not be included in the field but that the terms of its inclusion change de-pending on whether this inclusion results from a critical, an authorial, or a textual claim. Let us assume that *Dictée* can be classified as an Asian

American text owing to critical interventions, as Wong seems to indicate in her emphasis on the "changing frameworks of reception" of the text. Why would some critics want to (re)claim a text that earlier critics had rejected?

My argument here is that Asian American literary studies had reached a certain limit of capital accumulation, which was the internal contradiction in the field between its political legitimacy and its aesthetic/academic legitimacy. In order for the field to advance beyond this limit, it needed to reconfigure the relation between these two. *Dictée* facilitated a critique of identity politics and its aesthetics of realist representation and authentic (or positive) depictions. What "difference" made possible in this context was the elaboration of a politics of form rather than content, which meant that Asian American literary studies could recalibrate its scale of value so that it would correlate with the structures of value in the dominant cultural field. Although the inclusion of *Dictée* in the Asian American literary field enabled some of the capital that it had accumulated from the dominant aesthetic field to be siphoned off for Asian American literature, its greater purpose was to restructure the space of positions in the field to permit new mechanisms for the conversion and accumulation of capital.

This effort confronted the basic difficulty with *Dictée*, which is that it is extraordinarily resistant to easy incorporation into any field, especially those defined according to identity. For Asian American literary studies to wrest *Dictée* away from the field of the avant-garde, a claim had to be made for it on the basis of identity, as a text by an Asian American writer. At the same time, to conserve its revisionary potential for the field, this identity claim had to be reduced to its most schematic so that it would not interfere with the formalist arguments. If the main obstacle to *Dictée*'s incorporation into the Asian American literary field was its resistance to identity and representation, one solution would be to redefine the Asian American literary field in accordance with that very resistance. Asian American culture became the site not of the production of identity but of its deconstruction. In this way, *Dictée* was incorporated into the field and even became the field's exemplary instance. Indeed, the opening sentences of Lowe's essay on the book underscores the contradictions in this revaluation:

Theresa Hak Kyung Cha's *Dictée* proposes questions that engage and disturb desires—critical desire, disciplinary desire, incorporative desire. *An Asian American text*, a postcolonial text, and a woman's text, it evokes alternately a girlhood education in French Catholicism, a brief history of Korean nationalism during the Japanese colonial occupation, as well as episodes from the narrator's displaced adulthood as a Korean American immigrant and her return to a military-ruled South Korea.[61]

The invocation of desire—whose desires?—is striking here and is immediately followed by the assertion that *Dictée* is an Asian American text. It is, however, only because the adjective "Asian American" has been attached to the text that it is then possible to turn around and argue that *Dictée* in fact *displaces* Asian American identity.

Whatever symbolic value *Dictée* may have, it does not seem sufficient to account for its enormous impact on the field of Asian American literary and cultural studies, as well as Asian American studies as a whole. I agree with Wong that to understand these effects, we must situate the revisionary readings of *Dictée* in the larger historical context of the Asian American field. Wong argues that

> in the face of a radically recompositioned constituency, Asian American cultural nationalism became less and less able to specify a common political agenda and cultural identity around which the entire Asian American population could cohere. The respective needs—economic, social, political, cultural—of an increasingly diverse population which included fourth-generation Japanese American professionals as well as first-generation Hmong farmers could hardly be addressed or accommodated within a single oppositional program.
>
> With the advent of the new social movements of the 1980s—some centering on peoples: gays, lesbians, the physically challenged; others on issues: peace, ecology—came the dispersal of political allegiances which called into question the effectiveness of an oppositional strategy founded on the basis of racial identification alone. Asian American identity politics and the nationalist form it took began to founder in this welter of difference.[62]

This story of the fall of Asian America from the Eden of identity politics may provoke some skepticism. Whether Asian American cultural nationalism was ever able to "specify a common political agenda" is debatable. The sole example that Wong cites in her discussion of identity politics and cultural nationalism is *Aiiieeeee!* but as I will demonstrate in chapter 4, *Aiiieeeee!* was seen as apolitical by much of the more radical cultural left.

Moreover, many who participated in the Asian American movement dispute that it was based on "racial identification" alone.[63]

Most historical and sociological accounts offer a different narrative of the development of the panethnic Asian American political coalition, suggesting that initially it had only limited appeal among the general "Asian American" population and had to overcome some large obstacles in order to become widely recognized. Yen Le Espiritu observed that

> pan-Asianism has been primarily the ideology of native-born, American-educated, and middle-class Asians. Embraced by students, artists, professionals, and political activists, pan-Asian consciousness thrived on college campuses and in urban settings. However, it barely touched the Asian ethnic enclaves. When the middle-class student activists carried the enlarged and politicized Asian American consciousness to the ethnic communities, they encountered apprehension, if not outright hostility. Conscious of their national origins and overburdened with their day-to-day struggles for survival, most community residents ignored or spurned the movement's political agenda.[64]

At the very least, the notion that identity politics or cultural nationalism was ever able to unite a large segment of the Asian American population must be complicated. Although this observation does not obviate the argument for the necessity of a politics of difference, it does raise questions about how the political argument for the disruption of identity or representation has been extended to the domain of culture. If the waning of identity politics in the 1980s does not provide a plausible historical context for the revaluation of *Dictée*, then what would account for this critical moment?

Heterogeneity in and of itself is not a problem; it becomes a problem only when the heterogeneity of the Asian American population manifests itself in conflicting political priorities and agendas. Asian American cultural nationalism and the brand of identity politics espoused in *Aiiieeeee!* were less concerned with forcing a unitary identity on Asian Americans than they were with representing the unity of the theoretical class and the real class. The central issue, in other words, was that the radical politics of the Asian American movement was a minority ideology among the "Asian American" population in general. The various demographic changes in the Asian American community, along with the decline of the mass mobilizations of the 1960s and 1970s only made this disparity more apparent. The cultural nationalist solution to this problem was to institute a division between assimilationist Asians and nationalist Asian Americans, thereby excluding those who did not subscribe to authentic Asian American politics. This was credible as long as native-born Asian Americans were the majority, but with the tremendous growth in Asian immigration, this division threatened to exclude the majority of the Asian American population.

It was in this particular conjuncture, I argue, that the inclusion of *Dictée* in the Asian American literary field facilitated the reconceptualization of the relation between culture and politics, especially with regard to the question of representation. If the principal trope of the critical revaluations of *Dictée* was refusal, we might read this as an attempt to come to terms with the apparent "refusal" of much of the Asian American population to consent to their representation by the Asian American movement. My use of the term *refusal* is meant to encompass a range of responses from the outright rejection of Asian American politics to simple indifference. If Asian American identity politics sought to produce political unity through identity and culture, readings of *Dictée* proposed a new model for producing political subjects at the level of form rather than content. This new model evacuated the content of identity categories in order to recast them as purely formal identities, producing what we might call a *formal identity politics* (which may be a more specific permutation of strategic essentialism). In this way, Asian American politics can be liberated from the straitjacket of a narrowly defined identity or culture, even as it retains the identity category, because this identity has now been emptied and rendered completely abstract, which is to say, a purely structural effect.

Revisionary readings of *Dictée* offered a solution to the dilemma of claiming to represent those who refused to be represented by positing the defining feature of Asian American identity as the refusal of identity as such. Thus *Dictée* is the paradigmatic instance of nonrepresentative representation, but this construction appears to be noncontradictory only because Asian American identity is associated with content, whereas form is construed as nonrepresentational. As a result, Asian American identity must now be vested in texts that privilege form by opposing it to content. Form in itself simply refers to a particular relation among textual contents; the intentional use of formal structures and devices that deviate from the generic expectations of realist representation belongs to the aesthetic ideology called *formalism*, which has come to be the dominant ideology of the autonomous literary field, or the field of restricted production. If formal identity politics now operates in the field of restricted production, which is the field of cultural capital, then Asian American identity would seem to have an analogous relation to nominal Asian Americans as the field of restricted production has to the field of general production. That is, given the difficulties of its transmission to the larger Asian American population, the politics of the Asian American movement now reproduces itself through the mechanisms of the autonomous field in the university, which means that it has been transformed into a species of cultural capital. If this is indeed the case, it may help explain the apparent paradox in which the radical oppositional politics of the Asian American movement is now disseminated mainly at the most elite levels of the American educational system.

4

The Political Economy of
Minority Literature

"Asian American literature" as such can come into being only when there is a socially recognized category of identity and an institutionally defined literary field. As a subcomponent of the general field of Asian American identity, the Asian American literary field was formed amid intense political struggles over the definitions of the category. In large part, this was because no institutions were capable of sanctioning the legitimate definition of identity (or literature or research, and so forth) or of regulating access to the power to define legitimacy. This chapter retraces the struggles among the competing definitions of Asian American literature in the debates concerning two of the central texts of this period, *Aiiieeeee!* one of the first anthologies of Asian American literature published in 1974, and *The Woman Warrior*, published in 1975, the book that almost single-handedly catapulted Asian American literature from obscurity into public consciousness. The conflicts over such issues as authenticity and assimilation revolved around the legitimate definition of Asian American literature, but instead of rehearsing the particular issues, I will situate these struggles in the larger field of power relations in which they were defined. What follows is a descriptive and analytical, not a normative, account of certain definitions of Asian American literature. The point of this study is not to produce a better or more adequate definition of Asian American literature but to examine the general context in which these definitions were produced and the particular interests that shaped their articulation.

Any discussion of Asian American literature must begin, either implicitly or explicitly, by defining it and thus replicating in microcosm the same debates about categorization and identity that we already have examined. The starting point of my analysis is the conditions of belonging to the Asian American literary field. The most basic definition of Asian American literature is that it is literature written by Asian Americans, but because Asian American identity is not an ontological fact, identity cannot automatically qualify someone for inclusion in the field. Although we already have seen some of the critical claims made about *Dictée* that have been central to the history of Asian American literary studies, this chapter will investigate the kinds of claims that might be attributed to writers and texts. An authorial claim may consist of an explicit self-identification as an Asian American writer. This is, however, simply the minimal threshold of inclusion and tells us almost nothing about what it means to that writer to be an Asian American. In most cases, we can determine the details of that identification or positioning only in that writer's texts.

To ask how one becomes an Asian American writer is really to ask two distinct, though related, questions. First, what makes Asian American literature a field? And second, how does a writer or text come to be included in this field? To answer the first question, I argue that the field of Asian American literature is defined by autonomy from the community and that it is marked by the struggle over the legitimate mode of representation. In the dominant field, autonomy comes through a liberation from, or a refusal of, the burden of representation, but in the field of Asian American literature it can be achieved only through the *assumption* of representation. In other words, the Asian American literary field could not have been established without the possibility of representing Asian Americans. There must be a group of people who "need" representation (since they are not represented by the dominant field) in order for a literature to have to be created to represent them. It is the question of how to define that "need" that will become one of the central objects of struggle in the field.

In answer to the second question, writers belong to the Asian American literary field if their writing presents some implicit or explicit claim to represent Asian Americans. To say or think of oneself as an Asian American writer leads to two more questions: Who are Asian Americans, and what is my relationship to that group? The Asian American field and the dominant field are autonomous because they both are premised on a hierarchical and nonreciprocal relation. The difference, however, is the image that each relation of representation projects of Asian Americans as the object of representation. The dominant field demands the subsumption of particularity to universality, as in narratives of minorities developing into a correspondence to the majority.[1] In contrast, the Asian American literary field demands the construction of the Asian American as a resistant or counterhegemonic subject, partly for political reasons but also because a resistant constituency is the only one that provides a rationale for a separate Asian American literary field.

In the view of the *Aiiieeeee!* editors, the political function of Asian American culture is to define the community (that is, produce the Asian American subject). In the commercial field (or the field of general production), in contrast, the purpose of Asian American literature is to represent (in a purely descriptive or aesthetic sense) the community, or Asian American culture, hence the ethnographic imperative that many have identified in the dominant field (as in the prevalence of autobiography and so on). The editors of *Aiiieeeee!* clearly refused the latter form of representation in relation to the commercial field, which they identify as Orientalist. Seen from a different perspective, however, we might also say that the latter mode of representation is objectionable because it implies that one might actually have to account in some way for the desires of those who are represented, although this is certainly not the reason that the commercial field demands this form of representation.

To return to the question of autonomy, the first thing to note is that Asian American literature does not need autonomy from the market, since there is little "danger" (at least initially) of submission to the market. Rather, Asian American literature needs autonomy from the political demands of the community, for example, the demand for an activist and politically committed art, the kind of art that early critics such as Bruce Iwasaki espoused.[2] This is definitely not the kind of art in which the *Aiiieeeee!* editors are interested. In relation to the Asian American community, the *Aiiieeeee!* project is actually about carving out a space for the Asian American writer to represent the community in the way that he or she sees fit, rather than being obligated to represent the community in the way that it would like to be represented. This is the meaning of autonomy in the Asian American literary field—as well as in the dominant field—and it is connected to the particular relation of representation between the literary field and the community. Thus, we need to revise our understanding of the *Aiiieeeee!* project in order to grasp how its definitions of Asian American literature distinguish the field from both the dominant autonomous field and the Asian American community. What is instituted in the formation of Asian American literature as an autonomous field is a nonreciprocal relation of representation perhaps best encapsulated in the notion of "artistic freedom."

The Emergence of the Asian American Literary Field

The *Aiiieeeee!* anthology was originally published in 1974 by Howard University Press and was edited by Frank Chin, Jeffery Chan, Lawson Inada, and Shawn Wong. Although it was not the first anthology of Asian American literature, it was the most programmatic, the most polemical, and the most controversial. Much of the controversy stemmed from the editors' attempts to establish a set of political criteria by which to include or exclude works as authentically Asian American. These criteria then generated most of the discussion in literary studies about identity politics and cultural nationalism. The best-known issue here is the infamous exchange between Frank Chin and Maxine Hong Kingston over the publication of *The Woman Warrior* in 1975. Chin was perhaps the most vociferous critic of that text—but by no means the only one—charging that Kingston distorted the reality of Chinese and Chinese American culture (for example, by reinterpreting and revising various narratives from Chinese culture) and that in her depiction of sexism and patriarchy in Chinese culture she reaffirms a long history of representations of Oriental despotism that reinforce the cultural superiority of the West and emasculate Asian American men.

This exchange led to a profusion of critical commentary in Asian American studies, but without a systematic analysis of the Asian American literary field, there has been a general misrecognition of what was at stake in *Aiiieeeee!*[3] This misunderstanding was compounded by the general tendency to read the original *Aiiieeeee!* as more or less continuous with its successor, *The Big Aiiieeeee!* (published in 1991). In fact, the latter substantially modifies and to a large extent reverses several of the theses advanced in the former. To understand the reasons for the change in direction, we need to return to the first *Aiiieeeee!* While almost every discussion of this anthology has accepted its polemic at face value, as typical of the politicization of culture in the 1960s, critics failed to recognize that the editors' main concern was less to prescribe a politics of Asian American culture than to devise a theory of cultural production that would provide "serious art" with a political rationale. This intention becomes evident only when we resituate the *Aiiieeeee!* polemic in its historical context. Setting aside for the moment the editors' rhetoric, we can discern what they were arguing *for* by asking what they were arguing *against*. William Wei was one of the few commentators who recognized that in the context of the Asian American movement, the *Aiiieeeee!* editors did not belong to the radical wing of Asian American cultural politics. Instead, Wei aligned the

Aiiieeeee! group with the "aesthetic approach" to art rather than the "political approach," which was composed of artists and performers whose only purpose for art was social or political.[4] Their principal artistic objectives were consciousness raising and political mobilization, and they believed that culture could serve this function only if it were accessible to the masses.

Chris Iijima, one of the members of the early Asian American folk trio A Grain of Sand, recalled the group's attitude toward the music they played in the 1960s and 1970s:

> We were simply responding to what was going on around, about, and within us. It was an activity that found its meaning and purpose not intrinsically, but in relation to what it fed and what it was nurtured by. "Asian American culture" thirty years ago was, in essence, the cumulative political and ideological acts of many different Asian Americans contesting subordination in many different ways. All that we did was sing about it.[5]

Iijima denied that his role as an artist was special or distinctive, and he characterized Asian American culture as simply the reflection of the community's resistance to oppression. He then declared that "Asian American culture is too often defined backwards. That is, we tend to define it in terms of what artists do . . . rather than in terms of the collective and shared experience of people."[6] Defining art as what *artists* do is one of the main objectives in the introduction to *Aiiieeeee!* with its emphasis on the author's signature and the way that the status of the text depended on the author's identity.

In a 1971 essay predating *Aiiieeeee!* Bruce Iwasaki discusses some of the early works by Frank Chin and Lawson Inada. Iwasaki notes their complaints about the stereotypical language spoken by Asian characters in Orientalist depictions: "It is easy to see why they reject such stereotypes about the degree centuries of Eastern culture influence third generation Asian Americans," but then he remarks that Chin and Inada "seem to reject the culture too."[7] Iwasaki's criticism of what he sees as a reductive emphasis on language in the criticism and fiction of Chin and Inada exemplifies the kinds of attacks that the *Aiiieeeee!* editors appear to be anticipating.

> The problem isn't diction—or tone, style, accents, speech, or even language. They're off the mark . . . if they assert that the problem of Asian

Americans is that they mimic—either the classic Orient, black rhetoric, or white colloquialisms. Here Inada and Chin are responding to the majority culture's stereotypes instead of confronting the actual root problems of the Asian American community.

Again, we have the limitation, the absorbtion [*sic*], of both content and form. No matter how "universal" the language and style, a piece of literature will not convey a universal human experience as long as the community is used merely as source material. Employed in this way, the community becomes little more than "local color"—in writing, not at all less deplorable than an affected style. We are at the point where art touches society, for here artistic decisions are tied with moral, and finally, political decisions. And by ignoring this crucial interrelationship, Chin and Inada remain within the bounds that makes so much literature "safe."[8]

Instead, Iwasaki espouses the "merging of political action and literature," in which "literature and change no longer *describe* each other—they become the *same thing*."[9] How do literature and social change become the same? Although Iwasaki has no ready answer, he does offer an example of art that approaches this ideal, the music of A Grain of Sand, and he ends his essay by citing the lyrics of one of their songs in its entirety.

According to critics like Iijima and Iwasaki, the attempt to create "real" or "serious" art is irrelevant to the cultural-political work of mobilizing the masses. The introductory essays in *Aiiieeeee!* thus seem to respond to these kinds of criticisms by giving art a moral and political content, but their desire to establish Asian American literature as a domain of art much like the dominant autonomous literary field does not change, despite those who called for a "culture for the masses." Thus although the *Aiiieeeee!* editors' prescriptions for art seem superficially similar to the revolutionary view, they actually differ in a number of respects and in fact reverse the priority of politics over art. If this aim no longer seems apparent to academic readers, it may be because they inhabit essentially the same world as the editors and have a similar purpose: the political legitimation of autonomous activities.

How do the *Aiiieeeee!* editors proceed in their attempts to supply a political rationalization for art? A passage from the preface summarizes almost the entire argument:

Seven generations of suppression under legislative racism and euphemized white racist love have left today's Asian Americans in a state of self-contempt, self-rejection, and disintegration. We have been encouraged to believe that we have no cultural integrity as Chinese or Japanese Americans, that we are either Asian (Chinese or Japanese) or American (white), or are measurably both. This myth of being either/or and the equally goofy concept of the dual personality haunted our lobes while our rejection by both Asia and white America proved we were neither one nor the other. Nor were we half and half or more one than the other. Neither Asian culture nor American culture was equipped to define us except in the most superficial terms. However, American culture, equipped to deny us the legitimacy of our uniqueness as American minorities, did so, and in the process contributed to the effect of stunting self-contempt on the development and expression of our sensibility that in turn has contributed to a mass rejection of Chinese and Japanese America by Chinese and Japanese Americans.[10]

This argument is familiar to those in Asian American literary studies, but the peculiar logic of its rhetoric is not as self-evident as it may appear, especially with regard to the notion of "cultural integrity," which is one of the key concepts in *Aiiieeeee!* The preceding passage asserts that the cultural integrity of Asian Americans has been destroyed by the "racist love" of white American society and that this suppression was one of the means by which American society was able to keep Asian Americans in a state of subordination. The reason was that the lack of cultural integrity leads to self-contempt—or what others have called *disidentification*—and the political disintegration of the community. The solution to this problem, then, is to create a distinctive Asian American culture that will unite the community and presumably motivate political action.

The audacity of this thesis has rarely been fully appreciated, since it effectively proposes that "serious" literature is the answer to racism and the political disempowerment of the Asian American community. The usual interpretation is that culture should complement political action and not supplant it. This may be how other parties perceive the relation between culture and politics, but in *Aiiieeeee!* I would argue, culture competes with politics for legitimacy. The proposition that literature is the most effective response to racism is posed *against* the kind of cultural politics in which art must be subordinated to the needs of political mobilization. The import of this position usually is not recognized because in most Asian American literary criticism, *Aiiieeeee!* is either conflated with the more radical leftists or is simply made to stand for the prioritization of politics over art.[11] Moreover, those who claim that the *Aiiieeeee!* position is meant to accompany political mobilization must reckon with the deliberate silence surrounding any mention of actual political struggles in the community. There is no mention at all of labor issues, housing, poverty, lack of social services, or any of the other concrete problems confronting the community. The effects of racism and inequality are almost entirely reduced to the single vector of "self-contempt" and the lack of manhood. In this regard, the vociferousness of the polemic in *Aiiieeeee!* may be partly an attempt to appropriate some of the style and rhetoric of the more radical left in order to create the impression of political commitment.

In the preceding passage, the destruction of cultural integrity appears to be one of the main effects of racism, which is glossed as the denial of "the legitimacy of our uniqueness as American minorities." This phrase appears to refer to the refusal of Asian Americans' status as rightful Americans, but it does so in rather peculiar terms. What, for example, does "uniqueness" have to do with questions of racial identity? "Uniqueness" clearly derives from the literary field and is linked to the effort to produce a distinctive Asian American style and language, whereas "legitimacy" is the signifier of symbolic capital. We could translate the "legitimacy of our uniqueness" as the symbolic value of the specific capital of the Asian American field. Not surprisingly, the politics of *Aiiieeeee!* turn out to be the politics of representation, and the *Aiiieeeee!* theory of stereotypes and racist love is a strategic analysis of the politics of cultural capital. In order to rebuke the subordination of art to politics, the editors elaborate their theory of cultural integrity using the infamous division between authentic Asian American writers and assimilationist, "Americanized Asian" writers who cater to white audiences. Behind this division is the opposition between high and low culture, or the field of restricted production and the field of general production.

The primary effect of racism, as they have characterized it, is the destruction of cultural integrity, which in the *Aiiieeeee!* lexicon is code for literature. This effect can be seen in the absence not of Asian American writers in general but of "serious" writers. In the history of Asian American literature, a number of writers were quite successful but are rarely studied because they have been consigned to the ranks of the assimilationist, inauthentic writers (or for a related reason, that they aren't literary enough). The *Aiiieeeee!* editors assert that "only five American-born Chinese have published what can be called serious attempts at literature."[12] They are Pardee Lowe, Jade Snow Wong, Virginia Lee, Betty Lee Sung, and Diana Chang. Of these five, the editors maintained that the first four "were obviously manipulated by white publishers to write to and from the stereotype. Of these four, three do not consider themselves to be serious writers and welcomed the aid of editors."[13] They then cite the well-known example of Jade Snow Wong, whose editors deleted more than half of her *Fifth Chinese Daughter*. When Frank Chin asked Wong about this (in an interview quoted in *Aiiieeeee!*), Wong declared, "It's like selling to Gumps or sending to a museum. Everybody has a purpose in mind, in what they're carrying out. So, you know, you kind of have to work with them."[14] The editors' damning indictment is that "this was the talk of a good businesswoman, not a serious or very sensitive writer."[15]

The division between authentic and assimilationist writers mirrors closely the divisions between restricted and general production, in which literature constructs itself as such only by rejecting commercial success. Thus the tradition of authentic writers that *Aiiieeeee!* constructs is a tradition of failure. Not always an absolute or complete failure, but the romanticization of failure is certainly a large part of the reason why John Okada became the emblematic Asian American writer. Failure is the sign of authenticity because commercial success is cited as the mechanism of white domination by means of the theory of racist love, which posits that only those books that conform to white stereotypes of Asians will sell.[16] The notion of racist love, however, serves other, more important purposes because the phenomenon that it must ultimately explain is not the rejection of Asian American writers by the white audience but their rejection *by Asian American audiences.* What is rather surprising about the valorization of failure in *Aiiieeeee!* is that its critical apparatus presumes the antipathy of Asian American audiences to the very literary tradition that is supposed to represent them. The concept of self-contempt is the means by which the editors explain the antagonistic relation of the Asian American audience to "its" literature, although this calls into question the claim that the literature reflects or expresses the actual and authentic culture of Asian Americans. Instead, Asian American culture and identity are seen as a vanguard, as signposts of a future in which culture (in the sense of cultural production) and culture (in the sense of a way of life) might correspond. As we have seen, this is a future that has yet to be realized.

Here we return to the question of representation because if Asian American culture is not recognized as representative by those it claims to represent, in what sense can we say that it is "Asian American"? The central contradiction in *Aiiieeeee!* is the disparity between the repeated assertion that Asian American literature expresses a distinctive Asian American sensibility and the continual need to explain why Asian Americans themselves do not appreciate the literature.[17] This incongruity becomes most apparent in their discussion of *No-No Boy*, since its status as the great Asian American novel depends on its embodiment of an authentic Asian American sensibility, but this claim must be made against or despite its rejection by the Japanese American community. The editors thus produce two parallel readings of the book. One is that its greatness resides in the way that it "makes a narrative style of the Japanese American talk, gives the talk the status of a language, makes it work and styles it, deftly and crudely, and uses it to bring the unglamorous but more commonly lived aspects of Japanese American experience into the celebration of life."[18] The other reading is that *No-No Boy* "is an exploration of the universe of racial self-contempt."[19] Of course, it is possible to see these readings as describing different aspects of the text, its language and style, for example, as opposed to its narrative or characterizations. The difficulty arises from the implication that the first reading identifies what would make the book appeal to Asian American readers, while the second explains why the book did not in fact appeal to those readers.

The problem concerns the issue of categorization. That is, the conflict derives from the insistence in *Aiiieeeee!* on constructing and defining an *Asian American* literary tradition. Naming this literature as Asian American is to claim a relation between the writing and the people, but this claim continually clashes with the reality that there is apparently very little connection between the two. One might easily avoid this predicament by eliminating the phrase "Asian American" and just calling it "literature," so the question is why the editors did not do this. Alternatively, one could circumvent the issue by defining Asian American literature in terms of its content and subject matter rather than in terms of a theory of authorship based on a relation of representation. The editors understandably never explicitly acknowledge this contradiction in the introduction, nor do most of their critics. Still, what might account for their insistence on naming a literary tradition Asian American? The most obvious answer is that for Asian Americans who aspire to be writers but lack the necessary cultural capital, the alternative to competing in the dominant literary field is to form their own field. The problem, though, is that anyone can construct a category and constitute a literary tradition, but capital is what gives it substance, which in this case is capital derived from the political mobilization of Asian Americans.

Aiiieeeee! offers the paradigm for a literary field constituted by the conversion of political capital into cultural capital, in contrast with the more radical effort to mobilize culture for political action. The issue is not whether the *Aiiieeeee!* claim that Asian American literature gives expression to a culture or sensibility should be regarded as true or false but that the plausibility of the claim is inseparable from the effort to extract some of the capital accumulated by Asian American political activism. For the *Aiiieeeee!* editors, politics is less a matter of desire than necessity; that is, they do not want artistic freedom to be limited by political strictures. It is, however, what they need in order to have that art at all. The political foundation of Asian American literature means that the aspiration for an autonomous literary field confronts the antinomy of autonomy and representation. To claim a representative relation to a group is to open oneself to demands from that community, which may want to be represented in certain ways and not others. To give this power to the community is to allow them to impose limits and restrictions on the artist's creative freedom, thereby eroding the autonomy of the cultural field. To deny the community a voice in its own representation, however, would be to reduce it to mere "source material," which is the relation of representation that Iwasaki criticizes.

If the *Aiiieeeee!* editors need the community's political investment to initiate and sustain the Asian American literary field, community involvement also could threaten the autonomous development of the field so it must be mitigated or contained. I suggest that this is the work performed by the concept of "self-contempt," which is essentially a theory of racial false consciousness. Besides offering a convenient device for dismissing all criticism as the product of self-hatred, self-contempt also allows the editors to resolve the conflict between autonomy and representation. That is, the autonomy of the literary field is created by rejecting all external forms of control. The theory of self-contempt is an external projection of the field's rejection of community control, which inverts it as the community's rejection of the field. Indeed, the preface and introduction to *Aiiieeeee!* often portray writers and artists as the only Asian Americans who have an authentic sensibility. The audience, in contrast, is continually associated with rejection and self-contempt. "Authenticity," therefore, appears to be a quality always *lacking* in Asian Americans., and it names the aesthetic equivalent of the "real, best interests" of the represented, which the representative claims to follow even if the represented do not realize it themselves. In this regard, authenticity serves as a means of disciplining the community so that instead of subordinating art to politics, politics in *Aiiieeeee!* is a means of *subordinating the community to art.*

This is not simply a critical position in *Aiiieeeee!* but is realized most fully in the fiction and drama of Frank Chin, all of whose work before the publication of *Donald Duk* is obsessed with failure, particularly the failure of writers to achieve a representative relation to their community. This obsession is dramatized throughout Chin's early work in regard to gender and sexuality. The two prevalent motifs are the failed relations of fathers and sons and the Chinese American male protagonists' highly ambivalent relations with white women. About the former, the *Aiiieeeee!* editors declare that "a constant theme in Asian American literature from Pardee Lowe's *Father and Glorious Descendant* through *No-No Boy* to Frank Chin's play *The Chickencoop Chinaman* is the failure of Asian American manhood to express itself in its simplest form: fathers and sons."[20] The question is what "manhood" means in the *Aiiieeeee!* lexicon. Patricia Chu notes the gendered constructions of authorship in Chin's writing. The equation of authorship with masculinity derives from the gendering of the literary sphere as male, as opposed to the feminized domain of mass culture.[21] My argument is that gender offers a symbolic matrix to express ideas of authorship but that the content of these ideas comes primarily from the work of establishing and defining the Asian American literary field. This is not to minimize the sexism and misogyny prevalent in Chin's work, but it does suggest that these gender dynamics are overdetermined in complex ways. The imaginary rejection of the community contained in the theory of self-contempt, for example, is connected to the rejection of fathers or their failure to transmit authority to their sons. This break in the patriarchal line also means that because Asian American artists do not have the sanction of the community, they also have no responsibility to it.

The editors assert that

> the deprivation of language in a verbal society like this country's has contributed to the lack of a recognized Asian American cultural integrity . . . and the lack of a recognized style of Asian American manhood. These two conditions have produced the "house nigger mentality," under which Chinese and Japanese Americans accept responsibility for, rather than authority over the language and accept dependency.[22]

Manhood consists in the achievement of a distinctive language over which one possesses "authority." Like "cultural integrity," manhood is tied to the development of an authentic Asian American culture, and gender provides the terms in which the editors can talk about authorship while refuting associations of literature with an effete aestheticism. Masculinity signifies individual autonomy, which the editors continually present as the basis for the collective autonomy of Asian Americans. The implication is that artistic freedom is essential to community formation, rather than being a politically irresponsible individualism:

> Language is the medium of culture and the people's sensibility, including the style of manhood. Language coheres the people into a community by organizing and codifying the symbols of the people's common experience. Stunt the tongue and you have lopped off the culture and sensibility. On the simplest level, a man in any culture speaks for himself. Without a language of his own, he no longer is a man.[23]

As dubious as the last claim may be, it confirms that a "man" is identified here as someone with linguistic authority. In what sense, though, can a language be said to be "one's own"? What constitutes a relation of possession over language, which is by definition communal and constantly in flux? The issue here is less one of language than of authority; that is, language confers authority insofar as it constitutes a community that recognizes that authority.

If the duty of Asian American artists is not to represent the community in the way they would like, then what is their relation to the community? According to the editors, the task of the minority writer is either

> to legitimize his, and by implication his people's, orientation as white, to codify his experience in the form of prior symbols, clichés, linguistic mannerisms, and a sense of humor that appeals to whites because it celebrates Asian American self-contempt. Or his task is the opposite—to legitimize the language, style, and syntax of his people's experience, to codify the experiences common to his people into symbols, clichés, linguistic mannerisms, and a sense of humor that emerges from an organic familiarity with the experience.[24]

Rather than political representation (or the substantive representation of the community's needs and interests), *Aiiieeeee!* proposes that the role of the artist is to engage in the functions of legitimation and codification (or forms of classification that will produce the community as a discrete, coherent object amenable to representation), functions that we can rede-scribe as the objectification of culture in order to convert it into capital. What authorizes the artist to perform this function is a relation of representation to the Asian American community, based not on the consent of the represented but on the artist's inherent Asian American sensibility. This qualification, moreover, is capable of being judged only by those who already possess it, which seems to mean only other artists, thus exemplifying the very definition of the field of restricted production, which is production for other producers.

Ethnography as Capital Accumulation

Nearly two decades after the original *Aiiieeeee!* was published, its successor, *The Big Aiiieeeee!* came out in 1991. Most critics perceived the two anthologies as preoccupied with the same concerns, and many conflated their positions. In *The Big Aiiieeeee!* for example, the main issue was still the division between authentic and assimilationist artists, now expressed as the "real" and the "fake." The basis for these evaluations was completely reversed from the first book to the second, though, a fact that has not been adequately explained. The tentatively asserted Asian American sensibility in *Aiiieeeee!* which was defined *against* Asian identity, hardened in *The Big Aiiieeeee!* into an essentialized Asian American culture that maintains an unbroken continuity *with* Asia, in the "essential works of the universal Chinese and Japanese childhood."[25] What might account for this change of direction?[26] The cast of villains from the first *Aiiieeeee!* has expanded to include contemporary writers, most notably Maxine Hong Kingston, David Henry Hwang, and Amy Tan. The addition of these writers to the denigrated writers of the first anthology conceals the radical transformation in the sociohistorical contexts of the two groups' cultural production.

Aiiieeeee! begins with the premise that there is no serious Asian American literature, the lack of which is the result of racism. But in *The Big Aiiieeeee!* this premise no longer holds, because there now is an Asian American literary field. The problem, however, is that most readers and critics identify it with Kingston, Hwang, and, to a lesser extent, Tan, as well as a few others. Since the issue is no longer the necessity of creating an Asian American literary field against the commercial field, the definitions of authenticity and assimilation required a major revision. Although assimilation is still associated with work that reproduces stereotypes, the nature of the stereotype has shifted. That is, the stereotype in *Aiiieeeee!* was originally that of the Asian as a perpetual foreigner, part of whom remained bound to Asia and therefore ill suited to modern Western culture. The charge against Kingston, Hwang, and Tan, in contrast, was not that their work was too Asian but that it wasn't Asian enough. Chin's main complaint about Kingston, for example, pertained to her creative license regarding well-known Chinese stories and myths, as in her rewriting of the story of Fa Mulan.

> Kingston, Hwang, and Tan are the first writers of any race, and certainly the first writers of Asian ancestry, to so boldly fake the best-known works from the most universally known body of Asian literature and lore in history. And, to legitimize their faking, they have to fake all of Asian American history and literature, and argue that the immigrants who settled and established Chinese America lost touch with Chinese culture, and that a faulty memory combined with new experience produced new versions of these traditional stories. This version of history is their contribution to the stereotype.
>
> The lie of their version of history is easily proven by one simple fact: Chinese America was never illiterate. Losing touch with China did not result in Chinese Americans losing touch with "The Ballad of Mulan." It was and is still chanted by children in Chinatowns around the Western hemisphere. Losing touch with England did not result in English whites losing touch with the texts of the Magna Carta or Shakespeare.[27]

It is difficult to know how to interpret the last statement. If the name Shakespeare has become a cultural reference, Shakespeare's texts are known to most people only through school. Accordingly, the last sentence tries to equate an official culture disseminated in state institutions with a popular culture passed on spontaneously.

Whatever we make of Chin's theory of cultural essentialism, his indictment of "faking" means that he is attacking artistic freedom, the core principle of the autonomous literary field. The notion of authenticity elaborated in *The Big Aiiieeeee!* seems to draw on highly conservative articulations of tradition and the canon. It has a kind of continuity with the first *Aiiieeeee!* in the discursive linkages between its use of *sensibility* and the recourse to tradition and canon in *The Big Aiiieeeee!* For students of literature, these terms will immediately recall T. S. Eliot's critical writings, or such figures as Matthew Arnold or F. R. Leavis. In the more contemporary context, in the culture wars over multiculturalism and the canon, it isn't clear which side Chin would be on. Although he never stops denouncing the racism of European culture, his construction of Asian tradition (as the preceding passage illustrates) is based on the centrality of a cultural tradition to society that replicates the (largely imaginary) construction of Western culture that one finds in Eliot or William Bennett or Allan Bloom.[28] That Chin has read some literary theory is evident in passages such as the following:

> Freud found the keys to the subconscious and the dreams of Western man in Greek myth. For the literary critics of the world, he identified certain forms and certain themes, described their translation into other literature, poetry, and language of dreams, and traced them to their origins. The flow of the Western subconscious, from myth through literature, contributes to the place of books in the Western canon of literature.
>
> The Chinese do not need a Freud to find the books and myths containing the keys to the most deeply rooted, most fully grown Chinese subconscious. The Chinese people—in the Chinese marketplaces, toys, comic books, popular household curio shop and restaurant art and design—have already set the canon, kept it, taught it, and used it.[29]

Chin's use of an essentialized version of psychoanalysis reveals the extent to which the rhetorical politics in *Aiiieeeee!* has become a rigid policing of culture whose function is to draw boundaries around the Asian American literary field. Chin here enacts the production of Asian American literature as a countercanon, the very gesture that Guillory critiques.

Chin's theory of Asian American cultural production may have a monstrous quality to it, cobbled together as it is out of apparently disconnected ideas and intuitions. But I believe that whatever Kingston's, Hwang's, and Tan's transgressions, Chin's antipathy toward them has a more substantial reason than merely personal dislike or jealousy. Because the central issue for the Asian American literary field (as for any field) is the question of authorization or legitimacy, we will begin with that. In *Aiiieeeee!* the source of legitimacy (that is, symbolic capital) for the Asian American literary field was its representation of the community. *The Big Aiiieeeee!* revised these terms slightly so that instead of the community, it substituted the spirit of the community or its cultural tradition. This allowed Chin to avoid the problem of consent, or the artist's responsibility to the community. Instead of the false consciousness of self-contempt, we have the "real" consciousness of Chinese culture, which is now the responsibility of the Asian American artist to represent. In Chin's view, if Kingston, Hwang, and Tan are outcasts, I would argue that it is because they reject this responsibility of representation, of either the community or the culture. A more precise way to say this is that it is less a matter of rejecting the community than that their need for the community is obviated because they are able to exploit in their writing an alternative source of capital and hence authority.

A major obstacle for Asian Americans in the field of cultural production, I contend, has been the lack of symbolic capital. *Aiiieeeee!* responded to this problem by establishing a way to convert the political capital of community mobilization into cultural capital. There was an alternative source of capital, but it had to be rejected in order to make the Asian American literary field autonomous: the commercial field. All the writers branded as assimilationists in *Aiiieeeee!* were commercially successful, but their success signaled their betrayal. As the *Aiiieeeee!* editors persuasively argued, the value of Asian American writing in the commercial literary market depended on its production of "authentic" representations of an exotic Asian culture, with narratives that relied on figures serving as ethnographic informants, the kind of writing that Chin calls "food pornography." Although this was another source of capital for Asian American literature, the problem was that acquiring this capital risked exclusion from the autonomous field because it meant the subordination of literature to a representational content and the imperatives of the market. The solution to this dilemma that Kingston devised in *The Woman Warrior* was to produce a text structured in terms of the conflictual relation between form and content. I refer here to how the autonomous literary field objectifies certain kinds of content as "form" in relation to other kinds of content deemed as representational or referential. Despite Kingston's own statements, I contend that if *The Woman Warrior* represents anything, it is not Asian Americans but Asia. That is, at the level of content, the book reproduces the kinds of ethnographic representations that would make it marketable, while at the level of "form" it engages in a continuous critique and subversion of those representations.[30] This solution to the predicament of capital accumulation accounts for the complex disjunctions and dissonances in the text that have led so many critics to see *The Woman Warrior* as an example of postmodern writing. What Chin castigates as "faking," in other words, can be seen from another perspective as a deliberate textual principle of misrepresentation that encompasses a variety of strategies whose aim is to produce a nonrepresentative representation of Chinese culture.

The first objection to this interpretation is that Kingston herself explicitly names Chinese Americans in the passage that she often cites: "Chinese-Americans, when you try to understand what things in you are Chinese, how do you separate what is peculiar to childhood, to poverty, insanities, one family, your mother who marked your growing with stories, from what is Chinese? What is Chinese tradition and what is the movies?"[31] In directly addressing Chinese Americans, Kingston implicitly establishes some sort of relation to them. What relation this is remains to be seen. Nevertheless, this is the only point in the book where some segment of the audience is named, and Chinese Americans are never referenced again. Indeed, the term *Asian American* never appears at all. Even in the last chapter, in which the narrator is the central figure, the only other terms she uses to refer to herself besides "Chinese" are "American-Chinese" and "Asian." Note also that Kingston hyphenates Chinese-American here, but in her next book, *China Men*, she refers to unhyphenated Chinese Americans. The point is not that this somehow disqualifies her from consideration as an Asian American writer, but it does create the impression that the preceding passage was a later interpolation, perhaps as a response to Chin's early objections before the book's publication.

More important, in directly addressing Chinese Americans, the book asks an anthropological question: What is Chinese culture? Although the purpose of the question is to cast doubt on any definitive answer, in this framework "Chinese-Americans" remain defined by their relation to Chinese culture, even if that relation is one of "confusion" or, to put it in slightly different terms, misrepresentation. Kingston attributes this ignorance or confusion to Chinese Americans' distance from China, but reframing this relation in narrative terms suggests that ignorance is the means by which the book can distance itself from the responsibility of representing China or Chinese culture. Ignorance, after all, appears as such only in a desire to know. Otherwise, it would simply be indifference, say, or disinterest. Ignorance is thus a modulation of disinterest, and in *The Woman Warrior* it becomes the equivalent of self-contempt in *Aiiieeeee!* that is, the means of producing a disinterested or autonomous relation to the object of representation. Ignorance and confusion are the privileged tropes of style and form in the book—they are the origins of fiction itself—and they facilitate the book's metamorphosis of *Chinese culture* into *Asian American literature*.

Based on this analysis, we can hypothesize that in any text, the relation of the Asian American field to the autonomous field can be gauged as the relation of form to content. The relationship between form and content is complex, and my point here is not that this division actually exists but that it is produced by the dominant field. Thus it is an institutional fact. We can now look at the opposition between nationalism and assimilation as a conflict between competing constructions of the relation of form to content. We can also see Chin's complaint against Kingston as a charge that *The Woman Warrior* subordinates content to form. In fact, this subordination is thematized in various places in the book itself. One salient example is the image that opens the last chapter of the book, that of the knot so cruel that it blinds its maker. Kingston writes that "finally an emperor outlawed this cruel knot, and the nobles could not order it anymore. If I had lived in China, I would have been an outlaw knot-maker."[32] It is difficult to know what to make of this last comment, since at a literal level at least, it doesn't seem to make any sense. The reason that the knot is outlawed is because it is an example of the power of the nobility who are able to make their servants suffer only for their own pleasure. Why would the narrator declare a desire to make a knot so complicated that it may result in her own blindness?

The trope of the blinding knot seems deeply emblematic, and the general failure to recognize the literal illogic of this image also seems to mark a certain blindness in the criticism on the book, which is the failure to account fully for the problematics of representation. As a commentary on the book's own production, this passage thematizes the antithetical relation of form to content; the more complex the knot is, the greater the threat of blindness will be—to the artist. If we take sight as the privileged sense in the production of realist representation, then the renunciation of sight could figure the extravagance of the text's own formal structures to the necessity of that representation.[33] The book poses this relation in a more pointed manner, which is that form in *The Woman Warrior* is always the erasure or negation of a representational content, signaling the text's orientation toward the autonomous field. Since form in this mode always depends on a content that it tries to negate, the necessary but antagonistic complementarity of form and content reproduces the paradoxical (to use one of Kingston's favorite terms) relation of nonrepresentative representation.

Another image of the opposition of form and content comes in the pictures that the narrator draws when she is in grade school, ones that are entirely covered in black paint. Although her teacher is alarmed, the narrator explains that the black surface is meant to be a stage curtain, covering up all sorts of colorful images underneath. Like a modernist painting, the black facade enacts the erasure of all content by focusing the viewer's attention on the surface, not allowing access to any depth or interiority. It is striking that the narrator tells us that these paintings are in fact representational, even though the representations cannot be seen because the surface is opaque. These two tropes of the blinding knot and the opaque painting suggest that the book's formal complexity obscures or obstructs any clear view of its representational contents, but this does not mean that this strategy is entirely successful. The blackness of the paintings may also figure an emergent racialized self, but this would imply that race obstructs the narrator's true self from developing. I would argue in contrast that the antithesis of form and content in *The Woman Warrior* illustrates how Asian American racial identity occupies the level of form, as opposed to the Chinese identity that resides at the level of content. In this respect, far from exemplifying an identitarian developmentalism, *The Woman Warrior* actually prefigures the formalization of Asian American identity claimed for the critical intervention regarding *Dictée*.

The Anxiety of Representation

The specific representation (for example, of Asian Americans), though certainly relevant, is of less interest than a text's particular configuration of the relation of representation. This study attempts to delineate a literary analysis capable of elucidating the dynamic interplay of forces that position a text within the Asian American literary field, as well as the many ways in which specific texts struggle with and explore various relations of representation. Each text must be seen as emerging from a process of "becoming an Asian American writer," but this does not happen only once for each writer; it must be reenacted over and over again. There is no sense in which one becomes an Asian American once and for all, especially for writers. Each time a writer begins to write, he or she must repeat the same process of deciding on the various questions that mark the "Asian Americanness" of a literary text or its belonging in the Asian American field. Therefore, each text is the result of a unique set of determinations concerning these different parameters; only in this way is it possible to write anything new. Thus the Asian Americanness of a text is, at a certain level, only contingently related to the identity or identification of the author. Again, the point here is not to assess the extent to which a text or writer legitimately belongs to the field but to identify the particular configuration of variables that gives the text its specific Asian American identification or its claim to the Asian American literary field.

The object of an Asian American literary criticism is not a representation conceived as a static sign that can be read back to produce a detailed image of the model Asian American subject encoded in the text. This is not how representation works in the literary text. Rather, it seems to me that those texts most concerned with the problematics of Asian American identity reflect on, and struggle with, the question of representation in a specifically literary manner. The function of representation imposed on Asian American literary texts produces a pervasive thematics of the anxiety of representation. Unlike the dominant field, which is structured by the anxiety of influence and its attendant struggles over individuality, authority, and autonomy, the anxiety of representation confronts issues of politics, community, and reciprocity. Moreover, the anxiety of representation pertains not only to the political dimensions of culture but also to the dynamics of the literary field. What truly binds together texts of the Asian American field into what might in other terms be called a "tradition" is the necessity of engaging with the already constituted modes and forms of representation that comprise at any given moment the structure of the field.

In her survey of critical responses to *The Woman Warrior*, Laura Kang recognizes only half the problem when she suggests that

the "debate" over *The Woman Warrior* is symptomatic of the problem of delineating what counts as "Asian American literature," how "Asian American literature" always fails to stand for "Asian Americans." While the text has been an oft-cited touchstone, the demands and questions posed to its inability to be representative could be posed for all Asian American literature.[34]

The problem, as Kang points out, has to do with the disparity between the limits of Asian American literature and the boundaries of Asian America. If this descriptive representation is inadequate, the other half of the problematic of nonrepresentative representation, as I have argued, is that the text cannot concede the necessity of representation. If Asian American literature "always fails to stand for" Asian Americans, that is because it always must be measured in terms of that relation.

The opening chapter of *The Woman Warrior* demonstrates the problematic of representation that structures the entire book. "No Name Woman" begins with the mother of the narrator recounting the story of her aunt in China, who became pregnant while her husband was in America. As punishment for her adultery, the story maintains, the villagers destroyed their family home, and the aunt ended up committing suicide. The problem for the narrator, who wants to know more of this story, is that the family continues to punish the aunt by forgetting her, so the mother should not have told the narrator the story in the first place and will not tell her anything more about it. In order to recover the story of the aunt, the narrator must resort to her imagination, which means that she must represent the aunt, who is incapable of representing herself. The chapter begins with the mother's injunction that the narrator must not tell anyone what she is about to be told, but breaking this commandment replays the very act by which the Asian American literary field is inaugurated, as an act of writing what the community does not want told, an act authorized by the artistic freedom instituted in the dominant autonomous field. Although the book begins by assuming a representative authority against the community (which is narratively sanctioned as the representation of the aunt ostracized by the community), what the narrator quickly encounters when trying to give the aunt back her subjectivity are the considerably more complex questions of whether the aunt would want her story to be told at all and, if so, how.

Asking the question in these terms highlights the central tension in this chapter, as well as in the book as a whole, which is whose needs and interests the text will represent. What is the purpose for the narrator's retelling of the aunt's story? If it is to seek her "ancestral help" in defining an identity as a Chinese American woman, this appeal instead places the narrator in a complex relation of representation. She is, after all, exposing the aunt's shame for what is essentially a selfish purpose, her quandaries over her identity. The narrator, of course, has no responsibility to the aunt, both because she is dead and because the narrator fictionalizes her story. By reducing the aunt to a fictional contrivance in order to deal with her identity crisis, the narrator effects a kind of symbolic violence. Although this is not acknowledged, I would argue that this violence accounts for the ominous turn that the story takes at the end of the chapter, when the narrator must confront the consequences of telling the aunt's story.

The last section of the chapter begins with the narrator's admission that she has participated in the aunt's punishment: "In the twenty years since

I heard this story I have not asked for details nor said my aunt's name; I do not know it. People who can comfort the dead can also chase after them to hurt them further—a reverse ancestor worship."[35] The narrator's anxiety concerns the threat of ostracism from the family or community for exposing their secrets, but this fear somehow becomes displaced onto the aunt:

> My aunt haunts me—her ghost drawn to me because now, after fifty years of neglect, I alone devote pages of paper to her, though not origamied into houses and clothes. I do not think she always means me well. I am telling on her, and she was a spite suicide, drowning herself in the drinking water. The Chinese are always very frightened of the drowned one, whose weeping ghost, wet hair hanging and skin bloated, waits silently by the water to pull down a substitute.[36]

Although the threat of becoming the aunt's substitute seems to derive from the possibility that the narrator also might be ostracized as the aunt was, this passage clearly attributes that threat to the aunt herself, who may want revenge for the narrator's "telling on her." This suggests that the aunt may not like what the narrator has to say about her, since what the narrator offers are not goods for the afterlife but the revelation of her transgression. The fear of becoming a substitute is not the fear of expulsion from the community but the fear of becoming Chinese, because the aunt can be a credible threat only if the narrator is one of "the Chinese" who actually believes in ghosts. Moreover, by identifying the narrator as a nemesis, the aunt aligns her with the villagers.

The subtextual struggle between the representative and the represented becomes apparent here. That is, at the same time as the narrator is seeking to remake the aunt into a proto–Chinese American (the "ancestral help" she seeks), the aunt is also attempting to turn the narrator into a Chinese woman. This antagonism arises at the confluence of two diametrically opposed desires: the narrator wants to define her identity, but the aunt wants the narrator to tell the truth of her life. Although these two processes initially seem to be the same, the spectral eruption of the aunt marks the point at which they diverge, which is the antithetical relation between identity and *authority*. If the narrator's quest for identity depends on divining the truth of her aunt's life, the writer's authority depends on *not* having to tell the truth about Chinese culture. This is, after all, the province of nonfiction, but to write nonfiction as an Asian American is to be relegated to the commercial field. The narrator's relation to the aunt parallels her relation to her mother in that the mother's story is established as the "truth"—nonfiction—whereas the narrator's retellings of the story are fiction, or imagination.[37] It is only in *not* repeating the mother's story that she can become a writer, just as the book can be fiction only if it does not tell the truth about the aunt.

The question of identity that is ostensibly the central concern of the "autobiography" is thus opposed to the narrator's status as an author, a writer of fiction. This becomes evident in the passage I referred to earlier:

> It could very well have been, however, that my aunt did not take subtle enjoyment of her friend, but, a wild woman, kept rollicking company. Imagining her free with sex doesn't fit, though. I don't know any women like that, or men either. Unless I see her life branching into mine, she gives me no ancestral help.[38]

As it turns out, in seeking the aunt's ancestral help, the narrator must impose the normative assumptions of her own sociohistorical context on the aunt in order for their lives to connect. But this narrative assimilation destroys the alterity of the aunt's life, the truth of her story. What is the "ancestral help" that the narrator seeks here? It is not a matter of identity or subjectivity; it is the aunt's *story* that the narrator needs in order to become a writer—not the truth of her life. The narrator's sudden apprehension of the aunt derives from the realization that their relation entails a certain degree of exploitation and appropriation, but this anxiety is overcome by another, greater one, the anxiety of not being a writer. The fear of having to tell the truth about the aunt, the fear of being Chinese, is the fear of being reduced to a writer in the commercial field. Although the narrator begins by believing that she is in some way helping achieve justice for the aunt by telling her story, it eventually becomes clear that she is in a kind of antagonistic relation to the aunt. Justice requires that the narrator tell the story according to the aunt's interests, but the narrator's desire to be an author means that she must tell the story to fulfill her own interests. That is, the narrator's claim to represent the aunt requires no consent, both because the aunt is dead and so has no voice, but also because that is simply the way art works. It is unlicensed and needs no mandate other than the aesthetic.

The question of justice and its relation to representation is a major strand running throughout the book and is recapitulated at the end of the book, in the scene of the "reparation candy" that the narrator introduces with this admonition:

> You can't entrust your voice to the Chinese either; they want to capture your voice for their own use. They want to fix up your tongue to speak for them. "How much less can you sell it for?" we have to say. Talk the Sales Ghosts down. Make them take a loss.[39]

The following scene then illustrates how the narrator's voice was "captured" by the "Chinese" in the figure specifically of her mother. One day, a prescription is delivered to the narrator's family that is intended for another family. The mother thinks that this mistake will curse their family, so she forces the narrator to go to the pharmacy in order to get some reparation candy to stop the curse:

> "You get reparation candy," she said. "You say, 'You have tainted my house with sick medicine and must remove the curse with sweetness.' He'll understand."
>
> "He didn't do it on purpose. And no, he won't, Mother. They don't understand stuff like that. I won't be able to say it right. He'll call us beggars."
>
> "You just translate."[40]

The narrator "feels sick" at the thought of trying to convey the idea of curses and reparation candy to the pharmacists, but the mother thinks that all she needs to do is "just translate." The mother's theory of translation is one in which there exists exact equivalents—of words, concepts, values—but this theory describes a world in which there is no need for representation.[41] As this episode demonstrates, the need for representation arises only in contexts in which a direct translation is not possible, whether between different languages, different cultures, the literary field and the ethnic community, or the text and the world. The problem, as the narrator understands, is the almost absolute incommensurability between the reality of her mother's world and the pharmacist's reality. There is no possibility here of "just" translating, or perhaps we might say that what justice requires in this instance is not translation at all, but representation.

After the narrator is sent on her errand to retrieve the reparation candy, she recounts what happens:

"Mymotherseztagimmesomecandy," I said to the druggist. Be cute and small. No one hurts the cute and small.

"What? Speak up. Speak English," he said, big in his white druggist coat.

"Tatatagimme somecandy."

The druggist leaned way over the counter and frowned. "Some free candy," I said. "Sample candy."

"We don't give sample candy, young lady," he said.

"My mother said you have to give us candy. She said that is the way the Chinese do it."

"What?"

"That is the way the Chinese do it."

"Do what?"

"Do things." I felt the weight and immensity of things impossible to explain to the druggist.[42]

When she returns with the candy, the mother remarks, "See? . . . They understand. You kids just aren't very brave."[43] Of course, they don't understand at all, but the narrator has effectively engineered an outcome in which both sides believe they understand what the situation is even if those understandings do not overlap in the slightest. This is the work of representation in action. On the one hand, the representative serves as the point of articulation between otherwise incommensurable domains. On the other hand, it is the incommensurability of the two domains that makes representation necessary. Thus the representative always has a dual relation to that divide, simultaneously seeking to connect both sides while ensuring that they remain apart. In this instance, translation epitomizes that duality in that it fails and succeeds at the same time. That is, the task of the translator is to make the reader understand *something*, even if it has little or no relation to the original. The narrator produces a simulacrum of understanding, but in the process reinforces the mutual incomprehension that necessitates the translation in the first place.

Translation here is opposed to representation insofar as it signifies the possibility of adequation between two disparate registers. If the narrator could resolve the situation by "just translating," she would no longer be a representative, and the book would become *transcription* rather than *fiction*. The precariousness of the resolution in this scene, however, highlights the perils of representation and the possible consequences if it should fail. These consequences are nowhere more evident than in one of the book's best-known episodes, when the narrator confronts the quiet Chinese girl. Although this scene has been read in a variety of ways, I would argue that it is the signal moment of the anxiety of representation. In this scene, the question of speaking focuses solely on the relations of power between the two girls, one of whom violently attempts to coerce the other to speak. The quiet girl is commonly seen as a proxy for the narrator, with the narrator projecting onto the other those degraded or abjected aspects of the racialized and gendered self. To constrain the dynamics of this scene to the drama of self and other, however, would be to participate in the derealization of the other and her reduction to a mere shadow of the self, to abstract the text from the web of social relations in which it is embedded by the economy of representation in the Asian American literary field. But to read this scene as a displaced staging of the encounter between the text and the reader is to return to the other some of the materiality of the actual audience or community for whom the text attempts to speak and thus introduces the possibility of the audience's speaking back.

Indeed, what is most striking about this scene in the context of the relations of representation is the girl's very muteness. My point here is not that it is a misreading to view this scene in terms of self and other but that behind that drama other dynamics may be at work. Drawing on Gayatri Spivak's "Can the Subaltern Speak?" Colleen Kennedy questions how the achievement of voice in *The Woman Warrior* is bound up with narrative as a "discourse of mastery": "All the narratives within *The Woman Warrior* . . . share this feature: they demonstrate or promise control. However, control is always control *of*, and it is what the narrator gains her limited control of that keeps her from exerting it with impunity." Kennedy notes that in order for the narrator to speak, she must learn the discourses that marginalize her, thus becoming "painfully aware of the price of speech."[44] In the episode with the quiet girl, the narrator's sudden possession of speech allows her to occupy a position of power in relation to the other, who is even more silent than she is. Kennedy remarks that it is not incidental that this scene is central to the chapter in which "most critics recognize the artist's voice emerging" and that the narrator also "assumes that role when she is forced to make Chinese women speak—notably her drowned aunt and her mother, Brave Orchid."[45]

These comments reveal the deep ambivalence of the narrator's efforts to make the quiet girl talk. That is, the repeated injunction to talk is in some sense inseparable from its opposite, to shut up, or—what amounts to the same thing—to say only what you are told to say. The ambivalence inherent in the violence of speech reflects the paradox of representation, that the narrator's speech is possible only *because* of the other girl's silence. That is, the representative can speak only if the represented cannot speak for themselves; conversely, by speaking for them, the representative deprives the represented of the possibility of speaking for themselves. If the narrator's quest for voice is tied to the possibility of self-representation, the problem for minority artists is the extraordinary difficulty of separating *self*-representation from group representation. This is certainly one way to understand the mirroring between the two girls that is so central to this scene. The narrator's access to speech and self-representation is thoroughly confused with the narrator's representation of the other girl and her speech/silence.

The pervasive anxiety of indifference or identity is one factor motivating the narrator's hostility toward the other girl. Not only does the quiet girl follow her sister everywhere, but their parents kept her sister back so that she was in the same grade despite being a year older. The narrator comments:

> My younger sister was in the class below me; we were normal ages and normally separated. The parents of the quiet girl, on the other hand, protected both daughters. When it sprinkled, they kept them home from school. The girls did not work for a living the way we did. But in other ways we were the same.[46]

To be normal is to be separated, an individual; what the narrator fears is being the same, but being the "same" means being Chinese. In the middle of her torture of the quiet girl, the narrator declares: "If she had had little bound feet, the toes twisted under the balls, I would have jumped up and landed on them—crunch!—stomped on them with my iron shoes."[47] The girl, of course, does not have bound feet, but the narrator's projection of them onto her reveals her association of the girl with Chinese identity.

Finally, when the narrator begins to plead with the girl to talk, she tries to rationalize her actions by suggesting that she is acting in the girl's own interests: "If you don't talk, you can't have a personality. . . . You've got to let people know you have a personality and a brain. You think somebody is going to take care of you all your stupid life?"[48] The equation of talking with having a "personality" and a "brain" signifies the narrator's Americanization, but the question remains of *why* the girl needs to talk. The narrator gives two reasons: so she can get married and so she can get a job. As it turns out, the narrator tells us she was wrong about nobody's taking care of the quiet girl:

> Her sister became a clerk-typist and stayed unmarried. They lived with their mother and father. She did not have to leave the house except to go to the movies. She was supported. She was protected by her family, as they would normally have done in China if they could have afforded it, not sent off to school with strangers, ghosts, boys.[49]

To be Chinese here is to be supported, protected, enveloped by the family and community so that one does not have to talk. Thus the quiet girl is the opposite of the No Name aunt. Sameness signifies a threatening loss of individuality and voice, but it also offers a retreat from the anxiety of representation. These contradictory and ambivalent desires are conflated in the narrator's relation to the other girl, in which it becomes almost impossible to say whether the intent is to hurt or help her. As if to confirm this, immediately after her encounter with the quiet girl, the narrator is confined to her bed for a year and a half, afflicted with a strange malady that causes no pain or symptoms. If she has no pain or symptoms, we might well ask why she needs to stay in bed. The fact that this illness is never specified in the text seems to indicate its fantastic quality.

The narrator perceives this mysterious illness as retribution for her mistreatment of the quiet girl. If the illness is symptomatic of the narrator's guilt, she punishes herself by becoming like the girl, the very thing she strove to avoid. This episode serves as a kind of cautionary tale about the failure of representation. Coming after the chapter with Brave Orchid and Moon Orchid, the narrator's encounter with the quiet girl is perhaps the book's most intense expression of the anxiety of (mis)representation, illustrating the possible consequences of any mistake. The difference is that while Brave Orchid's actions led to her sister's madness, the narrator's actions resulted in her own affliction. Both episodes share the catastrophic failure of *political* representation; that is, problems arise when Brave Orchid and the narrator seek to make things happen in what they believe to be the best interests of those they represent. Although Moon Orchid's madness is clearly the result of Brave Orchid's actions, in the case of the quiet girl the narrator evades responsibility for her actions through her self-punishment, thus usurping the role of the victim. In fact, the incident with the quiet girl seems designed to demonstrate the impossibility of political representation, since the narrator's inability to convince the girl to talk signals her failure as a representative. If the quiet girl could talk, however, then the narrator would no longer have to speak for her. In either case, the effect is that the narrator is reduced to voicelessness.

What is the solution to the paradox of political representation? This is where the book returns to the trope of translation in order to separate political representation from aesthetic representation. The result of this separation is that Asian American literature becomes defined simply as writing that depicts Asian Americans (or purely descriptive representation), but the problem recurs of distinguishing between stereotypical Orientalist depictions of Asian Americans (whether by Asians or non-Asians) and "authentic" depictions, which is the problem that the *Aiiieeeee!* editors tried to address. In *China Men*, Kingston turns to history to solve this problem, but we have already seen the contradictions that arise in this effort. Without the stable ground of history, *The Woman Warrior* seems to return to a relativist aesthetics in which distinguishing between authentic and stereotypical representations is impossible. We must recall, though, that *The Woman Warrior* defines authenticity as fidelity to Chinese culture and locates that fidelity at the level of content or representation. The text's formal or aesthetic dimensions are associated with inauthenticity and infidelity, as is Asian American identity. Ultimately, the book's strategy on this issue is to reverse the hierarchy such that inauthenticity is shown to be more authentic than authenticity itself or betrayal turns out to be a higher form of loyalty.

This reversal becomes complete in the last section of the book, in which the narrator recounts the story of Ts'ai Yen. This section begins with a story told by the narrator's mother about the grandmother in China who loved to go to the theater. Bandits would follow the actors and raid houses that were empty while their occupants were at the performances. The grandmother was not deterred, however, and ordered the entire household to attend the performance. In addition, she left the house completely open. During the performance, the bandits struck the theater and almost carried off one of the narrator's aunts, except that she was left behind when they spied a more attractive victim. The entire family thus returned home unscathed, which was proof to the grandmother, as the narrator tells us, that "our family was immune to harm as long as they went to plays."[50] This story seems to perfectly encapsulate the main concerns of the book, since in choosing the theater over the home, the grandmother is expressing the book's own choice of the dominant field over the Asian American literary field. This reading is further bolstered by the opposition between the home as the site of material objects and the theater as the space of a pure art, and it lines up with the book's own prioritizing of form over content. The question is why the book cannot end with this story but must supplement it with the story of Ts'ai Yen.

On the most obvious level, the story of the grandmother is also the mother's, so the narrator seems compelled to revise it in some way, to signify on it. Looking again at this story, though, we might perceive other deficiencies. Another reading is that instead of concluding that the family is safe as long as they go to plays, the story might be seen as demonstrating that they are safe as long as they stick together. What enables the family to survive their incursion into the dangerous space of the theater is that they all go together. This reading suggests a strategy closer to that of *Aiiieeeee!* that Asian American writers must unite as a field in order not to be captured by the forces of the dominant field. Moreover, although the grandmother concludes that art will keep them safe, we could also say that the aunt was almost kidnapped because of the grandmother's selfish desires, which forced everyone to go. The implication is that art must continually negotiate the threat of being held hostage to an oppressive and fickle audience.

The narrator segues into her own retelling of the Ts'ai Yen story by saying that her songs might have been included in some of those performances. The other link is that Ts'ai Yen was abducted, just as the aunt's substitute was. The narrator's story thus shifts the focus from the grandmother who is the center of the community to the women who occupy its margins. Although the tale of Ts'ai Yen rewrites a number of the stories in the book, I shall examine its resonances with the Fa Mulan and reparation candy stories in particular. Both the last two stories emphasize the artist's responsibility to the community. As the narrator cautions, the "Chinese want to capture your voice." They are tales, we might say, of instructed representation. As in *Aiiieeeee!* the mother's story tries to teach the daughter the proper role of art and the artist, which is to keep the community safe, to reproduce the community and its identity. Ts'ai Yen, in contrast, is the other aunt, the No Name woman, whose transgression against the lines of patriarchal descent is redeemed in the end only because she is able to give her father Han descendants.

The last line of the story, and also of the book, is "It translated well,"[51] but what does translation mean in this context? *What* translates well? This line refers to the songs that Ts'ai Yen wrote among the barbarians, but "translation" here is obviously being used only in the most figurative way, since there is no translation anywhere in this episode. As I have suggested, if translation in *The Woman Warrior* signifies representation, then what forms of representation are inscribed in this story? Neither Ts'ai Yen nor her music represents anything. Ts'ai Yen is not a representative of China or Chinese culture or of the barbarians and their culture. As an exile, she becomes alien to both. The Chinese do not ransom her because she is Chinese but because she can continue her father's bloodline. Even though her music has now been reclaimed as part of Chinese culture, the daughter's story emphasizes that Ts'ai Yen's music would never have returned to China had it not been for her capacity for social reproduction, which is the same reason (apparently) that the barbarians kidnapped her in the first place, or at least kept her alive.

In refusing any form of representation, the story also ignores the question of identity. For instance, it seems telling that in contrast to the extended deliberations over the subjectivity of the No Name woman, the book is completely uninterested in Ts'ai Yen's subjective responses to her experiences.[52] By separating cultural production from social reproduction, the story of Ts'ai Yen imagines the birth of the aesthetic itself as an autonomous social domain. If Ts'ai Yen's value is her utility as an instrument of social reproduction, her cultural production occupies an entirely separate realm, one that exists nowhere in social space, like an "icicle in the desert."[53] The barbarians, as the book tells us, were "primitives" for whom the two senses of "culture" (as a way of life and as a domain of art) had not yet separated from each other. The barbarians' flutes originally were whistles that they attached to their arrows to frighten their enemies until, unaccountably, Ts'ai Yen one day discovers that the barbarians also use them to make music. The song that she sings to them is art in its purest form: it tells no story, seeks no audience, and conveys no meaning or purpose.

Although the book wants to imagine cultural production and social reproduction as discontinuous, it recognizes in the end that art needs to have some kind of value, since Ts'ai Yen's music survives only because she is of use to the community. There is, however, another kind of value in the story, which is the ransom paid for Ts'ai Yen's return. In a sense, this money simply realizes her social value as the daughter of an important scholar. What is the relation between this money and the capacity of her art to "translate well"? The ransom is not paid for her art, but both the money and the art derive from the capital that she embodies. To answer the question of what translates well, I would say "money," the general equivalent that enables the production of capital. Although *The Woman Warrior* strives to keep art and money in different spheres, "translation" here is understood as a locus of trade, of exchange, so that even if the Asian American artist would like to imagine herself as outside the community, she must continually confront the denied recognition that the source of aesthetic value for minority culture is the community's ransom.

5

Asian American Cultural Capital
and the Crisis of Legitimation

At its annual convention in 1998, held in Honolulu, the Association for Asian American Studies (AAAS) presented a fiction award to Lois-Ann Yamanaka for her novel *Blu's Hanging*. Immediately following the presentation, a resolution was introduced to rescind the award, based on the charge that Yamanaka's work contained stereotypical or racist depictions of Filipinos. The Honolulu convention was perhaps the most tumultuous in the short history of the AAAS (which was founded in 1979). The atmosphere was highly charged and even apocalyptic, with some participants intimating that the events taking place could mean the end of the association, if not the field as a whole. During a special emergency plenary session, supporters and critics of Yamanaka read statements followed by a general discussion. At the presentation of the award itself, three Filipina students from the high school where Yamanaka taught writing accepted the award on her behalf while many members of the audience, wearing black armbands, stood up and turned their backs to the stage. The vote was conducted by secret ballot and the resolution passed by a vote of 91 to 55. The award was withdrawn.

Nearly a decade after these events, it is striking that they appear to have been consigned to history, largely unremarked. Indeed, given the extremely painful nature of this episode, it is not surprising that it has been subject to a certain historical oblivion. The sparse commentary on *Blu's Hanging*, for example, reads the book as thematizing this trauma and forgetting in terms of "melancholia."[1] Although any attempt to return to this history threatens to reawaken the difficult memories associated with it, I do so because I am convinced that important lessons can be learned from it. Indeed, it is remarkable that so much of Asian American cultural studies, concerned as it is with the politics of culture, should simply ignore what has to have been the most significant political struggle over Asian

American culture in the past several decades. Even if theoretical analysis may not reveal anything that would prevent recurrences of such conflicts, I believe that the *Blu's Hanging* incident is an important test case for any theory of Asian American cultural politics.

My argument here is that the conflicts over *Blu's Hanging* were traumatic because they brought to the surface certain contradictions in the critical orthodoxy of Asian American literary studies and called into question some of the fundamental assumptions of the field as a whole. Critical commentary on *Blu's Hanging* has had difficulty grasping the underlying dynamics of the events or what their significance might be for Asian American studies or Asian American politics. I contend that one of the factors contributing to this incomprehension of the protests was the absence of a coherent theoretical account of representation in general and of stereotypes in particular. Although at the beginning of the movement, stereotype analysis was critical to Asian American cultural politics, it has since almost disappeared from the field. Thus, rather than approaching the stereotype as a conceptual category or an apparatus of discrimination, I believe that what is at stake in the notion of the stereotype is legitimacy itself. That is, even though the debate was a contest among competing interpretations, the question of whether or not its representations are stereotypical cannot be decided with reference to the text. Instead, this is a political question, so how one answers it depends to a large extent on one's relation to particular forms of capital.

After discussing this issue in more detail, I turn to an extended reading of *Blu's Hanging* in which I look at it in the history of protests over Yamanaka's previous work by reading *Blu's Hanging* as a response to her critics. Specifically, I argue that the Filipino characters in *Blu's Hanging*, the Reyes family and Uncle Paulo, are intended as allegorical representations of the protesters and as literal embodiments of the stereotypes that Yamanaka's critics accused her of creating. My point is not that they are stereotypical (since the question here is what defines a representation as a stereotype) but that these characters serve as figures for those in the local community who object to Yamanaka's representation of them. The main purpose in the book, then, is to establish Ivah's legitimacy as a representative of the community, and the various episodes in the book construct implicit comparisons between Ivah and other potential representatives in order to define the criteria for representative legitimacy as well as Ivah's fitness for that position.

If the *Blu's Hanging* episode foregrounds how stereotype analysis has become an illegitimate mode of reading in Asian American literary and cultural studies, we should retrace how this state of affairs has evolved because Asian American literary and cultural analysis could justifiably be seen as originating in the identification and critique of stereotypes. Indeed, the concept of the "Asian American" originated largely as a response to the stereotypical characterizations of "Orientals." Nevertheless, it is not surprising that the stereotype has dropped out of Asian American literary and cultural studies. As a theoretical concept, it is extraordinarily problematic and plagued by all kinds of definitional and logical difficulties. Consequently, the evaporation of theoretical inquiry into stereotypes has meant that investigations into a number of related issues and questions were simply dropped from the field's agenda.

As I observed in chapter 4, *Aiiieeeee!* emphasized authorial intention as the index of authenticity, which meant that reception could be conceived only as a reflection of the reader's own authenticity. Authenticity was the primary means by which Asian Americans contested stereotypical, Orientalist representations. But any evaluation of authenticity requires a realist theory of representation, as it is almost impossible to determine what a stereotypical or false representation is without some idea of what a realistic or accurate one is. The political evaluation of true and false images is associated mostly with identity politics and cultural nationalism, so the uproar over *Blu's Hanging* appeared to be simply another instance of the conflicts among modes of reading that privilege either political representation or aesthetic representation, identity or difference, realism or antirealism. Even though the current theoretical work in Asian American cultural studies construes these oppositions as aligned, the reality of the conflict over the fiction award blurs such neat dichotomies.

Many of the difficulties with the concept of the stereotype could be resolved if we could first define it or decide what makes something a stereotype. Despite the many answers to this question, all of them have eventually run into a conceptual or theoretical dead end, which no doubt accounts for much of the declining interest in the study of stereotypes. Furthermore, most psychological studies of stereotypes avoid this question because the examples they cite are presented as obviously or self-evidently stereotypical. Cultural studies, in contrast, are almost entirely devoted to identifying particular representations as stereotypical, but they usually offer little general theoretical reflection. This lack of definitional distinction became clear in the *Blu's Hanging* incident because the crux of the conflicts was not so much what makes a representation stereotypical as it was how we decide that something is *not* a stereotype. Surprisingly, this question has received almost no consideration in the entire body of research, even though it is central to many conflicts over charges of stereotypical representation.

I contend that the categorical dilemmas regarding stereotypes could be resolved if we regarded them as forms of practical knowledge in struggles among social groups. In other words, we would have to reframe the question of whether a particular representation is stereotypical as a question of why someone would perceive a depiction as stereotypical or not. Although research in psychology has linked stereotype formation to group identification, the *Blu's Hanging* incident demonstrates that group identification is also a function of the relations of representation between those who hold the position of representatives and those who must be represented. In other words, while most of the response to these events remains implicitly bound to the problem of identity, an analysis of representation can help explain how the conflicts between producers and consumers, or representatives and the represented, reveal an unrecognized dimension of the controversy to be the question of capital. The capacity to perceive a representation as stereotypical or not actually is a kind of capital, the capital of Asian American identity.

Before continuing, I will briefly recount the events in question. The controversy over *Blu's Hanging* was the culmination of a long-standing protest against the portrayal of Filipinos in Yamanaka's writing that began with the publication of her first book, *Saturday Night at the Pahala Theatre*.[2] Several of the poems in that book feature what many saw as stereotypical descriptions of Filipinos as sexual predators, although the speakers of the poems are adolescent girls, a fact that led some to claim that they were unreliable voices. When *Saturday Night* won the AAAS literary award in 1994, protests were raised, but there was no concerted effort to block the award. But when Yamanaka's next book, *Wild Meat and the Bully Burgers*, was again given the AAAS award in 1997, the level of dissent rose higher. Accordingly, the association's board decided to withdraw the award. As a result of the furor over that action, however, the board adopted a policy stating that it could not interfere with the decisions of the award committees. This policy was immediately put to the test when the following year's literary award committee again voted to give first prize to Yamanaka's third book, *Blu's Hanging*.

The debate over *Blu's Hanging* revolved in particular around one character, Uncle Paulo, a young Filipino man who sexually abuses his adolescent nieces and rapes the narrator's brother, Blu, in the book's climactic moment. Much of the interpretive dispute pertained to context, as the protesters pointed out that the depictions of Filipinos took on a heightened significance in the context of the history of interethnic relations in Hawai'i. The figure of Uncle Paulo seemed to recall too clearly the prevailing stereotypes of Filipinos as rapists and perverts. These stereotypes derived from the history of Hawai'i's plantations when Filipino men were imported as labor, forming large communities of single men. This spurred antagonism from other ethnic groups competing for a place in the plantation system; thus stereotypes of sexual deviance reflected the perceived economic threat of Filipino labor. Filipino Americans remain a disadvantaged group in Hawai'i, in contrast to Japanese Americans, who have the highest socioeconomic status and the most positions of political and economic power.[3]

These ethnic hierarchies further magnify Yamanaka's representations of Filipinos because Japanese Americans (as well as others) have had the power to perpetuate stereotypes of Filipinos, and not the reverse. In addition, the fact that most of the scholars in the AAAS are from the continental United States raises questions about the differing attitudes and perceptions of those from the continent, as opposed to Hawai'i. One salient indication that the award committee read *Blu's Hanging* in a continental American context rather than in a local Hawaiian framework can be seen in the announcement of their decision to give the fiction award to *Blu's Hanging*. In their statement, the committee labels Yamanaka a "native Hawaiian" writer, which, as many people in Hawai'i pointed out, is incorrect because Yamanaka is not native Hawaiian but local Japanese. Such a basic error reveals a lack of familiarity with Hawai'i's racial politics and the unequal circulation of knowledge that leads to disparate readings.

One reason that this controversy is important to me is that it produced an intense public debate in Hawai'i that made culture matter and that empowered many people to feel a sense of ownership over it. A continual stream of articles on Yamanaka led up to the convention, and the affair lingered in the media for quite a while afterward. It seems surprising, therefore, that the episode should have generated so little discussion in academic publications, since making culture matter and political empowerment are the avowed goals of so much committed political criticism. We can get a sense of the intensity of the responses provoked by the controversy from a few of the e-mails protesting the award.

For example, in a letter to members of the AAAS board, faculty in the ethnic studies department of the University of Hawaiʻi at Manoa, along with colleagues from other departments, wrote:

> The Board appears to be unaware that Yamanaka's writings about sup-posed Filipino American behaviors in Hawaii are just the latest version in a historical pattern of demeaning misrepresentations of Filipinos dis-pensed by academics, local comedians, radio disc jockeys, and the print media. These negative stereotypes all have contributed to the sense of "shame" that too many young Filipino Americans feel about being Fili-pino. By honoring Yamanaka's writings, the Board also has contributed to that sense of shame.[4]

The University of Hawaiʻi's Pamantasan Council, "an association of stu-dents, staff and faculty committed to fostering equal educational oppor-tunity for Filipino Americans in the UH system," declared to the AAAS board:

> Your recognition of Ms. Yamanaka's work contributes to the pervasive-ness of destructive and stereotypical views of Filipinos in particular, and Asian Americans in general. Such uninformed portrayals perpetu-ate negative stereotypes of Filipino Americans and undermine efforts to foster mutual respect and credibility within Hawaiʻi's multicultural community.[5]

Finally, Caroline Campos, a student at the University of Hawaiʻi, wrote:

> I volunteered earlier this year, to be a part of the undergraduate activities committee for the AAAS conference. I was told that AAAS is an entity that looked out for my best interests as a young Filipino woman in higher education. That is why it saddens me to hear the AAAS Fiction Award would even consider, let alone present, Lois-Ann Yamanaka's *Blu's Hang-ing* with the 1997 Book Award.
>
> This book is filled with negative stereotypes toward Filipinos that I and my peers find extremely offensive. It is difficult enough to stay confi-dent and proceed with my education without books of this nature insult-ing my ethnicity. By awarding this book, AAAS expresses to me as well as students across the nation that negative stereotypes deserve the highest recognition possible.[6]

From Political Representation to Cultural Representation

The debates over *Blu's Hanging* came to center on whether the book or its representations of Filipinos was racist. To focus on the issue of racism, however, implies the necessity of a definitive judgment, which has the effect of covering up or ignoring other important aspects and dynamics of the controversy. The debate over racial stereotypes in literature, for example, quickly became mired in the familiar oppositions of identity politics and cultural nationalism, on the one hand, and artistic freedom and aesthetic value, on the other. The conflict cannot be understood through these categories, and the emphasis on them reflects a failure to transform theory into practice by Asian American literary studies. Notions of difference and heterogeneity, for example, did not help bring together any of the opposing factions or facilitate a resolution. Only by tracing the larger social and institutional contexts of the controversy can we understand what motivated particular interpretations of the text. Accordingly, I will examine the charge of racism at the end of my analysis, instead of at the beginning.

I propose that we can move beyond identity by reexamining these events within a paradigm of representation, but only if we suspend any assumptions about the relation of culture to politics. Although the study of Asian American culture has always been a political project, that political impetus has sometimes narrowed scholarly inquiry, as one of the main objects of contention in the field was the question of what counted as legitimate politics. The establishment of political legitimacy, though, means excluding issues and approaches deemed illegitimate. Clearly, identity was at stake in the *Blu's Hanging* conflict—the identity of Filipino Americans and Asian Americans—but not as an attempt to impose or construct a unitary identity. Rather, my analysis begins from the premise that there are two sides, with opposing representations of social reality and the text. From this perspective, the central issue in the conflict is legitimacy. The question of identity was a matter of representation; that is, who was the legitimate representative of Filipino Americans? Could Filipino Americans be represented by other Asian Americans, or could they be adequately represented only by Filipino Americans? The conflict concerned the definitions of who "Filipino Americans" were, their identities and their interests. The book's representations of Filipinos became the site for a confrontation over the claims of the AAAS and other Asian American organizations to represent the interests of Filipino Americans as part of the panethnic Asian American coalition.

One of the striking aspects of the whole affair, for example, was how little, if any, political disagreement over the social conditions of Filipino Americans there was. Instead, the conflict was over competing representations of culture and its relation to social context, because the capacity to define the literary was the means by which one group would be able to establish itself as the legitimate representatives. Legitimacy is a function of symbolic capital, but the struggles concerned the kind of capital—political or cultural—that would define the value of literature and thus the legitimacy of representation. The specific readings advanced by various sides, then, can be understood initially in terms of the kind of capital that each tried to use in the struggle over representative legitimacy. The protesters interpreted the book in a realist matrix of true or false representations because this is how representation is understood *in the political field*. Conversely, the book's defenders tried to impose the standards of the cultural field regarding legitimate interpretations.

In examining the response of Asian American cultural producers, we can see the strategies that they used to circumscribe the arena of discussion. This response came primarily in the form of a petition drafted by the Japanese American writer David Mura which was widely circulated through e-mail and was signed by almost eighty Asian American writers and other artists:

1. I wish to protest the AAAS Board's decision in 1997 to ignore the choice of its 1997 literary awards committee to give a book award to Lois-Ann Yamanka [*sic*] for *Wild Meat and the Bully Burgers*. I also urge the Board to recognize the decision of its literary awards committee to give a book award to Yamanaka's *Blu's Hanging* in 1998.
2. I am concerned too with a reading of Yamanaka's work which ignores or misreads the way a fictional character or narrator functions in a literary work.
3. I also wish to reaffirm that writers often must, by the nature of their enterprise, upset and question prevailing views, evoke extreme and visceral reactions, and write in ways where ambiguity and complexity take precedence over "political correctness" or safe and comforting portraits of the world, our community, or the individuals who reside there.
4. I am also concerned with the way the AAAS has sometimes seemed to organize "witch hunts" against various writers. This is not to say that writers should be immune from criticism. Indeed, criticism is a necessary

> part of the creation of a literary culture. Perhaps, though, it might be helpful for people to look into the mechanism and psychological reasons why those within a community wish to tear someone from the community apart once they have become successful. Rather than encouraging literary variety and creativity and recognizing the difficulty of the tasks which writers and other artists perform, the AAAS seems at times to have been attempting to invoke comformity [*sic*] and silence.

This petition reveals the methods that were used to exclude certain kinds of readings, that is, those that "ignore or misread" the conventions of the literary field. This exclusion is then carried into the last paragraph in which Mura concedes that writers should not be immune from criticism but then immediately defines valid or legitimate criticism. What is valid criticism? The assertion that criticism is necessary to create a literary culture offers a clue; it is the advice or comments that *writers* give one another, the criticism of craft or form. The criticisms of nonwriters (regarding content), in contrast, are dismissed as the product of jealousy or personal vendettas. In the debates over *Blu's Hanging*, one of the key battles was defining the appropriate context of interpretation.

To restrict legitimate statements to the discourse of cultural producers, however, reveals the unequal terrain on which the debates took place. Because it was an academic context (that is, in the field of cultural production), the protesters had to contest the award as well as the various structures of legitimacy that upheld the award. These mechanisms became apparent in the way that the AAAS board responded to the protests. The board was in a difficult position as it attempted to negotiate between the two opposing sides. In 1997 when the literature award committee gave the award to Yamanaka for *Wild Meat and the Bully Burgers*, the board actually overturned the committee's decision in response to protests, and no award was issued that year. This action provoked a furor, as evident in the writers' misrecognition that the AAAS was somehow to blame for the continuing controversy over Yamanaka's works. This outcry prompted the board to seek a more neutral position, resulting in the policy that the board would not interfere in the decisions of the award committees, thus setting up the conditions that led to the confrontation over *Blu's Hanging*. As the protests over that book mounted the next year, the board tried to stick to its policy. My interest here is in making explicit some of the tacit assumptions underlying this policy.

Responding to the protests in a statement published in the AAAS newsletter, Yen le Espiritu, the president of the association, defended its actions:

> A central issue raised in the Board's deliberations over the Literary Award in 1997 was the relationship of the award committee(s) to the Board. Some board members felt that the decision about who receives an award should be left to the awards committee; others argued that the Board should make the final decision. Board members could not resolve these differing views in part because there was no formal Book Award Policy. After the Seattle Conference, as President of the AAAS, I appointed three board members to draft a book award policy to be discussed and voted on by the entire Board. Among other matters, this committee recommended that the Board should not have ratification power over the award committee's decisions. The rationale was that the Board already has the power to select the committee members whom they feel most appropriate to review the works of their peers. The Board should then trust the judgment of the committees and respect their autonomy, especially since they are the ones who have read, compared, and discussed the merits of the nominated titles, not the Board. To do otherwise would be giving the Board too much influence and control over the awarding process. After close to two months of active discussion over e-mail, nine Board members voted last June to adopt this book award policy, and one abstained. This near-unanimous vote reflected board members' belief that the integrity of the awards is contingent upon the autonomy of the award committees.[7]

When comparing the statements of the writers and the AAAS, it becomes evident that the writers were concerned with the legitimacy of the artwork itself (or its aesthetic value, which is embodied in the award), whereas the AAAS saw the main issue as the legitimacy of the process of selecting the award winner. This difference reflects the two kinds of capital at stake for each group—cultural and political—as well as the basis of legitimacy in each case, that is, the intrinsic merits of the representation as opposed to the valid selection of the representative.

While the protesters confronted the writers on the issue of aesthetic representation, they confronted the AAAS board in the contest over political representation. For example, as the protests mounted, members of the board who tried to broker a compromise became increasingly frustrated at the protesters' intractability. But this intractability may have resulted partly from the inability on all sides to identify the stakes in the conflict (an inability that was not simply the result of denial). Even the protesters tended to discount the matter of the award itself as simply a pretext for other, more important material issues, such as the social conditions of Filipino Americans or the marginalization of Filipino American scholars in Asian American studies. In response, the board proposed a series of measures to promote Filipino American studies, hoping that this would defuse the furor over the award. Although these promises did little to placate the protesters, the association did subsequently implement those measures. In retrospect, it seems apparent that the protesters could have accepted this compromise only at the cost of their political legitimacy, since they would have seemed to be trading the general interests of Filipino Americans for their own particular interests.

If we ask what the award had to do with Filipino Americans' material interests, the relation would seem to be an indirect one at best. The AAAS has no power to effect change in any domain except the academy, and any changes it might make there would directly affect only Filipino American academics. Because Filipino Americans had no material demands that might be subject to negotiation, the conflict centered on the award itself and the two basic options: award or no award. This constriction of a number of issues into a single choice thus appears to derive from the nature of the struggle as involving symbolic power rather than material resources. That is, if the object of the conflict was the legitimate representation of Filipino Americans, this conflict was shaped by the way the question of political representation was channeled through disputes over the legitimate interpretation of a literary text. These are, as we shall see, two different forms of legitimacy. Indeed, because the conflict took place in the *cultural* sphere, the question was defining *political* legitimacy in this context.

In the political sphere, the basis of legitimate representation theoretically depends on the consent of the represented, as expressed mainly through elections, the primary mechanism of accountability. The contest over the legitimate representative of Filipino Americans, though, was not decided by an election. There was, however, a vote: the vote for the fiction award. Without any other tangible index of power, this vote became the symbolic means by which one side might claim victory in the struggle over political representation. The complication was that in order to win the vote, each side had to produce a compelling interpretation of a literary text. Moreover, the voters were not members of the larger Filipino

American community but the constituency of the AAAS, all of whom were academics. The award could serve these multiple functions in large part because of the ambiguity of what it was intended to recognize. One of the persistent questions about the book awards, for example, concerns why the AAAS, a scholarly organization, presents awards for literature in the first place. Many participants believed that the conflict might have played out differently if the association had explained its rationale for the award and its criteria of evaluation. But the AAAS has never offered such an explanation.

This resistance to explanation, I argue, demonstrates that a certain indeterminacy is vital to the purpose of the award, which is the conversion of political into cultural capital. This indeterminacy arises from the refusal to specify whether the award was meant to serve a political or an aesthetic function, whether it was intended to reward a literary work's political value or aesthetic value. This is a distinction that Asian American cultural studies also refuses, by either denying that aesthetic value exists or insisting that the aesthetic and the political are continuous, so the equivocal intentions of the fiction award may be seen as congruent with the ambiguity of the meaning of "culture" in cultural studies. The division between politics and aesthetics, though, marked the line between the two opposing sides in the struggle over the fiction award. The protesters insisted that whatever its literary merits, the book was politically reprehensible, while its defenders tried to raise aesthetic value above the contingencies of popular reception. Thus although politics and aesthetics cannot be easily confined to separate spheres, this perception fails to account for the way that the division itself between politics and culture becomes a locus of struggle over the capital of the two fields.

The contest between politics and culture made clear that culture is the locus of those forms of legitimacy that are not "political." The book award policy's recourse to bureaucratic procedures and autonomy was obviously intended to remove politics from the award process, thus confirming that both literary and academic work belong to the larger field of cultural production.[8] This suggests that literature awards serve to shift the legitimacy of academic work in Asian American studies from politics to culture. The question is why the field needs cultural legitimacy rather than academic legitimacy, which would seem to be more relevant. The reason is that academic legitimacy cannot provide the ground for political claims, whereas culture offers a claim to representation that is *outside* or independent of the political field. Thus the peculiar status of the literature awards may be ascribed to the transition in the field from political representation to cultural representation.

Here cultural representation does not mean the representation of Asian Americans in culture but the *political representation of Asian American culture*. That is, as we saw in chapter 4 with the transition from *Aiiieeeee!* to *The Big Aiiieeeee!* the object of representative claims shifts from Asian American *people* to Asian American *culture*. In other words, the literature awards represent not the politics of Asian Americans but their culture. The crucial difference between these two objects is that a "culture" cannot contest one's representation, whereas people can. As a mode of political representation, culture is unaccountable; that is, those who are unhappy with the way they are represented in culture have no obvious or direct means by which to hold their representatives accountable. Thus the literature awards represent Asian Americans only through a series of metonymic connections, from a people to their culture to literature. Between the people and their representation, autonomous institutions intervene to insulate the representatives from the discontent of the represented. In the particular case of the fiction award, however, the possibility of rescinding the award through a vote provided a mechanism for the popular will to express itself, even if it was only (again) an *image* of the popular, as the membership of the association voted and not those presumably represented by the book.

In a straightforward political contest, power derives partly from the capacity to mobilize the most supporters. In a cultural conflict, however, success is not gauged by numbers but by which side can accumulate the greatest amount of legitimacy, or symbolic capital. Naturally, the protesters wanted to define the issue as political because they could capitalize on their popular support. One of the main factors in the protest was the lack of legitimacy accorded to Filipino American concerns, or their lack of cultural and symbolic capital. Politically, the two sides stood on relatively equal ground, but culturally, they confronted each other as legitimate and illegitimate antagonists because contesting the fiction award first required its delegitimation. Consequently, in the struggle over interpretation, the protesters had to advance an illegitimate interpretation of the text, since any legitimate interpretation would only confirm the award's legitimacy. To understand the cultural struggle at the core of the larger political contests, we now need to investigate the stereotype, the concept central to the debate. Most of the commentary on *Blu's Hanging* tends to discount the charge that the book contains stereotypical depictions of Filipino. In contrast, I want to ask what conditions need to prevail in order for the book to appear to be either stereotypical or not. The crux of the struggle, after all, was the same text, but one that the two sides read in diametrically opposed ways.

Stereotypes and the Legitimate Definition of the Literary

The *Oxford English Dictionary* defines *stereotype* as "a preconceived and oversimplified idea of the characteristics which typify a person, situation, etc.; an attitude based on such a preconception." This description does little to help us identify in any particular instance what is or is not a stereotype. An extended reading of the literature on stereotypes gives rise to the notion that one of the difficulties with any discussion of them is the implicit presupposition that the term *stereotype* actually denotes a distinct object. Indeed, the presumption that stereotypes exist leads to attempts to identify and define them, but such efforts continually run up against certain obstacles. Instead, I will begin with the most basic question: What makes something a stereotype? Or is there any way to distinguish between a stereotype and representations in general? If not, then on what basis would we continue to use the term if it is simply a synonym for cognition or knowledge? In the *Blu's Hanging* episode, this lack of definitional distinction also meant that there was no way to decide what is *not* a stereotype. Is it possible to produce some measure or criterion that could resolve this crucial political question?

As I have suggested, abandoning the discourse on stereotypes in Asian American studies in favor of other theoretical models meant that the problems that the concept produced were not investigated. What this meant in regard to the fiction award was that there was no effective way of responding to the charge of stereotyping because there was no theoretical paradigm within which to identify and analyze what actually constitutes a stereotype. In this regard, academic studies of stereotyping have diverged in ways that have obstructed certain avenues of investigation. Stereotypes, for example, have long been a central object of inquiry in social and cognitive psychology, but scholars in the humanities have largely disregarded this research, no doubt because of its emphasis on stereotyping as a cognitive process and because of the scientific and experimental basis of psychology as a discipline. Work in the humanities tends to focus on identifying and inspecting particular stereotypes, whereas social psychologists tend to answer more general questions about the processes by which stereotypes are formed. Consequently, the question of what defines a stereotype has been neglected in the humanities because of the political emphasis on asserting that certain images and ideas are stereotypical, leading to ad hoc forms of analysis. Social psychologists, in contrast, have avoided the question by taking the matter as self-evident and examining only those representations already generally accepted as stereotypical.

In cultural studies, the view of the stereotype as a biased or self-interested depiction is subsumed under the concept of ideology. Theories of ideology in British cultural studies developed in response to Marxist theories of culture and their relation to structures of power.[9] In the United States, one of the central texts in this transition was *Orientalism*, in which Edward Said examined the Oriental stereotype as a species of Foucauldian discourse by effectively banishing the referent. The principal difficulty with the stereotype in cultural studies is that its conception as an inaccurate misrepresentation relies on a realist epistemology because one can judge representational fidelity only if one has a stable object of comparison.[10] Thus the question of stereotypes in *Blu's Hanging* had to do not only with whether the depictions of Filipinos were accurate or distorted but also with who Filipino Americans are and what their situation is.[11]

The commitment of Asian American cultural studies to an antirealist and antiessentialist methodology meant that the accuracy of any representation could not be assessed. Instead, all representations were implicated in relations of power. Accordingly, the *Blu's Hanging* controversy highlighted one unfortunate consequence of such a position, which is that if "ideological representation" is simply a permutation of "stereotype," then everything is or can be a stereotype. Without any standard of judgment, there is no means by which one might say that a representation is not a stereotype. The failure to produce any clear criteria for identifying a stereotype thus seems tied to the inability of research in both the cultural and psychological fields to distinguish between valid and invalid representations of social groups. Insofar as stereotypes concern our ideas and perceptions of social categories, or groups—which, unlike natural categories, have no objective or substantive existence—then generalizations about a group cannot be wrong in any readily apparent manner or, what amounts to the same thing, *any* generalizations about a group are always wrong or inadequate in some way.

I argue that there is no objective basis on which to distinguish between true and false representations of groups, since their identity is what is at stake in struggles over legitimate representation. This does not mean, however, that the question of what is or is not a stereotype becomes moot or irrelevant. On the contrary, it is a deeply political question, but one connected to a problem made evident by J. C. Brigham, when he defined a stereotype as a "generalization made about [a] . . . group, concerning a trait attribution, which is considered to be unjustified by an observer."[12] The question of who determines what is or is not a justifiable attribution is precisely the issue; in academic studies, the scholastic point of view is privileged. This perspective, however, tries to identify the processes leading to the production of stereotypes in artificially constructed situations. By abstracting stereotypes from the concrete struggles in which they arise, such research fails to grasp that a stereotype appears as such only when someone (usually belonging to the group represented by the stereotype) *claims* that a particular representation is a stereotype.

After all, people who hold stereotypical ideas do not do so because they think that those ideas are wrong. Stereotypes induce credence because they are perceived as expressing some truth about the social world. They appear stereotypical only when someone begins to contest the veracity or objectivity of that idea or representation. It seems safe to say, for example, that no stereotype is universally recognized as false. The question then becomes, *who* thinks that a particular representation is false or stereotypical? Granted, some stereotypes are not the object of contestation (such as "the French are highly cultured and sophisticated"), but the very lack of objections indicates that such representations have little significant social impact (at least on the French). To suggest that stereotypes can be neutral or even positive seems misguided because they matter only when they are felt to be detrimental.[13] I propose that a "stereotype" is simply any representation that the group being represented perceives as negative.

At stake in social reality and the political struggles composing it is not the objective description of a group, which can be correct or accurate only if it can account for the particularities of each member, but the identity of the group, or the representation that enables the group to constitute itself and to act as a collective. Identities themselves are neither right nor wrong, accurate nor inaccurate representations of a group; they are only more or less efficacious in the mobilization, and therefore the realization, of the group. This does not mean that essentializing or exclusionary definitions of identity should not be critiqued; they certainly must be. But in political struggles over representation, the critique of one identity necessitates advancing another identity, another construction of the group.

Only from the scholastic point of view does it become possible to critique identity in the name of nonidentity.

As I have argued, Asian American identity is the stake of the struggles over representation in the Asian American field, which means that the truth or falsity of any construction of identity is the object of contention. Thus *every* representation of a group can be either true or false depending on the configuration of forces defining the group's social location. In the contest among representatives over the legitimate definition of Asian American identity, those who advance a particular representation will present it as true, and those who oppose it will construe it as false. A "stereotype" is any representation that an individual or group can credibly claim to be false. Most often, the term is used when one group disseminates representations of another. The lack of any special term for the opposite case, in which one group accepts its representation by another, demonstrates that this is the normative mode of political representation in a liberal democracy.

Therefore the question of whether *Blu's Hanging* is stereotypical has relatively little to do with the text itself but pertains to the political legitimacy of competing interpretations. In this respect, the contradictory nature of stereotypes reflects how they arise from illegitimate modes of thought; that is, they are cognitive mechanisms that apply the logic of the natural world to the social world by treating social groups as natural categories. Even the notion of the stereotype, we might say, emerges from categorical confusions and errors in negotiating the complex structures of modern societies. This is why cognitive theories mistake stereotyping for cognition itself, but stereotypes have little to do with information processing. Rather, they are the product of those who fail to understand the boundaries and rules that demarcate fields and so apply categories and procedures from one field to objects in another. This aspect of stereotypes seems to be obscured in academic investigations because scholarly work is directed toward producing the best (that is, the most legitimate) explanations and hence can recognize only those explanations that operate within the boundaries of correct methodologies. In the *Blu's Hanging* case, the primary categorical error was to apply the rules and assumptions of political representation to literary representation.

Whatever the merit of this account of stereotypes, it still does not offer a strategy for resolving conflicts such as those over the fiction award. In fact, to assert that any representation can be called a stereotype would seem to leave the domain of culture open to all sorts of political discontent, but one function of autonomy is to guard against such political reductionisms, as shown in the long history of complaints (from both the left and the right) against cultural representations in the United States alone. In this regard, the *Blu's Hanging* debates exhibited the typical pattern of such confrontations, which is a curious asymmetry. Since it is nearly impossible (for the reasons just enumerated) to directly refute the charge of stereotyping, the defenders of *Blu's Hanging* tried to redefine the question of whether it was stereotypical as whether the work was *good* literature or *bad* literature. Both sides presumed that by definition, literature could not be stereotypical. Thus one side essentially argued that the book was stereotypical and therefore bad literature, while the other side argued that the book was good literature and therefore could not be stereotypical, but these are not symmetrical arguments.

In returning to the conditions under which the book might appear to be stereotypical or not, we can see that the issue hinges on whether or not one perceives it to be *literature*. This suggests that those who accused the book of stereotyping did so because they did not read it within an interpretive frame appropriate to literary work. As Candace Fujikane notes, arguments concerning what were and were not properly literary readings sought to foreclose criticism of the book by separating qualified readers from those who were unqualified, thus "rendering local Filipinos as 'deficient' readers of literary texts and 'deficient' readers of race."[14] This helps explain one of the more mysterious aspects of the entire affair, which is the puzzling insistence of three separate AAAS committees on awarding prizes to Yamanaka's books, despite the ongoing protests. While some may see this as clear evidence of the literary quality of her work, the claim by the award committee that they were entirely unaware of the protests surrounding her work is striking. Although such obliviousness may be due partly to the way that the previous year's protests were kept quiet, it also raises larger questions about the continuing pattern of readings that failed to detect any stereotypical depictions in Yamanaka's writing. Does this mean that there were none? Some argued that this lack of awareness was due to the committee members' neglect of the racial dynamics in Hawai'i (even though one member of the committee was originally from there) or that it stemmed from the desire of continental Asian Americans to see Hawai'i as a genuinely multicultural society. I believe that more basic factors might account for the predilection of the award committees, namely, that as professional scholars of literature, the members of the committee were trained to *not* perceive stereotypes in a literary text.

This critical apparatus extends beyond the prior classification of *Blu's Hanging* as literature. The protesters, for example, also objected to the apparent double standard in which the critique of Orientalist stereotypes was seen as a vital aspect of Asian American cultural politics, whereas the allegation of stereotyping by Asian Americans met with considerably greater resistance. Whether or not one sees this disparity as hypocritical is connected to whether or not one considers the book to be stereotypical. The same readers who are incapable of recognizing the stereotypes in the book are also those who believe that stereotyping arises only in relations between non-Asians and Asians. These perceptions derive from the same vision of the social world (or what Bourdieu calls the "vision of divisions" that make up the social structure), and they provide concrete instances of the cultural capital of Asian American "identity." Identity in this case is a set of embodied dispositions, or habitus, enabling agents to recognize and display the particular vision of the social world identifying one as a legitimate representative of Asian Americans. To charge a work of Asian American *literature* with stereotyping *Asian Americans* reveals the lack of cultural capital that would preclude such a reading by those who have the legitimate means of appropriating legitimate Asian American culture.

The conflict over the fiction award thus was a conflict between those who possess capital—in this case, both the cultural capital and the political capital of Asian American identity—and those who do not. I have already suggested that the logic of stereotypes derives from the mode of representation of the political field, but my analysis also implies that the relation of the cultural field to the political field overall correlates with the relation of the field of restricted production to the field of general production in the cultural field. In general, the failure to perceive a text as literature means that one is reading it according to the protocols of the commercial field, which is what cultural studies rejects when it rejects realism, representation, and referentiality, as these all belong to the modes of consumption of the commercial field. To link the political field with the field of general cultural production simply shows that consumers of commercial products lack the cultural capital to appropriate the products of the restricted field. The readers who perceive stereotypes are also the same subjects who produce the political capital that representatives can accumulate but who lack the capital to represent themselves.[15] In this respect, the *Blu's Hanging* conflict differs from disputes like those between Chin and Kingston discussed in chapter 4. Those were debates among representatives, whereas at the core of the *Blu's Hanging* conflict was a contest between representatives and the represented.

I contend that what was at stake in the protests over the fiction award was less a demand for representation than a demand *not to be represented*. The defenders of *Blu's Hanging* could understand this only by misrecognizing it as censorship, because the ideology of artistic freedom states that it is illegitimate to demand to be represented aesthetically in specific ways. Therefore, those who are represented but who cannot represent themselves cannot refuse an aesthetic representation that they do not like, except to accuse it of being stereotypical. Another tactic might be to accuse a work of being bad art, but this presumes that one has the means of appropriating legitimate art and is therefore in a position to represent oneself. The concept of the stereotype is one of the few political mechanisms available to those who lack the cultural capital to present more "sophisticated" arguments and must therefore resort to arguments that are themselves illegitimate in the domain of legitimate art.

Ultimately, the *Blu's Hanging* episode offered a stark choice for Filipinos, the represented: was it better to be represented in a positive but illegitimate manner or to be represented in more "complex" ways, even if they were distressing or entirely reprehensible depictions? In other words, the question was whether they were to be represented in politically satisfactory but aesthetically devalued ways, or the reverse. The answer depends largely on the kind of capital one possesses. For those who lack cultural capital and therefore the means to appreciate literature, aesthetic value is not a form of capital that they can recognize or accumulate. Thus the most significant determining context of the conflict was the university itself, since it operates to conserve the scarcity of cultural capital and so must impose a relation of representation on all those sustained by it.

Sexuality and the Contest over Representative Respectability

Given the events surrounding *Blu's Hanging*, it might have been inevitable that critics would be tempted to read the novel in relation to those events, or even as commenting on them. Most of the commentary, however, has tended to circulate within the terms of the debates over identity and difference or heterogeneity. Viet Nguyen, for example, found the contentions dividing the local community in the book to be object lessons about the potential pitfalls in constructing a larger panethnic Asian American coalition. Erin Suzuki observed that "both the novel and the controversy surrounding it illustrate the way that the Asian American intellectual community must balance the need for a teleological political subjectivity (embodied by the upwardly-mobile Ivah) against the need for a critical, dissident 'bad subject,' such as Uncle Paulo."[16] Conversely, Kandice Chuh construed the debates over the text as an instance of the problematics of identity and difference in that the reduction of the text to the single vector of race excluded other dimensions, such as gender and "the failures of the heteronormative family."[17] Emily Russell offered a somewhat different perspective on the book by concentrating on the history of leprosy that was the Ogatas' hidden shame, but her reading also operates within the same paradigm in her argument that the obsession with a singular vision of the healthy body (politic) denies any value to disability as difference.

As incisive as these readings are, they tend to be bound by certain parameters of the text, locating it in an external relation to the events of the controversy and thus connecting them only in analogical or allegorical ways. Such readings distinguish between text and context. I believe not only that *Blu's Hanging* was motivated by the same concerns and issues as circulated in the debates but also that it can be seen as more or less directly participating in them. This claim is not as improbable as it may first appear, given that protests over the depictions of Filipinos in Yamanaka's writing began with the appearance of her first book. Thus it would hardly be surprising that Yamanaka's later books responded in some way to the criticisms of her work. Indeed, it would be more surprising if that were not the case. In any event, I contend that *Blu's Hanging* must be read in the context of the protests against her writing and that doing so offers a somewhat different perspective on the figure of Uncle Paulo, one that does not avoid the question of racism but offers new perspectives on it.

How is *Blu's Hanging* implicated in the controversies surrounding it? One explanation for the persistent appeal of Yamanaka's work to the AAAS's various award committees might be that it speaks directly to the "crisis of representation" in the field. Beginning with Yamanaka's own declarations that she had no conscious or overt racist intentions, then what in the logic of the narrative led to such an effect? I begin my analysis by arguing that the main point of contention in the book is Yamanaka's authority to represent the local community in Hawai'i. Framing the issue in this way enables us to recognize that Uncle Paulo poses a threat to Ivah precisely because he is the stand-in for those in the community who resist the text's representation.

Several critics have tried to recuperate the figure of Paulo, as Erin Suzuki does by arguing that instead of "denouncing the character of Uncle Paulo as a negative stereotype, we can also regard him as a resistant although delinquent subaltern who adamantly refuses to forgive and forget."[18] Somewhat ironically, this argument inserts the protests into the book by making Paulo their representative only to ignore the cause of the protests in the very same gesture by denying his stereotypicality. The problem with such a reading is that like Hans Holbein's painting *The Ambassadors*, we can see the shadow of death (or the protests) only from a vantage point obliquely situated with regard to Ivah's narration. In fact, the narrative of *Blu's Hanging* strives to prevent us from seeing things from Paulo's viewpoint if we are seeing him through Ivah, as a matter of perspective and also by reducing him to a two-dimensional caricature, which is one of the main reasons that he appears to be a stereotype in the first place. He exists as little more than a plot device in the narrative, but what is the purpose of this device? As a kind of mental exercise, it is possible to maintain both perspectives at once, but only in a purely conceptual nonspace. Moreover, the Manichaean characterization of Paulo reinforces this dichotomous relation to him, in which he is either a sexual predator and pedophile or the oppressed subaltern.

If Uncle Paulo is, as I am suggesting, the signifier of resistance to the book's representative regime, then it might seem obvious why the book would want to demonize him or prevent him from appealing to our sympathies. In order to understand what is at stake in Yamanaka's representation of local community and culture in Hawaiʻi, we need to contextualize the figure of Paulo within the larger symbolic economy of the book, beginning with his extended family. Despite Ivah's antagonism toward the Reyes girls, there exists an ambivalent relation of similitude and distancing between them. It seems fairly evident that Ivah's hostility toward the older Reyes girls in particular is due partly to her envy of them as well as to her barely concealed sense of being engaged in a competitive struggle with them. Both families, after all, are missing one parent while the other is either absent or barely functional, and the children are left largely to fend for themselves. Both families also hide secrets: the Reyes' secret is that they're half Japanese and their father has deserted them for his wife's second cousin, while the Ogatas' secret is that both their parents have leprosy.

The primary objects of the competition between Ivah and the two older Reyes daughters, Evangeline and Blendaline (or Vangie and Blendie, as Blu calls them), are Blu and Mitchell Oliveira, who is Portuguese but from El Segundo, California, so he can "talk really good haole English."[19] The most obvious register of this competition is sexuality, since Evangeline and Blendaline lure Mitchell and Blu away from Ivah primarily by engaging in oral sex with them. But if this is a competition, it isn't apparent how Ivah competes, since she does not engage in any sort of sexual activity with anyone, let alone Mitchell. Obviously it is not a competition for Mitchell, although he and Ivah do end up dating, it seems, by the end of the book. Rather, this is a struggle over "hearts and minds," or ideological hegemony. In fact, all of Yamanaka's writing up through *Blu's Hanging* is marked by its intense aversion to sexuality, despite the sometimes graphic descriptions of sexual acts. Most of the critical commentary has tended to address the sexuality in Yamanaka's work mainly in terms of sexual violence toward women, but in *Blu's Hanging*, and especially in the figure of Uncle Paulo, the anxieties surrounding sex make it unclear whether Ivah's revulsion to sex stems from the degrading incidents to which she (and we) are made witness or whether the pervasive sexual degradation in the book is an imaginary projection of her revulsion. Even though several of the characters (most notably Mitchell and Blu) describe their sexual experiences in almost ecstatic terms, Ivah's narrative presents a different point of view, as she sees her brother's relationship with Blendaline as leading to the same fate as that suffered by the cats, which is borne out by Uncle Paulo's assault.

From Ivah's perspective, sex can be only negative and threatening, and even though there certainly are understandable reasons for this, one of the more mysterious episodes in the text suggests that depictions of sex may be subject to certain imaginary distortions. Once when Ivah, Blu, and Maisie visit their mother's grave, they find a pie pan filled with what Ivah calls "childbearing stones." These are perfectly round stones capable of giving birth to child-stones. Ivah says, "When the mother-stone is about to give birth, I see the child-stone inside her with my own eyes. . . . The child-stone spins inside the mother-stone, a red and white swirl. . . . And when the child is born, there are no scars left on the mother-stone."[20] Introduced with no break in the narrative, the childbearing stones are presented as occupying the same textual reality as the children, although they are clearly perceived as fantastic. This introduction of fantasy into what is otherwise a mostly realist narrative appears to signal a breakdown in the lines dividing the "reality" of the narrative from the imaginary dimensions of Ivah's consciousness, a failure of censorship occasioned by anxieties of sexual and social reproduction.

The scars refer to the marks of pregnancy and childbirth, as well as the scars left by leprosy on the bodies of both her parents. As Blu comments, "Thass the miracle. . . . Even after all that, the Mama-stone no more scars and the babies perfect."[21] The childbearing stones recall the history of Ivah's parents, who met at the Kalaupapa leper colony in Hawai'i.[22] Even though her father, Bertram, and her mother, Eleanor, were happy there, they left because, as he tells her, "we wanted for prove to the world, everybody, that we could make perfect children, perfect."[23] The desire for offspring free of disease is connected by the stones to the fantasy of asexual reproduction that also is evoked here, in which Ivah and others see sexuality as a disease. One of the persistent images in Yamanaka's writing is of hickeys as a signifier of sexual promiscuity, which shows up in *Blu's Hanging* in the incident when Ivah's cousin, Lila Beth, is covered with hickeys and Bertram associates the shame of the red welts left by the hickeys with the red spots that are the first sign of leprosy. Perfect children, then, are free not just of the disease of leprosy but also of sexuality, as the image of immaculate conception signifies.

What accounts for this aversion to sexuality? Again, it is unclear what makes the Reyes girls so threatening. Apart from a few incidental references, they first appear in the middle of chapter 3, when Ivah declares that "our neighbors, Evangeline Reyes and her three sisters, make my brother's mouth water," and then she recounts some of the torture they inflict on cats.[24] Chapter 4 begins:

> Mama told me about Cat Haters. She said there's a breed who hate them because when cats get old, they know what you talk about, and they walk on hind legs like humans. They act like you, talk like you. Cat Haters, she said, are *Human Rats* like the Human Rats across the gully.[25]

Why do Human Rats hate cats? Ivah's mother explains that human rats hate cats because they become too similar to humans. The mother's story is one of transformation, but what kind of transformation? Psychoanalytic interpretations are not especially helpful here, as they tend to assimilate the death of the mother to the generalized loss or lack that is the basis of consciousness. For a more specific answer, we must attend to the mother's words.

In fact, chapter 4 is not particularly concerned with the Reyes girls, as there is little mention of them after the opening section. Most of the chapter is taken up with Ivah's memories of her mother, memories evoked by the reference to human rats. Although Eleanor and her death carry heavy symbolic freight in the book, little attention has been paid to what that might be. Beginning with the central issue of racist representations and stereotypes, it is striking that most of the children's apparently racist ideas can be traced directly back to their mother. This is most apparent in the episode with their neighbor, Clarence, who is black and whom Ivah and her siblings call "Kuro-chan." Clarence keeps a number of dogs, and the kids "adopt" one of them for Maisie. When their father finds out, he takes them to see Clarence so they can ask his permission to take the dog: "We walk to the Kuro-chan's house. Up the gravel driveway and Poppy tells Blu to knock it off. What the hell is he thinking, telling the rest of us about all Kuro-chans? 'You like grow up prej-dist, dammit, Blu?'"[26] Interestingly, we are not told what Blu was telling them about "all" Kuro-chans, only Poppy's response that it was prejudiced. This is the only time in the book that he raises the issue with the children, although it recurs in the arguments between Miss Ito and the two haole teachers, Miss Owens and Mrs. Nishimoto.

As it turns out, the reason that the children are afraid of Clarence is that "Mama used to tell Blu never to be bad to his sisters or Mama and Poppy or she'd call the Kuro-chan to take him away forever to his house with no springs on the screen door. 'And what the Kuro-chan does to little boys like you, Blu.'"[27] Her main concern here is to protect the kids from the sexual predators in the neighborhood, who also include Lerch and Mr. Iwasaki, the latter of whom at least does turn out to be a "pervert" who exposes himself to the kids, whereas it is clear that Clarence is not a threat. Nevertheless, for some reason, the children are unable to call him Clarence and continue to refer to him as the Kuro-chan, even though this nickname derives from the Japanese word *kuronbo*, a derogatory term for blacks. Although Eleanor does not explicitly assign the threat here to his being black, the conversations that she had with Ivah were littered with racial and ethnic stereotypes, from the nickname that she gives Ivah because her hair looks Samoan ("Ivah Kinimaka"), to her impersonations of haoles and Portuguese. None of these other stereotypes is refuted by anyone in the book, least of all Ivah.

The other advice that Eleanor gives Ivah is of particular interest, despite its apparent triviality. It is a litany of domestic tips and moral maxims including "No let one boy buy you clothes. Implies he *knows* your size, know what I mean?" and "No put too much water in the rice bumbye the bugga get mushy—buckshot better than sticky rice." Eleanor also instructs Ivah to wear a slip so the boys won't be able to see her panties, to wear clean panties with no holes in case she gets into a car accident, and to use the "bi-logical correct names" for body parts instead of their pidgin equivalents.[28] She also sings a little ditty: "Yellow on your panty, whadda you do? Yellow on your panty, whadda you do? Well, if you don't use regular Clorox, use Borax too."[29] It is apparent that the main emphasis of much of the mother's advice is the desire for middle-class respectability, suggesting that the Ogatas' aspiration to middle-class status is what separates them from the Reyes. Physical modesty and sexual abstinence, then, are coded as class markers, and the intense prohibitions against self-display and sexual activity that Ivah obeys indicate her desire to "better" herself, a discourse that derives from the mother.

As several critics have noted, Yamanaka's books are essentially *bildungs-roman* narratives that trace the maturation and development of their young female protagonists. Ivah goes through puberty midway through *Blu's Hanging*, in one of the book's most powerful scenes. In addition, Fujikane asserts that *Saturday Night at the Pahala Theatre* can be seen as narrating a "developmental model of feminist individualism" that "diminishes the other speakers in the collection who do not find liberation in written self-representation."[30] Similarly, Crystal Parikh notes the "developmental narrative" in *Blu's Hanging* that produces the "liberal, educated, autonomous ego" of Ivah as a normative subject.[31] Although the developmental impetus of the plot is evident in Ivah's departure for the Mid-Pacific Institute and (presumably) her accession to middle-class status, Yamanaka is acutely aware of the condemnations that such individual success may provoke, as evinced in the repeated accusations of betrayal and abandonment directed against Ivah. Conscious that her representative authority will not go unchallenged in the local community, Yamanaka's dilemma is how to construct a rationale that legitimates Ivah's representation but will also win the "consent" of those she seeks to represent, or at least will mitigate their resentment. The main burden of the narrative, therefore, is finding a way to reconcile individual freedom and success with responsibility to the community.

I contend that middle-class respectability is one of the major themes in all of Yamanaka's works, and it may be most obvious in her narratives' central opposition of sexuality and shame. Ivah is morally superior to the Reyes girls not for her abstinence but for her sensitivity to shame, whereas

Evangeline and Blendaline seem largely (but not completely) indifferent to the community's disapproval. The ability to exercise appropriate moral judgments identifies one as a member of the community because it entails being able to deploy its particular moral and ethical standards. In this regard, there are two aspects to the stereotypes that Eleanor declares. First, they are part of her effort to attain middle-class respectability, since the ability to discriminate comes from the internalization of racial hierarchy as the index of appropriate and inappropriate forms of conduct and values. Stereotypes attribute behaviors and beliefs to particular racial groups, thereby forming a hierarchical ranking of cultures in American society.

The second aspect of the stereotypes in Eleanor's discourse is that they display her credentials as a local. Ivah recalls characters that her mother would perform: "There was Hinalea Hammings, a big-talking haole who wanted to be Hawaiian. Vicky Ventura, stewardess for Malibu Airlines. Toiletta Paperu, so stupid, she didn't know how to wipe her own ass."[32] The first two characters are stereotypes that may register as such only in a Hawaiian context, but they also embody critiques of haoles who are ignorant of local culture and customs. While the performances of these two characters depend for their effect on the accuracy of the impersonation, the third character is a caricature, as her name indicates.

> Toiletta Paperu made us laugh till it hurt. Cutting people down like the ladies in Elvis' *Blue Hawaii*. With a real Portuguese accent, Toiletta would pronounce, "All the hula girls in *Blue Hawaii* look so haole, I swear, and they sappose to be Hawaiian? And all the Japanee and Chinee chicks, them too looking all haole. *Oh, please, Louise.* Haoles with black hair and heavy eyeliner so that they look like they get single eye. *Hel-lo.* . . . Like you seen France Nguyen on Hawaii Five-O trying for talk pidgin like yours truly with her Chinee accent: 'I dunno, McGarrett. You one dead mahimahi, you no watch out, bruddah.'"
>
> "Please, France," said Toiletta Paperu, "you betta off trying out for be Yuniyoshi's sista on *Breakfast at Tiffany's II*, or betta yet, Mrs. Livingston's aunty from Tokyo on *The Courtship of Eddie's Father*."

This is an extraordinarily complex moment in the text in which Eleanor satirizes an ethnic group considered marginally white, but the discourse that she attributes to Toiletta is a discourse of local cultural nationalism. That is, Toiletta mocks mainland Asian Americans who are supposed to play locals but lack local cultural authenticity. Her advice is that they instead play stereotypical Asian characters in the mainstream media. Although this is an assertion of her own local identity, Toiletta herself is Eleanor's satirical representation of the ambiguous status of Portuguese in the local community and their aspirations to whiteness.

At the same time, this passage is notable also for its mention of *Breakfast at Tiffany's*, the source of both the ridiculous Japanese character played by Mickey Rooney as well as the theme song ("Moon River") that Poppy plays over and over and even teaches to Blu. *Breakfast at Tiffany's* enacts a complicated ambivalence toward a fantasized ideal of heteronormative middle-class whiteness that seems somewhat incongruous coming from Poppy. The book never explains what hold the song has on him, although the lyrics ("Moon River, wider than a mile, / I'm crossing you in style some day") speak to any seemingly unattainable longing. Both the song and Eleanor's story of the human cats are narratives of metamorphosis and transition that are echoed throughout the book: the exile of Ivah's parents when they contract leprosy, their cure and return to "normal" society, Ivah's journey from the local community to the Mid-Pacific Institute, the passage from Hawai'i to the mainland, and others. Underlying all these crossings is the precarious ascent of the lower-class subject to an uncertain middle-class status, made more difficult in Ivah's case because she is trying to find a position in between where she can belong to both classes simultaneously. Thus "Toiletta Paperu" evokes the potential degradation of failing to achieve middle-class legitimacy while suffering the rejection of one's original community.

The story of the cats who grow up to become human narrates this transformation from being lower class to being respectable, which is equated with humanity itself. The reason that human rats hate them is jealousy, as expressed in accusations of betrayal, but in rejecting this transformation, the rats consign themselves to the domain of animals, or the lower class. In class warfare, working-class communities have always needed ways of enforcing class loyalty and solidarity, ranging from outright coercion and violence to moral censure and shame. *Blu's Hanging*, though, confuses the shame of lower-class status with the shame that the community tries to impose on deserters, rendering them indistinguishable or interchangeable. Indeed, the entire first half of the book consists of a series of episodes of shame, embarrassment, and humiliation, culminating in the scene when Ivah menstruates for the first time. After she figures out what is happening to her, she is too embarrassed to go to the store to buy any pads, so she uses a wad of napkins. In this book, her period happens to start the day before the big Christmas dance at school, at which Ivah was hoping that Mitchell would ask her to dance. She decides to go anyway, despite her period, but just as Mitchell finally asks her, Evangeline rushes over and accuses Ivah of having her "rags."

Ivah's embarrassment conflates several different kinds of shame: the shame of not having a mother who can help her, the shame of poverty and an ignorance associated with being lower class, the shame of failing to conform to a middle-class denial of embodiment, and the shame of public exposure of private matters. Much of this shame has to do with class norms of bodily discipline and the separation of public and private, but in the book, these norms are enforced by Evangeline Reyes, even though her public exposure invades Ivah's privacy and also reveals her own lack of manners. Blu, in contrast, understands the need for privacy, but at the same time, as he explains in his note to Ivah, when he buys her a "sanaterry belt and pads" for Christmas, "I not shame and I no care 'cause you got no mommy to tell you about birds and bees."[33] The problem with Blu is not exactly that he has no shame but that his desires easily overcome his shame, which is why he is susceptible to the influence of Blendie Reyes and ultimately becomes the victim of Uncle Paulo. In other words, he lacks sufficient discipline and self-mastery.

Obviously, both Blu and Mitchell are easily swayed by the sexual favors of the Reyes girls, although they eventually are brought back into the fold by shame and their own consciences. What is less evident are the meanings of sexuality in this book. When Mitchell confesses to Ivah what he has done, he says that "it feels like—like no pain. Like flying," and Blu, too, describes sexuality in metaphors of flight.[34] After Ivah discovers Blu and Blendaline together, she recounts this exchange with him:

It's a moment in my life that I will remember against my will forever. Him, tied on earth to me. There's no way for him to escape the house without a mother, the days and nights without a father. . . .

"I gotta fly, Ivah, anywhere in this world. . . . Why you no can just let me fly, hah, Ivah?"

The rope burns on his wrists and ankles aren't even healed. At night, he hangs on to a knotted sheet dangling from his window. . . . But tonight, I loosen the knots in the rope that tie him to me, and let the rope fall away. Fall from my brother, who has learned how to fly.[35]

Images of ropes are one of the most pervasive motifs in the book but they are often linked, as here, with sex and with flying, on the one hand, and with death, on the other. The title of the book encapsulates these paradoxical connotations in the images of Blu hanging by the neck and also hanging outside his window. Sexuality here marks Blu's passage into adulthood, but if he has learned how to fly, this does not mean that he knows where to go.

I would argue that sexuality in *Blu's Hanging* signifies sociality itself, or the need for social relations (which, in an earlier moment, Blu craves) and for community. But for Ivah, community is also the domain of death because it ties her to her lower-class origins and prevents her from leaving. If Blu has learned how to fly, this seems to be a flight toward death, in contrast with Ivah's departure, which is precisely not *flight* because she is not seeking to escape; she is bringing her family with her and she intends to return. Ivah and the Reyes girls compete for representative authority over the community in their lifestyles, practices that model strategies of self-improvement, for the Reyes are also class climbers. The main difference is that Ivah will pull herself up and her family with her, whereas the Reyes girls are forced to depend on men to raise their status. We may say generally that Ivah exemplifies individualistic and meritocratic strategies, whereas the Reyes use collectivist strategies. Collectivism is repudiated through its conflation with gender inequality and sexual violence, converting the shame of abandoning one's family and community into the shame of sexual exploitation and gender subordination. From the perspective of middle-class individualism, communally oriented practices can appear only as the loss of autonomy and submission to group conformity.

The effort to establish Ivah's representative legitimacy takes place along two axes, first, when the plot continually compares Ivah with other members of the community as a means of establishing her qualifications as a representative and, second, when it institutes a gendered division of representation. Ivah's continual refrain about being a "mama" emphasizes her representation as maternal rather than paternal. The adult men in the community are conspicuously absent from the narrative, and those that are mentioned are either sexual deviants or impotent and apathetic, as Ivah's own father is. What does it mean to represent the community as its mother? This is what the book seeks to establish through a series of comparisons between Ivah and the other women in the town. Even though her primary antagonists are the Reyes sisters, the book continually measures Ivah against other candidates for "mama," who are divided into two groups. Eleanor is the symbolic prototype of the legitimate mother, and her sister, Aunty Betty, exemplifies the illegitimate mother. Aunty Betty also is a human rat and is portrayed as hectoring and hypocritical. Her obsession with getting her daughter, Lila Beth, into a mainland college brands her as assimilationist and associates her with the haole teachers. Aunty Betty illustrates the dangers of taking respectability too far, for it alienates the very constituency whose approval Ivah is trying to win.

The representative ideal in the book is Miss Ito, Maisie's teacher, who is educated, attractive, and caring; she can also hang out with the locals and drink a beer. She occupies a position that is both within and above the community. As a model for Ivah, Miss Ito performs the exemplary act of representation, which is that she makes Maisie speak. This is one kind of claim made for Ivah's representative legitimacy in the book, that she has the ability (or the linguistic capital) to make the community speak, to give it a voice. As a mama, she knows what the community needs because she belongs to it, but at the same time, she is able to speak in the idiom of the dominant culture. Ivah, however, cannot claim credit for coaxing Maisie to talk, for that is Miss Ito's accomplishment. Instead, for Ivah, the real object of contention in the book is Blu, as the title indicates. Blu is just beginning to assert his independence, as we have seen, which means that he makes choices for which he is not prepared, and by protecting Blu from the consequences of his own choices, Ivah demonstrates that she is able to assume the responsibilities of being a mama.

The last section of the book after the scene with Blendaline joins two main narrative strands: one centers on Ivah's indecisiveness over whether to go to Mid-Pac, and the other largely consists of Blu's misadventures. The contrast between these two story lines allows the book to make several crucial points about Ivah's capability for mature representation. Blu, for example, gets them fired from their dog-washing job when he gets too emotionally involved with the dogs and tries to rescue one. Ivah, however, is able to overcome her antagonistic relation with Mrs. Nishimoto by taking the kids off her hands when she is about to reach the breaking point. When Mitchell is born again and tries to convince Ivah to attend church with him, Blu at first resists vehemently and calls Mitchell "stupid Portagee punk, stink ass, traitor with hickeys up his ass."[36] Once in church, though, Blu is quickly recruited to play the lead role in the church musical production, only to stop coming soon after the performance is over. Not only does Ivah assume a more distanced and noncommittal attitude toward religion, but this episode also demonstrates that she is capable of resisting even the "God Almightiest Handsomest Christian man from here to Kingdom Come," as she describes Jim Cameron, the haole missionary, and will not simply seize the first opportunity to assimilate into the dominant culture.[37]

More important, several incidents in the last part of the book involve money, from Mitchell's scheme to find valuable pennies to Blu's car- and dog-washing service. The first fails completely, but Blu's business succeeds despite Ivah's skepticism. When Blu tells Ivah that he got the idea from *Henry Reed's Babysitting Service*, she responds, "Thass *fiction*, like the librarian tell us every year. . . . You *nonfiction*, you moron. I no think going work."[38] Ivah's objection here links commerce to literature, and even though she is wrong that Blu's plan won't work, the book sides with her in the end because, as she says to Blu,

> "I dunno. . . . Maybe I still get Aunty Betty inside my head, know what I mean? How we no mo' class and we do what we like, how we like, with no manners. Thass kinda low-class to sell tickets. I mean, if we work for somebody, thass one thing, but for sell tickets? Thass the part I no like."[39]

Selling one's labor for a wage is acceptable, but selling services that one should perform as favors is low class, especially since Blu plans to target people at church, where, he reasons, they won't want to look cheap. Although this is impeccable logic, it is the logic of economism and the reduction of social relations to market relations. Despite Blu's arguments, Ivah continues to feel uneasy: "'I know but—' I pause and feel kind of disgusted and ashamed."[40] Ivah is mistaken here, since this is not the voice of Aunty Betty; it is the voice of the community attempting to resist commodification.

The reason that Blu comes up with this plan in the first place is that he wants badly to go to Honolulu with Ivah when she goes to Mid-Pac. Her disgust signals a kind of crisis, a crisis of denial. That is, Blu's commerce threatens to taint Ivah's opportunity with the stigma of self-interest, thus undoing her carefully constructed efforts to manifest her altruistic selflessness. In fact, in the climactic scene, Blu is at Uncle Paulo's house to wash his car. It is almost as if Blu must be punished for his entrepreneurial initiatives in order to preserve Ivah's disinterest and to distract us from the implications of his success. Moreover, if Blu actually became self-sufficient at this point, he would no longer need Ivah to take care of him. This would deprive her of her main reason for going to Mid-Pac, that she has to help support the family because her father is incapable of doing so. After Uncle Paulo rapes Blu, Ivah once again must assume the position of guardian over Blu, about whom she tells Maisie, "We gotta protect him from himself."[41]

Does this rape scene belong to fiction or nonfiction? Ivah assigns Blu to the realm of nonfiction, to which, I would argue, the Reyes girls and Uncle Paulo also belong, not because their representation is meant to correspond to reality but because nonfiction is the realm of crass self-interest as well as, paradoxically, community. Fiction, of course, signifies the disinterest to which Ivah, and the book, aspire, which is nowhere more evident than in what they do with the two thousand pennies. As Ivah explains,

> Blu says nothing's ever a waste. He tells Maisie to stand in the yard and hold up her hands, and he sprinkles the pennies onto her face as she spins and spins; she gathers the pennies in the scoop of her T-shirt like Easter eggs she finds in the grass.
>
> Blu takes the pennies to the county pool . . . and throws them on the glass surface of the water. They fall in slow motion through my fingers, tumbling to the bottom, where the three of us, cheeks full of air, gather the pennies. . . . When we rise to the surface, we see an explosion of pennies in the sunlight.[42]

Even if the pennies are worth no more than their stated face value, this passage manages to extract a kind of surplus value from them by converting them into art. Rather than the profit that Blu makes, the value that Ivah produces benefits the entire community and not just her alone. She transforms her pidgin English into poetry, something Blu cannot do, as his poems for Mrs. Ota attest. Unlike Blu, Ivah is not bound by pidgin and can "translate" between pidgin and standard English, as the narrative itself does.

At this point, we can return to the choice posed by the fiction award between aesthetic representation and political representation, or the choice between "literary" and "realist" representations. These are the same alternatives, we can now see, offered by the book itself. The antithesis of political representation and aesthetic representation is referenced in the division between fiction and nonfiction and figures directly in the book in the contrast between Ivah and the Reyes girls. If Ivah represents the community in the mode of fiction, the Reyes are assigned to the domain of nonfiction. We know that their representation is political rather than aesthetic because it is condemned to an endless quest for approval (or consent), which is why the Reyes can solicit the favor of the masses only by pandering to their lowest instincts rather than attempting to cultivate a more contemplative or *aesthetic* perspective on life, as Ivah does. The Reyes, in short, give people what they want, whereas Ivah knows what they need, which is the only license that she needs as a representative, because art does not require the consent of those it represents.

Ivah's refusal to engage in sexual activity shows that she does not need to seek the community's favor. Sexuality, then, connotes the Reyes' subordination to the popular will, but it is also the register of politics, power, and violence. Sexuality is what allows the book to yoke the Reyes' cruelty to animals with Uncle Paulo's violent assaults and Aunty Betty's obsession with shame and appearances. Uncle Paulo is allowed his one rant about prejudice against Filipinos (in a moment that is almost universally misread) because he is associated with ethnic nationalism, particularly with the futility and violence of political protest, which in the end is indistinguishable from the violence of domination. Ultimately, I argue, the book responds to the protesters by turning against them in the figure of Uncle Paulo the very weapon that it sees them as wielding, which is the *violence of the literal*.

To equate the literal with violence or power implies that the figurative is somehow free of the stigma of power, which is what the book tries to suggest, since almost all the narrative's symbolic and fantastic elements are meant to evoke innocence, whereas realism is the mode of violence and degradation. In her essay on *Blu's Hanging*, Candace Fujikane illuminates what that innocence covers up when she points out that the book's insistence on the Ogatas as the most downtrodden members of the community obscures their racial/ethnic privilege, pointing out that Ivah's entry to Mid-Pac is made possible by the relative privilege and status of the local Japanese community. Moreover, Fujikane notes that the book completely neglects the predominantly Native Hawaiian population on the island of Molokai, where it is set, and that this neglect also masks the status of local Japanese as settlers as well as the most powerful Asian ethnic community in Hawai'i.[43]

What lesson can we draw from the book and the events surrounding it? *Blu's Hanging* strives to legitimate Ivah's representation of the local community as superior because of its disinterest and innocence, but her representation means erasing the mechanisms of representation and their implication for relations of power. This is simply another way of describing the forms of denial imposed by both the academic and cultural fields in the production of disinterest and objectivity. Whether this erasure creates problems is the question that this book explores, but the significance of the controversy over *Blu's Hanging* is that it exposed the unexamined relations of representation as the determining matrix of the entire conflict. To return to the childbearing stones with which I began this discussion, the fantasy of virgin birth is one of a pure original innocence that could exist outside relations of power, which is the fantasy underlying the autonomy of the cultural and academic fields.

I shall conclude by pointing to one other convergence between the book and the controversy, which is the confrontation between two different ideological perspectives epitomized by Ivah and Blu. One of the central features of Blu's interpretations of social relations is that he continually views them as binary oppositions, for example, in his dichotomization of people into friends or enemies, them or us. Part of what ties Blu to Uncle Paulo is that they both share this Manichaean, nationalist view of the world. Similarly, Blu decides that he can't be a Christian because that would mean that his mother would be consigned to hell. The most salient instance can be found in the title itself, which doesn't refer directly to his rape by Uncle Paulo but to an earlier moment when Blu wants to play cowboys and Indians but has no one to cut him down when he (playing the bad guy) hangs himself (as the good guy). As he complains to Maisie, "I need somebody, just one guy, to be the bad guy."[44] Good guy or bad guy, heaven or hell, Baptist or Buddhist, blood or water: these are the oppositions that structure the world Blu lives in. Ivah, conversely, exhibits a less dualistic view of things; she is capable of seeing both sides and of looking at things through the eyes of even those with whom she disagrees. But this describes the ontology of liberalism. Ivah's more "mature" perspective is that of the classical liberal political subject and of the middle class. This is what she tries to teach Blu and the reader through the pedagogy of her narrative.

The problem is that Ivah, and the book, repeatedly confronts a world that is not so forgiving and that imposes mutually exclusive choices. Ultimately, she cannot remain in the community and, at the same time, achieve success in the dominant culture, which is the resolution that the book keeps trying to achieve but fails. The reason is that Ivah must finally confront the hard reality of interest, that the necessity of choosing is imposed by the investment that she must make in a particular field or a particular form of capital accumulation. The antinomy between the disinterested perspective of the public sphere and the antagonistic relations of interest also describes, I believe, the conditions that led to the conflict over the fiction award. The intractability of this conflict, it seems to me, had less to do with which side was right than with the deep investments and interests that spurred all sides, interests that were difficult to articulate and make explicit because of the denials imposed by the academic and cultural fields. The protests precipitated a crisis because they forced Asian American studies as a field to confront both its interests and the denials that sustained them.

Even though the AAAS strove to maintain a distanced and disinterested stance toward the conflict between the protesters and the writers, it was finally forced to confront the duality inscribed in the award itself, as the embodiment of interest and of capital, which was the duality imposed by the vote: yes or no. In the end, the award could not be simultaneously given and retracted. If reflexive analysis requires an investigation of the mechanisms of representation and the interests that motivate them, the difficulty of this task is compounded by the fact that in the case of fields such as the academic and cultural, interest is generally not personal, individual interest; it is collective interest, or the interest of the field, as well as perhaps the interest of the university. Have the interests of Asian American studies and the university become completely intertwined, or do they diverge in significant ways? That is the question I have explored in this book, but the answer can be collectively determined only by the field.

Coda

In her retrospective collection of talks and essays regarding the institutional and programmatic efforts in which she took part, Sucheng Chan provides some fascinating glimpses into the early history of Asian American studies at the University of California at Berkeley.

> During the mid-1970s, several sectarian groups whose members had different visions about what the "revolution" should accomplish struggled for control of the program. Many members of these groups worked as teaching assistants, research assistants, and fieldwork assistants in the program, but people not affiliated with us could also attend our meetings and participate in making decisions affecting Asian American Studies. In such an atmosphere of "ultrademocracy" there was no accountability whatsoever. . . .

Several of the groups saw the campus—specifically, the Asian American Studies Program—mainly as a source of funding for their activities off-campus and as a recruiting station for would-be adherents. Others, including myself, believed that an academic program had *its own needs* and should not be used to support groups that had *other agendas.* The never-ending struggles brought chaos to the Asian American Studies Program as hundreds, perhaps thousands, of people became involved and each individual or group staked a claim to the fragile academic turf.⁴⁵

Here we see the flip side of "community autonomy" and the struggles fought over program governance. One of the persistent themes in Chan's remarks was the lack of accountability resulting from community participation in the program, but I think we need to ask, accountable to what or to whom? Perhaps to the program's own needs, mainly the need for institutional survival, but at what point does this need begin to eclipse the other needs that the program was intended to serve? This was, of course, the question at the core of the intense factional struggles that Chan describes. One index of the trajectory of the field is that the book begins with Chan opposing those on the left and ends with her taking to task those on the right who want the field to become purely academic and to reject any political agenda entirely.

In the conflicts between revolutionaries and reformers, Chan clearly aligns herself with the latter:

Unlike many of my fellow political activists in the 1960s and 1970s who shouted, "Shut it down! Shut it down!" when they held demonstrations at various institutions of higher learning, I have, instead, always demanded, "Open it up! Open it up!" Opening up the institutions where I was employed meant that even as I and like-minded colleagues sought to change them in fundamental ways, we also accepted some of their core features and values.⁴⁶

What I find intriguing here is the opposition between "shutting it down" and "opening it up." Although this dichotomy is inadequate to chart the complex strategies and interests on both sides of these struggles, it does point to one of their basic features. Chan suggests that the difference between the two sides was the degree of institutional change that each perceived as necessary, whether the university required a total transformation or whether certain aspects of it should be retained. She does not specify the features and values that she thinks are worth preserving. Even less apparent are the intentions of the protesters who attempted to "shut down" the university. While some strikers may have sought to emulate the example of the Cultural Revolution in China, clearly the possibility of shutting down a single university, let alone the entire educational system, without the power of the state behind the effort, was remote at best. Most of the strike participants wanted to shut down the university in order to open it back up in a radically different configuration that would guarantee genuine access. The strategic conflict was over whether access could be achieved within the university's existing structure, as the reformers believed, or whether such access was possible only with its radical transformation.

Chan writes the history of the field as one of the victors, someone on the winning side, but we still need to ask, what meaning should we assign this victory? The reformists were right in that it was impossible to significantly transform even one university, much less the whole system of higher education, given its massive institutional inertia. But is this simply a historical fact, or does it imply, as Chan maintains, that some features and values of the university continue to be valuable? I suggest that this conflict of political ideologies can also be understood as strategies of cultural capital. That is, the opposition between "opening it up" and "shutting it down" reflects two strategies for overcoming the obstacles to Asian Americans' capital accumulation (discussed in chapter 2) that correspond to the dichotomy between those who already have some cultural capital and those who do not. The former, whose capital is certified by the university, would want to protect the institution guaranteeing that capital while agitating for changes that might enhance it. But for the latter, the quickest way to gain social parity is not to try to accumulate capital—a game in which they are always behind—but to devalue the capital of those above them. In this regard, the political struggle between reformists and revolutionaries was predetermined: those who had capital were able to survive in the academy, and those who did not were sooner or later expelled.

I am not proposing a determinist history of Asian American studies but simply indicating the limits imposed on the political project of the field by the institutional conditions of its existence. Contrary to Chan's assertions, "shutting it down" did not necessarily mean the destruction of either Asian American studies or the university as such, for the revolutionaries wanted a radical reconstruction of the university as a political rather than an academic institution. They wanted education to live up to the purpose that it had all along claimed, to provide all citizens with the basic capacity for democratic self-governance, a capacity that also had to include the means for economic self-sufficiency. On the face of it, these aims are not so different from those that Guillory pursues in his plan to rescue literary studies. The reason that Chan was so adamantly opposed to the revolutionaries did not pertain to their goals but to the means of achieving those goals. That is, to put politics ahead of academics would mean, in practice, expanding the popular functions of higher education to an extent that they would subsume the autonomous functions of research and scholarship, thus eroding faculty control and, *in this sense, destroying the university* in the form in which it existed in American society during the twentieth century. This is the unrecognized contradiction at the heart of Guillory's proposal, as well as of the university itself. As higher education undergoes major crises in the face of waning public funding, the question remains whether the research university as it exists now can sustain itself or whether it will be transformed by new ideological and institutional forms. I have tried to suggest here that greater attention to the history and origins of ethnic studies can offer important insights into the particular challenges that confront the university in the twenty first century.

Notes

INTRODUCTION

1. These tensions are documented in the special issue *Thinking Theory in Asian American Studies* (*Amerasia* 21, nos. 1–2 [1995]).

2. Fearing legal repercussions, the association's whole board resigned except for one graduate student who was assigned to incorporate and reconstitute the AAAS.

3. See Eithne Luibheid, "The 1965 Immigration and Nationality Act: An 'End' to Exclusion?" *positions* 5, no. 2 (1997):501–22, as well as Paul Ong, Edna Bonacich, and Lucie Cheng, eds., *The New Asian Immigration in Los Angeles and Global Restructuring* (Philadelphia: Temple University Press, 1994).

4. The recent acronyms APA (Asian Pacific American) and API (Asian Pacific Islander) are meant to signal the inclusion of Pacific Islander concerns under the Asian American rubric, but a growing number of Pacific Islanders are contesting their involuntary representation by Asian Americans.

5. Although some may disagree with this point, arguing that the study of literature, at least in the West, has always been tied to the formation of national cultures, we can, at the very least, say that such forms of representation operate in different ways with respect to "minority" versus "majority" cultures.

6. As this list suggests, the structure of nonrepresentative representation can be traced back to the seminal work of Gayatri Spivak. The trope of strategic essentialism in particular comes from her introduction to *Selected Subaltern Studies*, ed. Ranajit Guha and Gayatri Chakravorty Spivak (New York: Oxford University Press, 1988).7. See, for example, Yen Le Espiritu, *Asian American Panethnicity: Bridging Institutions and Identities* (Philadelphia: Temple University Press, 1992); Pei-te Lien, *The Making of Asian American through Political Participation* (Philadelphia: Temple University Press, 2001); and Nazli Kibria, "College and Notions of 'Asian American,'" *Amerasia* 25, no. 1 (1999):29–51.

8. See Pierre Bourdieu, *The Logic of Practice* (Stanford, CA: Stanford University Press, 1990).

9. For the sake of curiosity, and also to avoid the impression that I am simply trying to evade the issue, I will answer one question that always comes up by

214 Notes to the Introduction

saying that I voted to revoke the fiction award and stand by that decision. This book arose in part out of my efforts to explain why.

CHAPTER 1

1. Viet Thanh Nguyen, *Race and Resistance: Literature and Politics in Asian America* (New York: Oxford University Press, 2002), v.

2. As these terms indicate, the references for Nguyen's analysis come from the work of Yen Le Espiritu and Aihwa Ong. In transferring these theoretical paradigms, however, Nguyen fails to identify the significant points of friction among them, as well as with the work of Bourdieu that he introduces. Ong's account of flexible citizenship derives from postmodern analyses that assert the development of a new stage of global capitalism in terms of what is called *flexible accumulation*, whereas Espiritu's analysis of panethnic entrepreneurship derives from the particular context of American race relations within which the Asian American category arises from a panethnic social movement.

3. Nguyen, *Race and Resistance*, 5.

4. According to Pierre Bourdieu, *The Logic of Practice* (Stanford, CA: Stanford University Press, 1990), 122,

> The theory of strictly economic practices is a particular case of a general theory of the economy of practices. Even when they give every appearance of disinterestedness because they escape the logic of "economic" interest (in the narrow sense) and are oriented towards nonmaterial stakes that are not easily quantified, as in "pre-capitalist" societies or in the cultural sphere of capitalist societies, practices never cease to comply with an economic logic. The correspondences which are established between the circulation of land sold and bought back, revenge killings "lent" and "redeemed," or women given and received in marriage . . . require us to abandon the economic/noneconomic dichotomy which makes it impossible to see the science of "economic" practices as a particular case of a science capable of treating all practices, including those that are experienced as disinterested or gratuitous, and therefore freed from the "economy," as economic practices aimed at maximizing material or symbolic profit.

See also Pierre Bourdieu, "The Economy of Symbolic Goods," in his *Practical Reason: On the Theory of Action* (Stanford, CA: Stanford University Press, 1998).

5. Louis Althusser, "Ideology," in his *Lenin and Philosophy, and Other Essays* (New York: Monthly Review Press, 1972), 174, italics in original.

6. Pierre Bourdieu and Loïc J. D. Wacquant, *An Invitation to Reflexive Sociology* (Chicago: University of Chicago Press, 1992), 70.

7. Omi and Winant note the lack of politics in cultural nationalism, while Manning Marable comments that both integrationist and separatist forms of

racial politics rely on symbolic representation, or the way that the success of one minority can be made to stand for the success of the group as a whole.

8. John Guillory, *Cultural Capital: The Problem of Literary Canon Formation* (Chicago: University of Chicago Press, 1993), 3.

9. Guillory asserts, for example, that

the project of legitimizing noncanonical works in the university produces an irresolvable contradiction between the presentation of these works as equal in cultural value to canonical works, and at the same time as the embodiment of countercultural values which by their very definition are intended to delegitimize the cultural values embodied in canonical works. (*Cultural Capital*, 47)

This contradiction appears, however, only if one posits that literature constitutes a single form of capital or is defined according to a single standard of value.

10. Guillory, *Cultural Capital*, 21.

11. Ibid., 54, italics in original. The question, of course, is whether giving people a "right" to the means of production and the consumption of cultural works is really an effective or efficient solution to the problem of social inequality.

12. Guillory's appropriation of Gramsci here is not unproblematic, since apart from the question of interpretation, given that his notes were written in prison, Gramsci seems to have been concerned primarily with the production of organic intellectuals of the working class, rather than with democratic access to education. There is also the issue that Gramsci's educational agenda derives from a Marxist theory that is in some ways at odds with Bourdieu's conception of the forms of capital making up the social structure, from which the notion of cultural capital derives.

13. Guillory, *Cultural Capital*, 55, italics in original.

14. Ibid., 337.

15. See Karl Marx et al., *The German Ideology* (New York: International Publishers, 1972).

16. Guillory, *Cultural Capital*, 339.

17. Ibid., 339. Lest we think that the end of capital spells the end of the canon, Guillory takes pains to emphasize that to the contrary, in a situation of universal access to the means of consumption of aesthetic objects,

canonical works could not be experienced as they so often are, as lifeless monuments, or as proofs of class distinction. Insofar as the debate on the canon has tended to discredit aesthetic judgment . . . it has quite missed the point. The point is not to make judgment disappear but to reform the conditions of its practice. (340)

These sentences make apparent that the purpose of the retention of cultural capital in Guillory's argument is the preservation of the canon.

18. Guillory claims to derive both the persistence of cultural capital and the universality of the aesthetic from Bourdieu in a passage that is worth quoting

because it raises the question of Bourdieu's rather complex relation to culture and the cultural field. Guillory argues that with the disentanglement of cultural capital from the reproduction of social inequality,

> what we call canon formation would then become a much larger part of social life, because not restricted to the institutions of the materially advantaged. Bourdieu has recently made this implication of his argument more explicit, in response to readings of his work which impute to it an evaluative relativism he has never endorsed. (*Cultural Capital*, 339)

Guillory then goes on to cite this passage from Bourdieu:

> Verbally to deny evaluative dichotomies is to pass a morality off for a politics. The dominated in the artistic and intellectual fields have always practiced that form of radical chic which consists in rehabilitating socially inferior cultures or the minor genres of legitimate culture. . . . To denounce hierarchy does not get us anywhere. What must be changed are the conditions that make this hierarchy exist, both in reality and in minds. We must . . . work to *universalize in reality the conditions of access* to what the present offers us that is most universal, instead of talking about it. (Bourdieu and Wacquant, *An Invitation*, 84–85, italics in original)

Guillory's argument is that high art is truly universal and that aesthetic experience is the basis on which one can objectively know that, but this does not quite seem to be Bourdieu's position. First, Bourdieu's explicit point here is not that he is an aesthetic universalist but that he distinguishes between value judgments about social phenomena and descriptions of those phenomena. His goal, for example, is not to say whether the distinction between high and low art should or should not exist; the fact is that it does exist and he wants to understand it. Moreover, to say simply that it should not exist does not do anything to eliminate the concrete practices and institutions that perpetuate the division. While Bourdieu does view high art as more universal, he defines universality specifically as a product of the history of the functioning of autonomous fields and not, as Guillory would have it, of a universal aesthetic experience.

19. If Guillory's somewhat sensational declaration of the end of literature has any truth, we may do well to look back to the beginning of the academic study of literature in the United States a little more than a century ago. Gerald Graff reminds us that it was only in the last decades of the nineteenth century that literature in American colleges began to be studied as "literature" and not something else (Greek and Latin, oratory, rhetoric, and so on). In the general perception, "the idea had hardly arisen that the literature of one's own language needed to be taught in formal classes instead of being enjoyed as part of the normal experience of the community" (Gerald Graff, *Professing Literature: An Institutional History* [Chicago: University of Chicago Press, 1987], 19). The question is how and why the flourishing extracurricular literary culture of American colleges came be to absorbed into the educational institution. The retreat of literary culture into

the university may in fact have been a response to its potential devaluation. Since literary culture was public and essentially unrestricted, the only requirement was literacy. With the expansion of literacy, therefore, any literate person could acquire that culture, thus diminishing its value for the upper classes. The educational institution, in contrast, offered a much more effective means of restricting access to that culture, hence preserving its value. The retreat into the institution, however, also meant a loss of social relevance and value. These conditions seem very similar to the situation that Guillory outlines.

20. Guillory, *Cultural Capital*, 7.

21. Ibid., 57–58, italics added.

22. Ibid., 56.

23. Ibid., 54.

24. See Pierre Bourdieu, "The Forms of Capital," in *Handbook for Theory and Research for the Sociology of Education*, ed. John G. Richardson (Westport, CT: Greenwood Press, 1985), 241–58; and Pierre Bourdieu and Jean Claude Passeron, *Reproduction in Education, Society and Culture* (Beverly Hills, CA: Sage, 1977).

25. Guillory, *Cultural Capital*.

26. Michael Omi and Howard Winant describe this process as rearticulation in their *Racial Formation in the United States: From the 1960s to the 1990s*, 2nd ed. (New York: Routledge, 1994).

27. Glenn Omatsu explores the rise of Asian American neoconservatives who are opposed to racial discrimination in "The 'Four Prisons' and the Movements of Liberation."

28. Kandice Chuh, *Imagine Otherwise: On Asian Americanist Critique* (Durham, NC: Duke University Press, 2003), 4.

29. Ibid., 9.

30. Ibid., 10–11, italics in original.

31. Given the contextual and shifting nature of identity, there is, of course, no definitive measure by which to assess this gap, although some sociological studies attest to the large divergence in terms of identity and politics in various particular Asian American populations. See Yen Le Espiritu, *Asian American Panethnicity: Bridging Institutions and Identities* (Philadelphia: Temple University Press, 1992); Pei-te Lien, *The Making of Asian America through Political Participation* (Philadelphia: Temple University Press, 2001); as well as Pei-te Lien, M. Margaret Conway, and Janelle Wong, eds., *The Politics of Asian Americans: Diversity and Community* (New York: Routledge, 2004); and Nazli Kibria, "College and Notions of 'Asian American,'" *Amerasia* 25, no. 1 (1999):29–51.

32. Pierre Bourdieu, *Practical Reason: On the Theory of Action* (Stanford, CA: Stanford University Press, 1998), 11.

33. Chuh reiterates this point when she declares that part of the work of Asian American studies

must be to undermine persistently the multicultural, positivist narratives of otherness that suggest a concrete knowability. That, for me, demands a deconstructive account of "Asian American," a move toward embracing the *a priori* subjectlessness of discourse. Such an account works to *unify* Asian American studies by holding the category "Asian American" under erasure so that its provisional nature and its constructedness cannot be forgotten. (*Imagine Otherwise*, 26, italics added)

34. Nguyen, *Race and Resistance*, 6–7, italics in original.

35. Nguyen's account, however, also succumbs to this problem because he universalizes "flexible accumulation" as the mode of Asian American cultural production instead of recognizing that the particular modes and strategies of accumulation must be deciphered for each text and for various historical contexts. Chapter 4 elaborates this point in my analysis of *The Woman Warrior*.

36. Bourdieu, *Practical Reason*, 31 italics in original.

37. Chuh, *Imagine Otherwise*, 4.

38. On relational analysis, see especially the important essay "Social Space and Symbolic Space" in Bourdieu's *Practical Reason*, as well as "Social Space and Symbolic Power" in *In Other Words*, and "The Practice of Reflexive Sociology" in *An Invitation to Reflexive Sociology*.

39. Iris Marion Young, "Ruling Norms and the Politics of Difference: A Comment on Seyla Benhabib." *Yale Journal of Criticism* 12, no. 2 (1999):416.

40. Iris Marion Young, *Justice and the Politics of Difference* (Princeton, NJ: Princeton University Press, 1990), 3–4.

41. Ibid., 5.

42. Ibid., 157.

43. Ibid., 184.

44. Ibid., 190.

45. Stuart Hall, David Morley, and Kuan-Hsing Chen, eds., *Stuart Hall: Critical Dialogues in Cultural Studies* (New York: Routledge, 1996), 45, italics in original.

46. Susan Koshy, "The Fiction of Asian American Literature," *Yale Journal of Criticism: Interpretation in the Humanities* 9, no. 2 (1996):342.

47. For a fascinating discussion of elections and the use of lots as a means of assigning political office in classical Athens, see Bernard Manin, *The Principles of Representative Government* (Cambridge: Cambridge University Press, 1997).

48. Bourdieu, "The Scholastic Point of View," in *Practical Reason*, 127–28.

49. Bourdieu refers to this as "epistemocentrism," or the ethnocentrism of the scholastic point of view.

50. Chuh, *Imagine Otherwise*, 27, italics in original.

51. Bourdieu, *The Logic of Practice*, 118. Bourdieu develops the concept of symbolic capital from his analysis of precapitalist economies, which are not necessarily temporally before capitalism but before the establishment of a self-perpetuating capitalist economy. Arguing that one cannot apply categories and concepts

(such as interest, investment, or capital) that are the products of capitalism to those economies that are not capitalist, Bourdieu notes that "everything takes place as if the specificity of the 'archaic' economy lay in the fact that economic activity cannot explicitly recognize the economic ends in relation to which it is objectively oriented" (*The Logic of Practice*, 113). The apparent contradiction here is that archaic economies are still economies and thus susceptible to economic analyses that presume capitalist categories and relations, but Bourdieu's point is that it is the very denial or misrecognition of the "economic" organization of social relations that is the specific principle of the precapitalist economy. Symbolic systems in modern societies perform the essential function of legitimating the structure of social relations and the exercise of power and domination by disguising the "interested" (that is, economic) nature of relations and practices and making them appear disinterested and natural.

52. Bourdieu, *The Logic of Practice*, 126.

53. As Derek Robbins comments, "'legitimate culture' is only such *by virtue* of its dominance rather than of any intrinsic quality. Bourdieu and Passeron are careful to say that 'in any given social formation,' legitimacy is nothing other than a function of dominance." See Derek Robbins, *Bourdieu and Culture* (Thousand Oaks, CA: Sage, 2000), 118.

54. What would happen, for example, if instead of "identity" in this discussion, we substituted "power"? We then would be talking about power and the negation of power, but there is no such thing as the negation of power. Power can be negated only through the exercise of power.

CHAPTER 2

1. In his historical overview of the Asian American movement, Glenn Omatsu argues that the keywords of the 1960s were *consciousness, theory, ideology, participatory democracy, community,* and *liberation,* in contrast with those of the 1990s, which were *advocacy, access, legitimacy, empowerment,* and *assertiveness.* See Glenn Omatsu, "The "Four Prisons" and the Movements of Liberation: Asian American Activism from the 1960s to the 1990s," in *The State of Asian America: Activism and Resistance in the 1990s,* ed. Karin Aguilar-San Juan (Boston: South End Press, 1994), 30.

2. The withering away of representation by mobilization is the scenario that Michael Hardt and Antonio Negri strive to project in their *Multitude: War and Democracy in the Age of Empire* (New York: Penguin, 2004).

3. Lane Ryo Hirabayashi and Marilyn C. Alquizola, "Whither the Asian American Subject?" in *Color-Line to Borderlands: The Matrix of American Ethnic Studies,* ed. Johnnella E. Butler (Seattle: University of Washington Press, 2001), 171.

4. Lane Ryo Hirabayashi and Marilyn C. Alquizola, "Asian American Studies: Reevaluating for the 1990s," in *The State of Asian America: Activism and*

Resistance in the 1990s, ed. Karin Aguilar-San Juan (Boston: South End Press, 1994), 354.

5. This structure most likely derived from the model of area studies, since the original demand of the Third World strike was for a school of ethnic area studies. For accounts of the establishment of the first Asian American studies programs, see William Wei, *The Asian American Movement: Asian American History and Culture* (Philadelphia: Temple University Press, 1993); Karen Umemoto, "'On Strike!' San Francisco State College Strike, 1968–1969: The Role of Asian American Students," in *Contemporary Asian America : A Multidisciplinary Reader*, ed. Min Zhou and James V. Gatewood, 2nd ed. (New York: New York University Press, 2007), 49–79; and Yen Le Espiritu, *Asian American Panethnicity: Bridging Institutions and Identities* (Philadelphia: Temple University Press, 1992). Sucheng Chan's collection of essays entitled *In Defense of Asian American Studies: The Politics of Teaching and Program Building. The Asian American Experience* (Urbana: University of Illinois Press, 2005) offers an extremely interesting (and partisan) perspective on many of the issues I discuss in this chapter from someone who was instrumental in the development of the field.

6. Hirabayashi and Alquizola, "Asian American Studies," 356, italics added.

7. Ibid., 360.

8. Fabio Rojas, *From Black Power to Black Studies: How a Radical Social Movement Became an Academic Discipline* (Baltimore: Johns Hopkins University Press, 2007), 61.

9. Ibid., 214.

10. William H. Orrick and the U.S. National Commission on the Causes and Prevention of Violence, *College in Crisis; a Report to the National Commission on the Causes and Prevention of Violence* (Nashville: Aurora Publishers, 1970), 103.

11. Leo Litwak and Herbert Wilner, *College Days in Earthquake Country; Ordeal at San Francisco State, a Personal Record* (New York: Random House, 1971), 82.

12. Ibid., 104.

13. Of the twelve members appointed to the first board of overseers for Harvard (est. 1636), seven were alumni of Cambridge, one was an alumnus of Oxford, and the remaining four were relatives of Cambridge graduates. See Lawrence Cremin, "College," in *Ashe Reader on the History of Higher Education*, ed. Lester F. Goodchild, Harold S. Wechsler, and Association for the Study of Higher Education (Needham Heights, MA: Ginn Press, 1989), 28–41.

14. See John R. Thelin, *A History of American Higher Education* (Baltimore: Johns Hopkins University Press, 2004), 7–13.

15. These problems, in particular, stemmed from the centralization of authority, the lack of parity with the University of California, the lack of financial flexibility, and the lack of faculty voice. See Orrick and the U.S. National Commission, *College in Crisis*, 13–21.

16. This situation resulted from the reorganization of the state colleges under the California Master Plan of 1960, legislation that was intended to rationalize the chaotic system of higher education in California by instituting an educational hierarchy in which students would be tracked to the University of California system, the state colleges, or community colleges, depending on their skills and preparation. Not only did this relegate the state colleges to second-class status, but it also pushed more poorly prepared minority students into the lower tiers of the system. The declining enrollment of black students at SF State became increasingly apparent throughout the 1960s. For a more extensive discussion of the master plan and its impact on SF State, see Orrick and the U.S. National Commission, *College in Crisis*, 13–21.

17. Orrick and the U.S. National Commission, *College in Crisis*, 33.

18. Hirabayashi and Alquizola, "Asian American Studies," 353–54.

19. Ibid., 357–58.

20. Ibid., 361.

21. Ibid., 360.

22. Rojas, *From Black Power to Black Studies*, 215.

23. Ibid.

24. Orrick and the U.S. National Commission, *College in Crisis*, 79.

25. For a more extensive account of this history, see James D. Anderson, "Training the Apostles of Liberal Culture: Black Higher Education, 1900–1935," in *Ashe Reader on the History of Higher Education*, ed. Lester F. Goodchild, Harold S. Wechsler, and Association for the Study of Higher Education (Needham Heights, MA: Ginn Press, 1989), 455–77.

26. For a more extensive description of the black studies curriculum, see Rojas, *From Black Power to Black Studies*, 61–64.

27. Orrick and the U.S. National Commission, *College in Crisis*, 103.

28. Rojas, *From Black Power to Black Studies*, 167–68.

29. Orrick and the U.S. National Commission, *College in Crisis*, 102.

30. Phil Hardimon, "Black Educators Need Support," *Black Liberator* 2 (1969):2. Quoted in Rojas, *From Black Power to Black Studies*, 42.

31. Orrick and the U.S. National Commission, *College in Crisis*, 91.

32. Ibid.

33. Ibid.

34. Ibid., 86.

35. Quoted in Orrick and the U.S. National Commission, *College in Crisis*, 109.

36. One of the most succinct descriptions of cultural capital can be found in Pierre Bourdieu, "The Forms of Capital," in *Handbook for Theory and Research for the Sociology of Education*, ed. John G. Richardson (Westport, CT: Greenwood Press, 1985), 241–58.

37. In fact, as Wei notes in *The Asian American Movement*, 5, many historical accounts of the Third World strike leave out Asians altogether, a fact that does

not reflect their relatively small numbers so much as the continuing invisibility of Asian Americans in the U.S. racial order.

38. Pierre Bourdieu, *Homo Academicus* (Stanford, Calif.: Stanford University Press, 1988).

39. Bourdieu, "The Forms of Capital," 249.

40. Bourdieu comments that

if the internal competition for the monopoly of legitimate representation of the group is not to threaten the conservation and accumulation of the capital which is the basis of the group, the members of the group must regulate the conditions of access to the right to declare oneself a member of the group and, above all, to set oneself up as a representative . . . of the whole group, thereby committing the social capital of the whole group. ("The Forms of Capital," 251)

41. See Pei-te Lien, Margaret Conway, and Janelle Wong, eds., *The Politics of Asian Americans: Diversity and Community* (New York: Routledge, 2004).

42. See Pierre Bourdieu and Loïc J. D. Wacquant, *Invitation to Reflexive Sociology* (Chicago: University of Chicago Press, 1992), 23–24 and 79–83.

43. Ibid., 82.

44. Wacquant makes this argument in *Invitation to Reflexive Sociology*.

45. In contrast to Bourdieu, this is the argument of Lloyd and Thomas with respect to English working-class opposition to the school system, as discussed in chapter 1. Such arguments, deriving from Deleuze and Guattari and, to some extent, Foucault, have become widely received in postcolonial and ethnic studies.

46. Pierre Bourdieu, "For a Scholarship with Commitment," in his *Firing Back: Against the Tyranny of the Market 2* (New York: New Press, 2003), 21.

47. Bourdieu, *Invitation to Reflexive Sociology*, 84–85, italics in original.

CHAPTER 3

1. Michael Omi and Dana Takagi, "Thinking Theory in Asian American Studies," *Amerasia* 21, nos. 1–2 (1995):xi.

2. The one notable exception is Sau-ling C. Wong, who, in her article "Denationalization Reconsidered: Asian American Cultural Criticism at a Theoretical Crossroads," *Amerasia* 21, nos. 1–2 (1995):1–27, defends the identity politics of the 1960s, but she is less concerned with theory per se than with issues of nationalism and transnationalism.

3. Both Lane Ryo Hirabayashi, "Back to the Future: Re-Framing Community-Based Research," *Amerasia* 21, nos. 1–2 (1995):103–18; and Paul Takagi and Margot Gibney, "Theory and Praxis: Resistance and Hope," *Amerasia* 21, nos. 1–2 (1995):119–26 address the question of Asian American studies' relationship to the community, although in somewhat different ways. Takagi and Gibney in

particular offer insights into the "relevance" of academic work to the needs of various segments of the community.

4. John Guillory, "The Sokal Affair and the History of Criticism," *Critical Inquiry* 28 (2002):474.

5. On the evolution of literary studies in the United States, see Gerald Graff, *Professing Literature: An Institutional History* (Chicago: University of Chicago Press, 1987). On the history of the idea of research, see Roger L. Geiger, *To Advance Knowledge: The Growth of American Research Universities, 1900–1940* (New York: Oxford University Press, 1986); and John R. Thelin, *A History of American Higher Education* (Baltimore: Johns Hopkins University Press, 2004).

6. These anxieties are apparent in the special issue of *Amerasia* in that the debate over theory seems to end up being an argument internal to the social sciences. That is, the most polemical arguments for and against the "political necessity" of poststructuralist theory come from an anthropologist and a historian, respectively, whereas most of the literary critics refute the notion of the divisiveness of theory.

7. Gordon Chang, "History and Postmodernism," *Amerasia* 21, nos. 1–2 (1995):92.

8. Ibid., 90.

9. Ibid., 91.

10. Ibid. Chang confirms this point when he declares that "historical work, including the most untheoretically informed, narrative history, should/will remain the central resource for Asian American Studies, for it will be, as it always has been, an irreplaceable well-spring for artistic, critical (including postmodern criticism itself), social, anthropological and other thoughtful work" (Chang, "History and Postmodernism," 92).

11. Chang, "History and Postmodernism," 93.

12. Lisa Lowe, "On Contemporary Asian American Projects," *Amerasia* 21, nos. 1–2 (1995):41. Lowe's refusal of the dichotomization of theory and politics is echoed in the special issue *Thinking Theory* by such scholars as David Palumbo-Liu and Dorinne Kondo.

13. Guillory, "The Sokal Affair and the History of Criticism," 485.

14. Lowe, "On Contemporary Asian American Projects," 42.

15. See, for example, Stuart Hall's comments in "Cultural Studies and Its Theoretical Legacies," in *Cultural Studies*, ed. Lawrence Grossberg, Cary Nelson, and Paula A. Treichler (New York: Routledge, 1992), 277–86.

16. Omi and Takagi, "Thinking Theory in Asian American Studies," xiv.

17. One can certainly perceive this response to the work by the pioneering critics in Asian American literary studies, such as, first, Elaine Kim and then Sau-ling Wong, King-Kok Cheung, and Stephen Sumida.

18. This passage comes from Lowe's original essay, published in *Diaspora* 1,

no. 1 (1991):24–44. The version of this essay that is republished in *Immigrant Acts* omits the sentence describing hybridity as concealing identity.

19. Kent Ono's article in the *Amerasia* issue also points to the lingering essentialisms in both Lowe's and Butler's articles. See Ono, "Re/signing 'Asian American': Rhetorical Problematics of Nation," *Amerasia* 21, nos. 1–2 (1995):67–78.

20. Judith Butler, "Contingent Foundations: Feminism and the Question of 'Postmodernism,'" in *Feminists Theorize the Political*, ed. Judith Butler and Joan Wallach Scott (New York: Routledge, 1992), 15, italics in original. Butler does not consider the question of how to make claims "in the name of women" through forms of representation other than descriptive.

21. Ibid., italics in original.

22. Ibid., 16.

23. As I argued in chapter 1, this is the world envisioned in Guillory's thought experiment at the end of his *Cultural Capital*.

24. Although the critique of identity has common roots in gender/women's studies and ethnic studies, the body in the former is the corollary of the category of identity in the latter in that they both seem to signify a nationalist or separatist politics that must be excised in order for the field to gain legitimacy in the university.

25. See Fabio Rojas, "The Life and Death of Black Studies Programs," in his *From Black Power to Black Studies: How a Radical Social Movement Became an Academic Discipline* (Baltimore: Johns Hopkins University Press, 2007), 93–129.

26. Rojas, *From Black Power to Black Studies*, 168.

27. Chuh provides one of the most forceful elaborations of this discourse, although it has become nearly orthodox in Asian American cultural studies.

28. Paul Wong, Meera Manvi, and Takeo Hirota Wong, "Asiacentrism and Asian American Studies?" *Amerasia* 21, nos. 1–2 (1995):138.

29. Of course, their work is distinguished by its interdisciplinary aspirations, as Palumbo-Liu has been a member of history, East Asian studies, and comparative literature departments; and Kondo is an anthropologist who has moved into performance studies and is a playwright as well. See David Palumbo-Liu, ed., *The Ethnic Canon: Histories, Institutions, and Interventions* (Minneapolis: University of Minnesota Press, 1995); his *Asian/American: Historical Crossings of a Racial Frontier* (Stanford, CA: Stanford University Press, 1999); and his *Streams of Cultural Capital: Transnational Cultural Studies*, coedited with Hans Ulrich Gumbrecht (Stanford, CA: Stanford University Press, 1997). Also see Dorinne Kondo, *Crafting Selves: Power, Gender, and Discourses of Identity in a Japanese Workplace* (Chicago: University of Chicago Press, 1990); and her *About Face: Performing Race in Fashion and Theater* (New York: Routledge, 1997).30. See Rojas, *From Black Power to Black Studies*, 198–99. In his contribution to the *Amerasia* issue, Keith Osajima offers anecdotal evidence supporting Rojas's observation: "Most Asian American scholars in the social sciences adhere closely to the normative

standards set forth in traditional academic disciplines . . . such as the value of objective positivist science in the search for universal laws and reductionist explanatory models." See Keith Osajima, "Postmodern Possibilities: Theoretical and Political Directions for Asian American Studies," *Amerasia* 21, nos. 1–2 (1995):82.

31. Trow's essay is actually a conservative attack on ethnic studies, which he views as a threat to the autonomy of the university. Nevertheless, his analysis offers interesting insights into the structures of autonomy.

32. Omatsu's essay is in fact cited in Lowe's, Hirabayashi's, and Ono's articles in the *Amerasia* special issue. Of these, Ono is the only one who raises any questions regarding the article.

33. Glenn Omatsu, "The 'Four Prisons' and the Movements of Liberation: Asian American Activism from the 1960s to the 1990s," in *The State of Asian America: Activism and Resistance in the 1990s*, ed. Karin Aguilar-San Juan (Boston: South End Press, 1994), 20.

34. Ibid., 51.

35. Lane Ryo Hirabayashi and Marilyn C. Alquizola, "Whither the Asian American Subject?" in *Color-Line to Borderlands: The Matrix of American Ethnic Studies*, ed. Johnnella E. Butler (Seattle: University of Washington Press, 2001), 171.

36. Ibid., 181.

37. They seem to have chosen this somewhat random collection of texts to emphasize that literature can be historical and representational and still be inclusive of gender, sexuality, and ethnic diversity.

38. Hirabayashi and Alquizola, "Whither the Asian American Subject," 182.

39. Laura Hyun Yi Kang, *Compositional Subjects: Enfiguring Asian/American Women* (Durham, NC: Duke University Press, 2002), 3.

40. The notion of a disciplinary regime references Foucault, while Kang characterizes "trenchant interdisciplinarity" as "an agonistic but nevertheless situated relation to prevailing disciplinary forms of knowledge formation and reproduction" (*Compositional Subjects*, 20).

41. Kang, *Compositional Subjects*, 115.

42. Ibid., 150.

43. Ibid., 67.

44. Lisa Lowe, *Immigrant Acts: On Asian American Cultural Politics* (Durham, NC: Duke University Press, 1996), 34–35.

45. Ibid., 35, italics in original.

46. Ibid.

47. Ibid., 27.

48. Ibid., 29.

49. Ibid., 30.

50. Ibid., 100.

51. Ibid., 111.

52. Ibid., 31.

53. Elaine Kim, *Asian American Literature: An Introduction to the Writings and Their Social Context* (Philadelphia: Temple University Press, 1982), xv.

54. Ibid., 32.

55. Shelley Wong, "Unnaming the Same: Theresa Hak Kyung Cha's *Dictée*," in *Writing Self, Writing Nation: A Collection of Essays on* Dictée *by Theresa Hak Kyung Cha*, ed. Hyun Yi Kang, Norma Alarcón, and Elaine H. Kim (Berkeley, CA: Third Woman Press, 1994), 103.

56. Lisa Lowe, "Unfaithful to the Original: The Subject of *Dictée*," in *Writing Self, Writing Nation*, ed. Norma Alarcón and Elaine H. Kim (Berkeley, CA: Third Woman Press, 1994), 37.

57. Wong, "Unnaming the Same," 103–4.

58. Lowe, "Unfaithful to the Original," 63.

59. Anne Anlin Cheng, "Memory and Anti-Documentary Desire in Theresa Hak Kyung Cha's *Dictée*," *MELUS* 23, no. 4 (1998):119. Cheng argues that it is possible to read an identity and a politics in *Dictée* despite its apparent resistance to such readings. "Cha's critique of the 'ready-made' image of the marginalized subject disturbs the tenets of representation on which the ideology of the ethnic bildung rests. I propose that the 'form' of *Dictée* effects a historical and cultural reconstruction that enacts, simultaneously, a critique of that reconstruction" (120).

60. Sue J. Kim, "Apparatus: Theresa Hak Kyung and the Politics of Form," *Journal of Asian American Studies* 8, no. 2 (2005):163.

61. Lowe, "Unfaithful to the Original," 35–36, italics added.

62. Wong, "Unnaming the Same," 132.

63. See Omatsu, "The 'Four Prisons'"; William Wei, *The Asian American Movement: Asian American History and Culture* (Philadelphia: Temple University Press, 1993); and Fred Ho, Carolyn Antonio, Diane Fujino, and Steve Yip, eds., *Legacy to Liberation: Politics and Culture of Revolutionary Asian Pacific America* (San Francisco: Big Red Media, 2000).

64. Yen Le Espiritu, *Asian American Panethnicity: Bridging Institutions and Identities* (Philadelphia: Temple University Press, 1992), 50. Pei-te Lien also notes that "when the pan-Asian consciousness was finally formed in the late 1960s, it was limited to a specific constituency whose legitimacy to represent the opinions of the community was almost immediately challenged because of the huge and continuous stream of newcomers from Asia beginning at that same time." See Pei-te Lien, *The Making of Asian America through Political Participation*, 50.

CHAPTER 4

1. Lisa Lowe, *Immigrant Acts: On Asian American Cultural Politics* (Durham, NC: Duke University Press, 1996); and David Lloyd, *Anomalous States: Irish*

Writing and the Post-Colonial Moment (Durham, NC: Duke University Press, 1993).

2. For example, Iwasaki cites a poem by Joann Miyamoto as the most committed kind of Asian American art. This is how he characterizes what is valuable about her art (also included are the first two stanzas of the poem):

Joann Miyamoto is a radical activist in New York, working in the Latin and Asian communities. With Chris Ijima, they [*sic*] write and sing original revolutionary songs. The following is an example. We do not think it is merely a "political poem." It represents an entire community's experience. This may not be the poetry of the burning brush [*sic*], but it is a worthy piece of Asian American writing. Hopefully, the direction of Asian American writing too.

(meant to be read aloud)

when I was young
kids used to ask me
what are you?
I'd tell them what my mom told me
I'm an American
chin chin Chinaman
you're a Jap!
flashing hot inside
I'd go home
my mom would say
don't worry
he who walks alone
walks faster

people kept asking me
what are you?
and I would always answer
I'm an American
they'd say
no, what nationality?
I'm an American
that's where I was born
flashing hot inside
and when I'd tell them what they wanted to know
Japanese . . .
Oh I've been to Japan.

See Bruce Iwasaki, "Response and Change for the Asian in America: A Survey of Asian American Literature," in *Roots: An Asian American Reader*, ed. Amy

Tachiki and the University of California Los Angeles Asian American Studies
Center (Los Angeles: Continental Graphics, 1971), 98.

3. Almost all works on Asian American literary studies refer to the two *Aii-
ieeeee!* anthologies. Some of the main responses are Elaine H. Kim, *Asian American Literature: An Introduction to the Writings and Their Social Context* (Phila-
delphia: Temple University Press, 1982); Sau-ling Cynthia Wong, *Reading Asian
American Literature: From Necessity to Extravagance* (Princeton, NJ: Princeton
University Press, 1993); King-Kok Cheung, *Articulate Silences: Hisaye Yamamoto,
Maxine Hong Kingston, Joy Kogawa* (Ithaca, NY: Cornell University Press, 1993);
Jinqi Ling, *Narrating Nationalisms: Ideology and Form in Asian American Litera-
ture* (New York: Oxford University Press, 1998); David Leiwei Li, *Imagining the
Nation: Asian American Literature and Cultural Consent* (Stanford, CA: Stanford
University Press, 1998); Lowe, *Immigrant Acts*; Leslie Bow, *Betrayal and Other
Acts of Subversion: Feminism, Sexual Politics, Asian American Women's Litera-
ture* (Princeton, NJ: Princeton University Press, 2001); Rachel Lee, *The Ameri-
cas of Asian American Literature: Gendered Fictions of Nation and Transnation*
(Princeton, NJ: Princeton University Press, 1999); and Kandice Chuh, *Imagine
Otherwise: On Asian Americanist Critique* (Durham, NC: Duke University Press,
2003).

4. Wei writes, "Frank Chin, father of modern Asian American literature, pio-
neered in the development of Asian American culture, paving the way for the
aesthetic approach." See William Wei, *The Asian American Movement: Asian
American History and Culture* (Philadelphia: Temple University Press, 1993), 67,
italics added.

5. Chris Iijima, "Pontifications on the Distinction between Grains of Sand and
Yellow Pearls," in *Asian Americans: The Movement and the Moment,* ed. Steve
Louie and Glenn Omatsu (Los Angeles: UCLA Asian American Studies Center
Press, 2006), 4.

6. Ibid., 6.

7. Iwasaki, "Response and Change for the Asian in America," 97.

8. Ibid., 97–98.

9. Ibid., 98.

10. Frank Chin et al., eds., *Aiiieeeee! An Anthology of Asian American Writers*
(New York: Meridian, 1997).

11. One example is David Leiwei Li, who simply misrecognizes Iwasaki's relationship to the *Aiiieeeee!* editors when he aligns them as sharing the same political conception of culture. See Li, *Imagining the Nation*, 34.

12. Chin et al., eds., *Aiiieeeee!* 12.

13. Ibid., 13.

14. Ibid., 14.

15. Ibid.

16. This requires, for example, a critical recuperation of commercially

successful writers, such as Carlos Bulosan or Diana Chang, to explain why their success does not disqualify them from consideration.

17. About their anthology, the editors declare, for example, that "the age, variety, depth, and quality of the writing collected here proves the existence of Asian American sensibilities and cultures that might be related to but are distinct from Asia and white America" (Chin et al., eds., *Aiiieeeee!* xiii).

18. Chin et al., eds., *Aiiieeeee!* 26.

19. Ibid., 30.

20. Ibid., 35.

21. Chu draws on Nina Baym's seminal article, "Melodramas of Beset Manhood." See Patricia P. Chu, *Assimilating Asians: Gendered Strategies of Authorship in Asian America* (Durham, NC: Duke University Press, 2000).

22. Chin et al., eds., *Aiiieeeee!* 24–25.

23. Ibid., 37.

24. Ibid., 23–24.

25. Jeffery Paul Chan et al., eds., *The Big Aiiieeeee! An Anthology of Chinese American and Japanese American Literature* (New York: Meridian, 1991), xv.

26. When asked about this complete shift in critical orientation, Shawn Wong replied that the editors of *Aiiieeeee!* realized they were wrong and needed to include Asian immigrant writers in their genealogy of Asian American literature (personal communication).

27. Frank Chin, "Come All Ye Asian American Writers of the Real and the Fake," in *The Big Aiiieeeee!: An Anthology of Chinese American and Japanese American Literature*, ed. Jeffery Paul Chan, Frank Chin, Lawson Inada, and Shawn Wong (New York: Meridian, 1991), 3.

28. Allan David Bloom, *The Closing of the American Mind: How Higher Education Has Failed Democracy and Impoverished the Souls of Today's Students* (New York: Simon & Schuster, 1987).

29. Chin, "The Real and the Fake," 33–34.

30. See Sau-ling Cynthia Wong, "Autobiography as Guided Chinatown Tour? Maxine Hong Kingston's *The Woman Warrior* and the Chinese-American Autobiographical Controversy," in *Multicultural Autobiography: American Lives*, ed. James Robert Payne (Knoxville: University of Tennessee Press, 1992), 248–79.

31. Maxine Hong Kingston, *The Woman Warrior: Memoirs of a Girlhood among Ghosts* (New York: Vintage Books, 1989), 5–6.

32. Ibid., 163.

33. I refer here to Sau-ling Wong's elaborations of these terms that she extracts from *The Woman Warrior* itself. See Wong, *Reading Asian American Literature*.

34. Laura Hyun Yi Kang, *Compositional Subjects: Enfiguring Asian/American Women* (Durham, NC: Duke University Press, 2002), 67–68.

35. Kingston, *The Woman Warrior*, 16.

36. Ibid.

37. In "Shaman," the narrator declares of her mother: "A practical woman, she could not invent stories and told only true ones." On the relation of autobiography to literature and history, see Kang, *Compositional Subjects*, 66.

38. Kingston, *The Woman Warrior*, 8.

39. Ibid., 169.

40. Ibid., 170.

41. The book seems to refer to this notion of translation in this passage.

42. Ibid., 170–71.

43. Ibid., 171.

44. Colleen Kennedy and Deborah Morse, "A Dialogue with(in) Tradition: Two Perspectives on *The Woman Warrior*," in *Approaches to Teaching Kingston's The Woman Warrior*, ed. Shirley Lim (New York: Modern Language Association of America, 1991), 122–23.

45. Kennedy and Morse, "A Dialogue with(in) Tradition," 123. They remark that "if *one* voice emerges at the end of *The Woman Warrior* . . . it is certainly not Brave Orchid's. In fact, her voice becomes the discourse to be resisted. Ironically, if what is to be excluded in this book is the patriarchy, it is excluded only as it is embodied in other women" (123–24, italics in original).

46. Kingston, *The Woman Warrior*, 172.

47. Ibid., 178.

48. Ibid., 180.

49. Ibid., 182,

50. Maxine Hong Kingston, *China Men* (New York: Vintage Books, 1989), 207.

51. Ibid., 209.

52. Sau-ling Wong remarks that Kingston neglects one of the most prominent features of Ts'ai Yen's story, which is her tremendous sorrow at leaving her two sons.

53. Kingston, *China Men*, 208.

CHAPTER 5

1. See Crystal Parikh, "Blue Hawaii: Asian Hawaiian Cultural Production and Racial Melancholia," *Journal of Asian American Studies* 5, no. 3 (2002):199–216; Erin Suzuki, "Consuming Desires: Melancholia and Consumption in *Blu's Hanging*," *MELUS* 31, no. 1 (2006):35–52; and Kandice Chuh, *Imagine Otherwise: On Asian Americanist Critique* (Durham, NC: Duke University Press, 2003).

2. For a more detailed chronology of events, consult the appendix to Candace Fujikane, "Sweeping Racism under the Rug of 'Censorship': The Controversy over Lois-Ann Yamanaka's *Blu's Hanging*," *Amerasia Journal* 26, no. 2 (2000):158. My understanding of the controversy owes a great deal to the important work of Fujikane, who was directly embroiled in the protests at the local level in Hawai'i. See also Candace Fujikane, "Reimagining Development and the Local in Lois-

Ann Yamanaka's *Saturday Night at the Pahala Theatre,*" in *Women in Hawai'i: Sites, Identities, and Voices,* ed. Joyce N. Chinen, Kathleen O. Kane, and Ida Yoshinaga (Honolulu: University of Hawai'i Press, 1997), 40–61.

3. See Candace Fujikane, "Asian Settler Colonialism in Hawai'i," *Amerasia Journal* 26, no. 2 (2000):xv; and Jonathan Okamura, "Social Stratification," in *Multicultural Hawai'i: The Fabric of a Multiethnic Society,* ed. Michael Haas (New York: Garland, 1998), 185–204.

4. Ibrahim Aoude, e-mail message dated April 17, 1998.

5. The University of Hawai'i's Pamantasan Council, e-mail message dated June 3, 1998, signed by thirty-seven members.

6. Caroline Campos, e-mail message dated June 11, 1998, also signed by fourteen other members of the AAAS conference student planning committee.

7. Statement from Yen le Espiritu, president of the AAAS, published in the *AAAS Newsletter* 15, no. 2 (1998).

8. Ironically, the recourse to a single book award policy undermines the evaluation of the book according to specifically literary criteria. By assimilating *Blu's Hanging* to academic criteria, the book award policy unintentionally reduces the literary value of the text by submitting it to judgment by critics rather than writers.

9. See Raymond Williams, *Marxism and Literature* (Oxford: Oxford University Press, 1977); and also Stuart Hall, "Cultural Studies and Its Theoretical Legacies," in *Cultural Studies,* ed. Lawrence Grossberg, Cary Nelson, and Paula A. Treichler (New York: Routledge, 1992), 277–86; Stuart Hall, "The Problem of Ideology: Marxism without Guarantees," in *Stuart Hall: Critical Dialogues in Cultural Studies,* ed. David Morley and Kuan-Hsing Chen (London: Routledge, 1996), 25–46; and Stuart Hall, "Gramsci's Relevance for the Study of Race and Ethnicity," *Journal of Communication Inquiry* 10, no. 2 (1986):5–27.

10. This quandary already appears in *Orientalism,* since as Pickering comments, "if Orientalism consists of its constructed representations, then it can be appraised on this basis, but it cannot misrepresent what it has only constructed." See Michael Pickering, *Stereotyping: The Politics of Representation* (New York: Palgrave, 2001), 154. The problem of the referent was subsequently elaborated in Gayatri Spivak's essay "Can the Subaltern Speak?" in *Marxism and the Interpretation of Culture,* ed. Cary Nelson and Lawrence Grossberg (Urbana: University of Illinois Press, 1988), 271–313, in which she questions the ways that "speaking" or self-representation was constructed in a Western colonial episteme so that the true voice of the non-Western subaltern was simply unrepresentable in the discourses of Western modernity.

11. Antiessentialism begins with the recognition that there is no single Filipino identity, but this argument could be advanced on both sides of the debate, as an argument both that the depiction of Filipinos in *Blu's Hanging* reduced the multiplicity of Filipino identities to a singular depiction and that because there is

more than one depiction of Filipinos and of sexual predators in the book, those were not stereotypes.

12. J. C. Brigham, "Ethnic Stereotypes." *Psychological Bulletin* 76 (1971):31.

13. The salient instance with regard to Asian Americans is the model minority image, although many people think of it as positive and therefore not a stereotype, the effort to identify it as a stereotype revolves around its negative effects on Asian Americans and their place in American society.

14. Fujikane, "Sweeping Racism," 46.

15. Yamanaka completely fails to understand the inability of the protesters to represent themselves when she asserts that they should write their own stories; if they could write their own stories, then they wouldn't be reduced to criticizing hers.

16. Erin Suzuki, "Consuming Desires," 50. See also Viet Thanh Nguyen, *Race and Resistance: Literature and Politics in Asian America* (New York: Oxford University Press, 2002), 157–66.

17. Chuh, *Imagine Otherwise*, 142.

18. Suzuki, "Consuming Desires," 50. Both Parikh and Chuh suggest similar readings of Uncle Paulo.

19. Lois-Ann Yamanaka, *Blu's Hanging* (New York: Bard, 1998), 23.

20. Ibid., 177.

21. Ibid., 178.

22. For a history of leprosy in Hawai'i, see Emily Russell, "Locating Cure: Leprosy and Lois-Ann Yamanaka's *Blu's Hanging*," *MELUS* 31, no. 1 (2006):53–80.23. Yamanaka, *Blu's Hanging*, 144.

24. Ibid., 28.

25. Ibid., 34, italics in original.

26. Ibid., 16.

27. Ibid., 14.

28. Ibid., 18.

29. Ibid., 35–36.

30. Fujikane, "Reimagining Development," 47.

31. Parikh, "Blue Hawaii," 208.

32. Yamanaka, *Blu's Hanging*, 39.

33. Ibid., 101.

34. Ibid., 155.

35. Ibid., 162.

36. Ibid., 212.

37. Ibid.

38. Ibid., 237, italics in original.

39. Ibid., 238.

40. Ibid.

41. Ibid., 253.

42. Ibid., 225.

43. See Fujikane, "Sweeping Racism," 42.

44. Yamanaka, *Blu's Hanging*, 30.

45. Sucheng Chan, *In Defense of Asian American Studies: The Politics of Teaching and Program Building. The Asian American Experience* (Urbana: University of Illinois Press, 2005), 9–10, italics added.

46. Ibid., xv.

Bibliography

Aguilar-San Juan, Karin. *The State of Asian America: Activism and Resistance in the 1990s*. Race and Resistance Series. Boston: South End Press, 1994.

Althusser, Louis. *Lenin and Philosophy, and Other Essays*. New York: Monthly Review Press, 1972.

Anderson, James D. "Training the Apostles of Liberal Culture: Black Higher Education, 1900–1935." In *Ashe Reader on the History of Higher Education*, ed. Lester F. Goodchild, Harold S. Wechsler, and Association for the Study of Higher Education, 455–77. Ashe Reader Series. Needham Heights, MA: Ginn Press, 1989.

Asian Women United of California. *Making Waves: An Anthology of Writings by and about Asian American Women*. Boston: Beacon Press, 1989.

Bloom, Allan David. *The Closing of the American Mind: How Higher Education Has Failed Democracy and Impoverished the Souls of Today's Students*. New York: Simon & Schuster, 1987.

Bourdieu, Pierre. *Distinction: A Social Critique of the Judgement of Taste*. Trans. Richard Nice. Cambridge, MA: Harvard University Press, 1984.

———. *The Field of Cultural Production: Essays on Art and Literature*. Ed. Randal Johnson. New York: Columbia University Press, 1993.

———. *Firing Back: Against the Tyranny of the Market 2*. New York: New Press, 2003.

———. "The Forms of Capital." In *Handbook for Theory and Research for the Sociology of Education*, ed. John G. Richardson, 241–58. Westport, CT: Greenwood Press, 1985.

———. *Homo Academicus*. Stanford, CA: Stanford University Press, 1988.

———. *In Other Words: Essays Towards a Reflexive Sociology*. Trans. Matthew Adamson. Stanford, CA: Stanford University Press, 1990.

———. *The Logic of Practice*. Stanford, CA: Stanford University Press, 1990.

———. *Practical Reason: On the Theory of Action*. Stanford, CA: Stanford University Press, 1998.

———. *The Rules of Art: Genesis and Structure of the Literary Field*. Trans. Susan Emanuel. Stanford, CA: Stanford University Press, 1995.

Bourdieu, Pierre, and Jean Claude Passeron. *Reproduction in Education, Society and Culture*. Beverly Hills, CA: Sage, 1977.

Bourdieu, Pierre, and Loïc J. D. Wacquant. *An Invitation to Reflexive Sociology*. Chicago: University of Chicago Press, 1992.

Bow, Leslie. *Betrayal and Other Acts of Subversion: Feminism, Sexual Politics, Asian American Women's Literature*. Princeton, NJ: Princeton University Press, 2001.

Boyle, Kay. *The Long Walk at San Francisco State, and Other Essays*. New York: Grove Press, 1970.

Brigham, J. C. "Ethnic Stereotypes." *Psychological Bulletin* 76 (1971):15–38.

Brown, Nicholas, and Imre Szeman, eds. *Pierre Bourdieu: Fieldwork in Culture*. Culture and Education Series. Lanham, MD: Rowman & Littlefield, 1999.

Butler, Johnnella E. *Color-Line to Borderlands: The Matrix of American Ethnic Studies*. Seattle: University of Washington Press, 2001.

Butler, Judith. *Bodies That Matter: On the Discursive Limits of "Sex."* New York: Routledge, 1993.

———. "Contingent Foundations: Feminism and the Question of 'Postmodernism.'" In *Feminists Theorize the Political*, ed. Judith Butler and Joan Wallach Scott, 3–21. New York: Routledge, 1992.

Butler, Judith, John Guillory, Kendall Thomas, and English Institute, eds. *What's Left of Theory? New Work on the Politics of Literary Theory*. New York: Routledge, 2000.

Butler, Judith, and Joan Wallach Scott. *Feminists Theorize the Political*. New York: Routledge, 1992.

Cha, Theresa Hak Kyung. *Dictée*. Berkeley: University of California Press, 2001.

Chan, Jeffery Paul, Frank Chin, Lawson Inada, and Shawn Wong, eds. *The Big Aiiieeeee! An Anthology of Chinese American and Japanese American Literature*. New York: Meridian, 1991.

Chan, Sucheng. *In Defense of Asian American Studies: The Politics of Teaching and Program Building*. The Asian American Experience. Urbana: University of Illinois Press, 2005.

Chang, Gordon. "History and Postmodernism," *Amerasia* 21, nos. 1–2 (1995):89–93.

Cheng, Anne Anlin. "Memory and Anti-Documentary Desire in Theresa Hak Kyung Cha's *Dictée*." *MELUS* 23, no. 4 (1998):119–33.

Cheung, King-Kok. *Articulate Silences: Hisaye Yamamoto, Maxine Hong Kingston, Joy Kogawa*. Reading Women Writing. Ithaca, NY: Cornell University Press, 1993.

———, ed. *An Interethnic Companion to Asian American Literature*. Cambridge: Cambridge University Press, 1997.

Cheung, King-Kok, and Stan Yogi. *Asian American Literature: An Annotated Bibliography*. New York: Modern Language Association of America, 1988.

Chiang, Mark. "Aesthetics and the Crisis of Asian American Cultural Politics in the Controversy over Blu's Hanging." In *Literary Gestures: The Aesthetic in Asian American Writing*, ed. Rocio G. Davis and Sue-Im Lee, 17–34. Philadelphia: Temple University Press, 2006.

Chin, Frank. *Bulletproof Buddhists and Other Essays*. Honolulu: University of Hawai'i Press / Los Angeles: UCLA Asian American Studies Center, 1998.

———. *The Chickencoop Chinaman; and, the Year of the Dragon: Two Plays*. Seattle: University of Washington Press, 1981.

———. *The Chinaman Pacific & Frisco R.R. Co.: Short Stories*. Minneapolis: Coffee House Press, 1988.

———. "Come All Ye Asian American Writers of the Real and the Fake." In *The Big Aiiieeeee!: An Anthology of Chinese American and Japanese American Literature*, ed. Jeffery Paul Chan, Frank Chin, Lawson Inada, and Shawn Wong, 1–92. New York: Meridian, 1991.

———. *Donald Duk : A Novel*. Minneapolis: Coffee House Press, 1991.

———. *Gunga Din Highway: A Novel*. Minneapolis: Coffee House Press, 1994.

Chin, Frank, Jeffrey Paul Chan, Lawson Fusao Inada, and Shawn Wong, eds. *Aiiieeeee! An Anthology of Asian American Writers*. New York: Meridian, 1997.

Chu, Patricia P. *Assimilating Asians: Gendered Strategies of Authorship in Asian America*. New Americanists. Durham, NC: Duke University Press, 2000.

Chuh, Kandice. *Imagine Otherwise: On Asian Americanist Critique*. Durham, NC: Duke University Press, 2003.

Chuh, Kandice, and Karen Shimakawa. *Orientations: Mapping Studies in the Asian Diaspora*. Durham, NC: Duke University Press, 2001.

Cremin, Lawrence. "College." In *ASHE Reader on the History of Higher Education*, ed. Lester F. Goodchild, Harold S. Wechsler, and Association for the Study of Higher Education, 28–41. Needham Heights, MA: Ginn Press, 1989.

Espiritu, Yen Le. *Asian American Panethnicity: Bridging Institutions and Identities*. Philadelphia: Temple University Press, 1992.

———. "From the AAAS President." *AAAS Newsletter* 15, no. 2 (1998):5–6.

Fujikane, Candace. "Asian Settler Colonialism in Hawai'i." *Amerasia Journal* 26, no. 2 (2000):xv.

———. "Reimagining Development and the Local in Lois-Ann Yamanaka's *Saturday Night at the Pahala Theatre*." In *Women in Hawai'i: Sites, Identities, and Voices*, ed. Joyce N. Chinen, Kathleen O. Kane, and Ida Yoshinaga, 40–61. Honolulu: University of Hawai'i Press, 1997.

———. "Sweeping Racism under the Rug of 'Censorship': The Controversy over Lois-Ann Yamanaka's *Blu's Hanging*." *Amerasia Journal* 26, no. 2 (2000):158.

Fuss, Diana. *Essentially Speaking: Feminism, Nature and Difference*. New York: Routledge, 1989.

Gates, Henry Louis. *"Race," Writing, and Difference*. Chicago: University of Chicago Press, 1986.

——. *The Signifying Monkey: A Theory of Afro-American Literary Criticism.* New York: Oxford University Press, 1988.

Gee, Emma. *Counterpoint: Perspectives on Asian America.* Los Angeles: Asian American Studies Center, University of California, 1976.

Geiger, Roger L. *To Advance Knowledge: The Growth of American Research Universities, 1900–1940.* New York: Oxford University Press, 1986.

Ghee, Lim Teck, ed. *Reflections on Development in Southeast Asia.* Singapore: ASEAN Economic Research Unit, Institute of Southeast Asian Studies, 1988.

Goodchild, Lester F., Harold S. Wechsler, and Association for the Study of Higher Education. *Ashe Reader on the History of Higher Education.* Ashe Reader Series. Needham Heights, MA: Ginn Press, 1989.

Gooding-Williams, Robert, ed. *Reading Rodney King / Reading Urban Uprising.* New York: Routledge, 1993.

Graff, Gerald. *Professing Literature: An Institutional History.* Chicago: University of Chicago Press, 1987.

Gramsci, Antonio, Quintin Hoare, and Geoffrey Nowell-Smith. *Selections from the Prison Notebooks of Antonio Gramsci.* New York: International Publishers, 1972.

Grossberg, Lawrence, Cary Nelson, and Paula A. Treichler, eds. *Cultural Studies.* New York: Routledge, 1992.

Guha, Ranajit, and Gayatri Chakravorty Spivak, eds. *Selected Subaltern Studies.* New York: Oxford University Press, 1988.

Guillory, John. *Cultural Capital: The Problem of Literary Canon Formation.* Chicago: University of Chicago Press, 1993.

——. "The Sokal Affair and the History of Criticism." *Critical Inquiry* 28 (2002):470–508.

Hall, Stuart. "Cultural Studies and Its Theoretical Legacies." In *Cultural Studies,* ed. Lawrence Grossberg, Cary Nelson, and Paula A. Treichler, 277–86. New York: Routledge, 1992.

——. "Gramsci's Relevance for the Study of Race and Ethnicity." *Journal of Communication Inquiry* 10, no. 2 (1986):5–27.

——. "The Problem of Ideology: Marxism without Guarantees." In *Stuart Hall: Critical Dialogues in Cultural Studies,* ed. David Morley and Kuan-Hsing Chen, 25–46. London: Routledge, 1996.

Hall, Stuart, David Morley, and Kuan-Hsing Chen, eds. *Stuart Hall: Critical Dialogues in Cultural Studies.* New York: Routledge, 1996.

Hamilton, Alexander, James Madison, John Jay, and Max Beloff. *The Federalist; or the New Constitution.* Oxford: Blackwell / New York: Macmillan, 1948.

Hardt, Michael, and Antonio Negri. *Empire.* Cambridge, MA: Harvard University Press, 2000.

——. *Multitude: War and Democracy in the Age of Empire.* New York: Penguin, 2004.

Harvey, David. *The Condition of Postmodernity: An Enquiry into the Origins of Cultural Change*. Oxford: Blackwell, 1989.

Hinton, Perry R. *Stereotypes, Cognition, and Culture*. Psychology Focus. Philadelphia: Psychology Press, 2000.

Hirabayashi, Lane Ryo. "Back to the Future: Re-Framing Community-Based Research." *Amerasia* 21, nos. 1–2 (1995):103–18.

Hirabayashi, Lane Ryo, and Marilyn C. Alquizola. "Asian American Studies: Reevaluating for the 1990s." In *The State of Asian America: Activism and Resistance in the 1990s*, ed. Karin Aguilar-San Juan, 351–64. Boston: South End Press, 1994.

———. "Whither the Asian American Subject?" In *Color-Line to Borderlands: The Matrix of American Ethnic Studies*, ed. Johnnella E. Butler, 169–202. Seattle: University of Washington Press, 2001.

Ho, Fred, Carolyn Antonio, Diane Fujino, and Steve Yip, eds. *Legacy to Liberation: Politics and Culture of Revolutionary Asian Pacific America*. San Francisco: Big Red Media, 2000.

Hwang, David Henry. *FOB and Other Plays*. New York: New American Library, 1990.

———. *M. Butterfly*. New York: New American Library, 1989.

Iijima, Chris. "Pontifications on the Distinction between Grains of Sand and Yellow Pearls." In *Asian Americans: The Movement and the Moment*, ed. Steve Louie and Glenn Omatsu, 2–15. Los Angeles: UCLA Asian American Studies Center Press, 2006.

Iwasaki, Bruce. "Response and Change for the Asian in America: A Survey of Asian American Literature." In *Roots: An Asian American Reader*, ed. Amy Tachiki and University of California Los Angeles Asian American Studies Center, 89–100. Los Angeles: Continental Graphics, 1971.

Jameson, Fredric. *The Political Unconscious: Narrative as a Socially Symbolic Act*. Ithaca, NY: Cornell University Press, 1981.

———. *Postmodernism, or, the Cultural Logic of Late Capitalism*. Post-Contemporary Interventions. Durham, NC: Duke University Press, 1991.

JanMohamed, Abdul R., and David Lloyd, eds. *The Nature and Context of Minority Discourse*. New York: Oxford University Press, 1990.

Kang, Laura Hyun Yi. *Compositional Subjects: Enfiguring Asian/American Women*. Durham, NC: Duke University Press, 2002.

Kang, Laura Hyun Yi, Norma Alarcón, and Elaine H. Kim, eds. *Writing Self, Writing Nation: A Collection of Essays on* Dictée *by Theresa Hak Kyung Cha*. Berkeley, CA: Third Woman Press, 1994.

Karagueuzian, Dikran. *Blow It Up! The Black Student Revolt at San Francisco State College and the Emergence of Dr. Hayakawa*. Boston: Gambit, 1971.

Kennedy, Colleen, and Deborah Morse. "A Dialogue with(in) Tradition: Two Perspectives on *The Woman Warrior*." In *Approaches to Teaching Kingston's*

The Woman Warrior, ed. Shirley Lim, 121–30. New York: Modern Language Association of America, 1991.

Kibria, Nazli. "College and Notions of 'Asian American.'" *Amerasia* 25, no. 1 (1999):29–51.

Kim, Elaine H. *Asian American Literature: An Introduction to the Writings and Their Social Context*. Philadelphia: Temple University Press, 1982.

———. "Home Is Where the *Han* Is: A Korean American Perspective on the Los Angeles Upheavals." In *Reading Rodney King / Reading Urban Uprising*, ed. Robert Gooding-Williams, 215–35. New York: Routledge, 1993.

Kim, Elaine H., Lilia V. Villanueva, and Asian Women United of California. *Making More Waves: New Writing by Asian American Women*. Boston: Beacon Press, 1997.

Kim, Sue J. "Apparatus: Theresa Hak Kyung and the Politics of Form." *Journal of Asian American Studies* 8, no. 2 (2005):143–69.

Kingston, Maxine Hong. *China Men*. New York: Vintage Books, 1989.

———. "Cultural Mis-Readings by American Reviewers." In *Asian and Western Writers in Dialogue: New Cultural Identities*, ed. Guy Amirthanayagam, 55–65. London: Macmillan, 1982.

———. *The Woman Warrior: Memoirs of a Girlhood among Ghosts*. New York: Vintage Books, 1989.

Kondo, Dorinne. *About Face: Performing Race in Fashion and Theater*. New York: Routledge, 1997.

———. *Crafting Selves: Power, Gender, and Discourses of Identity in a Japanese Workplace*. Chicago: University of Chicago Press, 1990.

———. "Poststructuralist Theory as Political Necessity." *Amerasia* 21, nos. 1–2 (1995):95–100.

Koshy, Susan. "The Fiction of Asian American Literature." *Yale Journal of Criticism: Interpretation in the Humanities* 9, no. 2 (1996):315–46.

Laclau, Ernesto, and Chantal Mouffe. *Hegemony and Socialist Strategy: Towards a Radical Democratic Politics*. London: Verso, 1985.

Larrain, Jorge. "Stuart Hall and the Marxist Concept of Ideology." In *Stuart Hall: Critical Dialogues in Cultural Studies*, ed. David Morley and Kuan-Hsing Chen, 47–70. New York: Routledge, 1996.

Lee, Rachel. *The Americas of Asian American Literature: Gendered Fictions of Nation and Transnation*. Princeton, NJ: Princeton University Press, 1999.

Li, David Leiwei. *Imagining the Nation: Asian American Literature and Cultural Consent*. Stanford, CA: Stanford University Press, 1998.

Lien, Pei-te. *The Making of Asian America through Political Participation*. Philadelphia: Temple University Press, 2001.

———. *The Political Participation of Asian Americans: Voting Behavior in Southern California*. Asian Americans. New York: Garland, 1997.

Lien, Pei-te, M. Margaret Conway, and Janelle Wong, eds. *The Politics of Asian Americans: Diversity and Community.* New York: Routledge, 2004.

Lim, Shirley. *Approaches to Teaching Kingston's* The Woman Warrior. Approaches to Teaching World Literature 39. New York: Modern Language Association of America, 1991.

Lim, Shirley, Mayumi Tsutakawa, and Margarita Donnelly. *The Forbidden Stitch: An Asian American Women's Anthology.* Corvallis, OR: Calyx Books, 1989.

Ling, Jinqi. *Narrating Nationalisms: Ideology and Form in Asian American Literature.* New York: Oxford University Press, 1998.

Linmark, R. Zamora. *Rolling the R's.* New York: Kaya Production, distributed by Distributed Art Publishers, 1995.

Litwak, Leo, and Herbert Wilner. *College Days in Earthquake Country; Ordeal at San Francisco State, a Personal Record.* New York: Random House, 1971.

Lloyd, David. *Anomalous States: Irish Writing and the Post-Colonial Moment.* Durham, NC: Duke University Press, 1993.

Lloyd, David, and Paul Thomas. *Culture and the State.* New York: Routledge, 1998.

Lowe, Lisa. "Heterogeneity, Hybridity, Multiplicity: Marking Asian American Differences." *Diaspora* 1, no. 1 (1991):24–44.

———. *Immigrant Acts: On Asian American Cultural Politics.* Durham, NC: Duke University Press, 1996.

———. "On Contemporary Asian American Projects." *Amerasia* 21, nos. 1–2 (1995):41–52.

———. "Unfaithful to the Original: The Subject of *Dictée*," in *Writing Self, Writing Nation,,* ed. Norma Alarcón and Elaine H. Kim, 35–69. Berkeley, CA: Third Woman Press, 1994.

Lowe, Lisa, and David Lloyd. *The Politics of Culture in the Shadow of Capital. Post-Contemporary Interventions.* Durham, NC: Duke University Press, 1997.

Luibheid, Eithne. "The 1965 Immigration and Nationality Act: An 'End' to Exclusion?" *positions* 5, no. 2 (1997):501–22.

Manin, Bernard. *The Principles of Representative Government.* Cambridge: Cambridge University Press, 1997.

Marable, Manning. *Beyond Black and White: Transforming African-American Politics.* New York: Verso, 1995.

Marx, Karl. *The Eighteenth Brumaire of Louis Bonaparte.* New York: International Publishers, 1964.

Marx, Karl, Friedrich Engels, and C. J. Arthur. *The German Ideology.* New York: International Publishers, 1972.

McGarty, Craig, Vincent Yzerbyt, and Russell Spears. *Stereotypes as Explanations: The Formation of Meaningful Beliefs about Social Groups.* Cambridge: Cambridge University Press, 2002.

Morley, David, and Kuan-Hsing Chen, eds. *Stuart Hall: Critical Dialogues in Cultural Studies*. New York: Routledge, 1996.

Newfield, Christopher, and Ronald Strickland, eds. *After Political Correctness: The Humanities and Society in the 1990s*. Politics and Culture. Boulder, CO: Westview Press, 1995.

Nguyen, Viet Thanh. *Race and Resistance: Literature and Politics in Asian America*. New York: Oxford University Press, 2002.

Okamura, Jonathan. "Social Stratification." In *Multicultural Hawai'i: The Fabric of a Multiethnic Society*, ed. Michael Haas, 185–204. New York: Garland, 1998.

Omatsu, Glenn. "The 'Four Prisons' and the Movements of Liberation: Asian American Activism from the 1960s to the 1990s." In *The State of Asian America: Activism and Resistance in the 1990s*, ed. Karin Aguilar-San Juan, 19–69. Boston: South End Press, 1994.

Omi, Michael, and Dana Takagi. "Thinking Theory in Asian American Studies." *Amerasia* 21, nos. 1–2 (1995):xi–xv.

Omi, Michael, and Howard Winant. *Racial Formation in the United States: From the 1960s to the 1990s*. 2nd ed. New York: Routledge, 1994.

Ong, Aihwa. *Flexible Citizenship: The Cultural Logics of Transnationality*. Durham, NC: Duke University Press, 1999.

Ong, Paul, Edna Bonacich, and Lucie Cheng, eds. *The New Asian Immigration in Los Angeles and Global Restructuring*. Philadelphia: Temple University Press, 1994.

Ono, Kent A. "Re/signing 'Asian American': Rhetorical Problematics of Nation." *Amerasia* 21, nos. 1–2 (1995):67–78.

Orrick, William H., and the U.S. National Commission on the Causes and Prevention of Violence. *College in Crisis; a Report to the National Commission on the Causes and Prevention of Violence*. Nashville: Aurora Publishers, 1970.

Osajima, Keith. "Postmodern Possibilities: Theoretical and Political Directions for Asian American Studies," *Amerasia* 21, nos. 1–2 (1995):79–87.

Palumbo-Liu, David. *Asian/American: Historical Crossings of a Racial Frontier*. Stanford, CA: Stanford University Press, 1999.

———, ed. *The Ethnic Canon: Histories, Institutions, and Interventions*. Minneapolis: University of Minnesota Press, 1995.

———. "Theory and the Subject of Asian American Studies." *Amerasia* 21, nos. 1–2 (1995):55–65.

Palumbo-Liu, David, and Hans Ulrich Gumbrecht, eds. *Streams of Cultural Capital: Transnational Cultural Studies*. Stanford, CA: Stanford University Press, 1997.

Parikh, Crystal. "Blue Hawaii: Asian Hawaiian Cultural Production and Racial Melancholia." *Journal of Asian American Studies* 5, no. 3 (2002):199–216.

Park, Josephine Nock-Hee. "'What of the Partition': *Dictée's* Boundaries and the American Epic." *Contemporary Literature* 46, no. 2 (2005):213–42.

Pickering, Michael. *Stereotyping: The Politics of Representation*. New York: Palgrave, 2001.

Pitkin, Hanna Fenichel. *The Concept of Representation*. Berkeley: University of California Press, 1967.

Richardson, John G., ed. *Handbook for Theory and Research for the Sociology of Education*. Westport, CT: Greenwood Press, 1985.

Robbins, Derek. *Bourdieu and Culture*. Thousand Oaks, CA: Sage, 2000.

Rojas, Fabio. *From Black Power to Black Studies: How a Radical Social Movement Became an Academic Discipline*. Baltimore: Johns Hopkins University Press, 2007.

Roof, Judith, and Robyn Wiegman. *Who Can Speak? Authority and Critical Identity*. Urbana: University of Illinois Press, 1995.

Russell, Emily. "Locating Cure: Leprosy and Lois-Ann Yamanaka's *Blu's Hanging*." *MELUS* 31, no. 1 (2006):53–80.

Simpson, Caroline Chung, David L. Eng, and Wendy Ho. "Response by the Fiction Award Committee." *AAAS Newsletter* 15, no. 2 (1998):6–7.

Spivak, Gayatri Chakravorty. "Can the Subaltern Speak?" In *Marxism and the Interpretation of Culture*, ed. Cary Nelson and Lawrence Grossberg, 271–313. Urbana: University of Illinois Press, 1988.

———. *In Other Worlds: Essays in Cultural Politics*. New York: Routledge, 1988.

———. *Outside in the Teaching Machine*. New York: Routledge, 1993.

Sumida, Stephen H. *And the View from the Shore: Literary Traditions of Hawai'i*. Seattle: University of Washington Press, 1991.

Suzuki, Erin. "Consuming Desires: Melancholia and Consumption in *Blu's Hanging*." *MELUS* 31, no. 1 (2006):35–52.

Tachiki, Amy, and University of California Los Angeles Asian American Studies Center, eds. *Roots: An Asian American Reader*. Los Angeles: Continental Graphics, 1971.

Takagi, Dana, and Michael Omi. "Introduction: Thinking Theory in Asian American Studies." *Amerasia* 21, nos. 1–2 (1995):xi–xv.

Takagi, Paul, and Margot Gibney. "Theory and Praxis: Resistance and Hope." *Amerasia* 21, nos. 1–2 (1995):119–26.

Tan, Amy. *The Joy Luck Club*. New York: Vintage Books, 1991.

Thelin, John R. *A History of American Higher Education*. Baltimore: Johns Hopkins University Press, 2004.

Trow, Martin. "Reflections on the Transition from Mass to Universal Higher Education." *Daedalus* 99, no. 1 (1970):1–42.

Tsui, Kitty. *Breathless: Erotica*. Ithaca, NY: Firebrand Books, 1996.

Umemoto, Karen. "'On Strike!' San Francisco State College Strike, 1968–1969: The Role of Asian American Students." In *Contemporary Asian America: A Multidisciplinary Reader*, ed. Min Zhou and James V. Gatewood, 49–79. New York: New York University Press, 2007.

Veysey, Laurence R. *The Emergence of the American University*. Chicago: University of Chicago Press, 1965.

Wei, William. *The Asian American Movement: Asian American History and Culture*. Philadelphia: Temple University Press, 1993.

Williams, Raymond. *Keywords: A Vocabulary of Culture and Society*. Rev. ed. New York: Oxford University Press, 1985.

———. *Marxism and Literature*. Oxford: Oxford University Press, 1977.

Wong, Paul, Meera Manvi, and Takeo Hirota Wong. "Asiacentrism and Asian American Studies?" *Amerasia* 21, nos. 1–2 (1995):137–47.

Wong, Sau-ling Cynthia. "Autobiography as Guided Chinatown Tour? Maxine Hong Kingston's *The Woman Warrior* and the Chinese-American Autobiographical Controversy." In *Multicultural Autobiography: American Lives*, ed. James Robert Payne, 248–79. Knoxville: University of Tennessee Press, 1992.

———. "Denationalization Reconsidered: Asian American Cultural Criticism at a Theoretical Crossroads." *Amerasia* 21, nos. 1–2 (1995):1–27.

———. *Maxine Hong Kingston's* The Woman Warrior: *A Casebook*. New York: Oxford University Press, 1999.

———. *Reading Asian American Literature: From Necessity to Extravagance*. Princeton, NJ: Princeton University Press, 1993.

Wong, Sau-ling Cynthia, and Stephen H. Sumida. *A Resource Guide to Asian American Literature*. New York: Modern Language Association of America, 2001.

Wong, Shelley. "Unnaming the Same: Theresa Hak Kyung Cha's *Dictée*." In *Writing Self, Writing Nation: A Collection of Essays on* Dictée *by Theresa Hak Kyung Cha*, ed. Hyun Yi Kang, Norma Alarcón, and Elaine H. Kim, 103–40. Berkeley, CA: Third Woman Press, 1994.

Yamamoto, Hisaye, and King-Kok Cheung. *Seventeen Syllables*. New Brunswick, NJ: Rutgers University Press, 1994.

Yamanaka, Lois-Ann. *Blu's Hanging*. New York: Bard, 1998.

———. *Saturday Night at the Pahala Theatre*. Honolulu: Bamboo Ridge Press, 1993.

Young, Iris Marion. *Justice and the Politics of Difference*. Princeton, NJ: Princeton University Press, 1990.

———. "Ruling Norms and the Politics of Difference: A Comment on Seyla Benhabib." *Yale Journal of Criticism* 12, no. 2 (1999):415–21.

Zhou, Min, and James V. Gatewood, eds. *Contemporary Asian America : A Multidisciplinary Reader*. 2nd ed. New York: New York University Press, 2007.

Index

Academic freedom. *See* Freedom

Aesthetic: experience, 35–36; value, 36, 184, 205–6. *See also* Politics

Affirmative action, 37, 115

Afrocentrism, 110

Aiiieeeee!, 19, 134–35, 139, 141–56, 168–69, 175, 185

Alquizola, Marilyn, 60–62, 71–72, 117–19

Althusser, Louis, 27

Amerasia (journal). See *Thinking Theory in Asian American Studies*

Anderson, James D., 221n25

Antonio, Carolyn, 226n63

Anxiety of representation. *See* Representation, anxiety of

Aoude, Ibrahim, 231n4

Apparatus, 131–32

Area studies. *See* Asian Studies

Arnold, Matthew, 153

Asante, Molefi, 110

Asiacentrism, 110

Asian American: community, 6–7, 24, 42, 54, 60, 62, 98, 112, 115–17, 119, 141, 150–51, 202–5, 209; demographics, 6–7, 19; field, 10, 12–14, 21, 54, 55, 86–87, 89, 117–18, 159, 189; identity, 14, 18, 40, 45–46, 48–50, 58, 88, 98, 117, 128, 137, 139, 176, 189, 191; movement, 6, 8, 14–5, 18, 20, 29, 85, 115, 135, 137,

142; as term, 6, 13, 49, 51, 54, 55. *See also* Community, autonomy

Assimilation, 84, 136, 139, 146, 147, 152, 155, 203–4

Assimilationist ideal, 48

Association for Asian American Studies (AAAS), 1–3, 5, 12, 45, 93–94, 173, 176–84, 190, 193, 208, 213n2; fiction award, 1, 4–5, 12, 93–94, 173, 176, 178, 180–84, 192

Asian studies, 11

Autonomy: of aesthetic, 8, 100; of Asian American Studies, 5–6, 60–63, 57, 72; of faculty, 5, 9, 11, 59–60, 65, 70–73; of literary field, 141, 149; of university, 5, 70–72

Baym, Nina, 229n21

Bennett, William, 37, 154

Big Aiiieeeee! The, 152–54, 185

Black Panthers, 66–67, 76

Black Students Union (BSU), 18, 63, 65–70, 76, 78; demands of, 63

Black studies, 3, 18, 57, 63–68, 73–74, 77, 79, 107–9, 111, 113. *See also* Curriculum

Bloom, Allan, 154

Blu's Hanging, 1–4, 20–21, 42, 45, 93–94, 173–81, 185–87, 189–93, 196, 198, 200, 202, 206

Bonacich, Edna, 213n3

Bourdieu, Pierre, 8–10, 15–17, 23,
    26–28, 30, 34, 37, 42, 51, 79, 81,
    84, 90–92, 116, 184, 191, 215n8,
    217n24
Bow, Leslie, 228n3
Brigham, J. C., 188
Bulosan, Carlos, 229n16
Bush, George W., 5
Butler, Judith, 104–6

Cambridge University, 69
Campos, Caroline, 178
Canon, 8, 31–33, 35–39, 41–42; "wars,"
    17, 24, 30, 129
Cha, Theresa, 19, 96, 120, 131–33
Chan, Jeffery, 142
Chan, Sucheng, 208–11, 220n5
Chang, Diana, 147, 229n16
Chang, Gordon, 98–102, 108–10
Cheng, Anne, 131
Cheng, Lucy, 213n3
Cheung, King-Kok, 223n17, 228n3
Chin, Frank, 19, 142–44, 147, 150,
    153–54, 157, 192
Chinese Exclusion Act, 6
Chu, Patricia, 150
Chuh, Kandice, 3–4, 42, 45, 52, 55,
    193, 224n27, 228n3, 230n1, 232n18
Civil rights, 74–75, 115
College in Crisis, 69
Community: autonomy, 9, 11, 17, 60,
    209; education, 73, 107; commodi-
    fication, 26
Consciousness, 13, 57, 73–74, 77, 116,
    143, 154–55
Conway, M. Margaret, 88, 217n31
Credentialization, 37–38, 41, 80, 84–
    85, 114, 129
Cremin, Lawrence, 220n13
Crisis of representation. *See*
    Representation
Critical Filipino Studies Collective, 5

Cultural nationalism, 2, 19, 29, 44, 58,
    96, 112, 114; and aesthetics, 127,
    129, 175, 179; and Asian Americans,
    134–36; and Asian American stud-
    ies, 71–73; and Black studies, 74–75;
    and cultural capital, 85; local, 199
Curriculum: Black studies: 57, 74; clas-
    sical, 97; core, 34; liberal arts, 58,
    74, 113

Deleuze, Gilles, 222n45
Dictée, 19, 96, 120, 125, 129–35, 136,
    158
Du Bois, W. E. B., 74

Eliot, T. S., 153–54
Espiritu, Yen le, 182, 213n6, 214n2,
    217n31, 220n5, 226n63
Experimental College, 57, 63, 65, 70,
    74, 113

Feminism, 44, 96, 99, 104
Fiction award (AAAS), 1, 4–5, 12,
    93–94, 173, 176, 178, 180–84, 192
Field, 23–24, 26–29, 52
Filipino American Studies Caucus, 5
Foucault, Michel, 222n45, 225n40
Freedom: academic, 5–6; artistic, 141,
    151, 153, 179; of speech, 5
Freud, Sigmund, 154
Fujikane, Candace, 190, 198, 206,
    230n2, 231n3
Fujino, Diane, 226n63
Fuss, Diana, 48

Garrett, Jimmy, 66, 78
Geiger, Roger, 223n5
Gibney, Margot, 222n3
Governance: of Asian American stud-
    ies programs, 9, 60–61, 209; of col-
    leges and universities, 3, 69
Graff, Gerald, 216n19, 223n5

About the Author

MARK CHIANG is an Associate Professor in the Department of English at the University of Illinois at Chicago.